T.W. HUNT

MELANA HUNT MONROE

The HOPE of GLORY

SEEING THE WORLD

FROM HEAVEN'S VIEW

NAVPRESS

Discipleship Inside Out®

Discipleship Inside Out®

NavPress is the publishing ministry of The Navigators, an international Christian organization and leader in personal spiritual development. NavPress is committed to helping people grow spiritually and enjoy lives of meaning and hope through personal and group resources that are biblically rooted, culturally relevant, and highly practical.

For a free catalog go to www.NavPress.com
or call 1.800.366.7788 in the United States or 1.800.839.4769 in Canada.

Hunt, T. W., 1929-
  The hope of glory : seeing the world from heaven's view / T.W. Hunt and Melana Hunt Monroe.
    p. cm.
  ISBN 978-1-61521-732-8
  1. Hope—Religious aspects—Christianity. 2. Christianity—Essence, genius, nature. I. Monroe, Melana Hunt. II. Title.
  BV4638.H86 2013
  248.4—dc23
                              2012031719

Printed in the United States of America

1 2 3 4 5 6 7 8 / 18 17 16 15 14 13

*To Steve Monroe, who did the most
to inspire the writing of this book.*

Contents

Preface   11

PART I: LEARNING TO SEE FROM HEAVEN'S VIEW

CHAPTER 1: The Advantages of Seeing from Heaven's View   17
    God Wants Us to See from His View
    The World's View Versus Heaven's View
    Heaven's View and Our Earthly Existence
    Heaven's View of Our Identity
    Heaven's View of Our Relation to God

CHAPTER 2: Heaven's View Establishes Heavenly Priorities   33
    The Three Great Frameworks of God's Design
    The First Framework: Creation
    The Second Framework: Redemption
    The Third Framework: Bringing His Children to Glory
    God's Use of Process in Perfecting Us

CHAPTER 3: Heaven's View Begins with Relationships   59
    Placing the Process on the Right Basis
    The Two Fundamental Relationships of Christianity
    Loving in the Right Priority
    Loving Other Human Beings
    The Contexts of Our Earthly Love for One Another

CHAPTER 4: Seeing Glory from a New Viewpoint   85
    The Outer Glories of Heaven
    The Inner, Greater Glories

CHAPTER 5: Heaven's View Sees Christ in Us   107
    Our Stature Derives from the Indwelling Christ
    We Imitate Christ's View of Himself
    The Hope of Christ Within Us Enlivens the Present

CHAPTER 6: Heaven's View Sees Us Realizing God's Attributes in Our Lives   125
    God's Personal and Supernal Attributes Are Related
    Heaven's View Realizes the Emotions of God in Us
    Becoming Like God in His Personal Qualities
    Desirable Attributes That God Does Not Have
    The Surprising Road to Glory

PART II: APPLYING HEAVEN'S VIEW IN OUR LIVES

CHAPTER 7: From Heaven's View, Limitations Help Us Grow   147
    Facing Our Limitations
    Purposes of Limitations
    Limitations Teach Us the Nobility of Humility
    The Main Purpose of Limitations: Our Overcoming

CHAPTER 8: How Heaven Views Evil   165
    The Presence of Evil in the World
    The Heart and the Spirit Determine Our Character
    The Invasion of Sin in Our Lives
    The Temptation of Christ
    Heaven's View Is Ultimate

CHAPTER 9: Heaven's View of Our Crucible   193
    Universality of the Crucible
    What Goes On in the Refining Process
    The Crucible Requires Time
    Purposes of the Crucible

CHAPTER 10: Heaven's View of Suffering   211
    Earthbound Views of Suffering
    The Opposite View: Heaven's Perspective
    Different Kinds of Suffering
    Beyond Restoration: Suffering Allowed by God to Test, Prove, and Teach
    Heaven's Instructions for Going Through Suffering

CHAPTER 11: The Noblest Miracle of Heaven: Grace   239
    What Grace Is
    The Nature of Grace
    Applying the Grace of God
    How Grace Works
    We Appropriate Grace Through Faith

CHAPTER 12: Heaven's View of Glory   257
    From Here to Eternity
    God Shares His Glory with Us
    Elements of Glory
    The Glories of Eternity Future (or Graduation Day)

Afterword   281
    Death as a Threat — Our First Cancer
    Comfort in the Midst of the Threat — Our Second Cancer
    Growth out of the Threat — Our Third Cancer
    A New Paradigm

About the Authors   295

[I pray] that He would grant you, according to the riches of His glory, to be strengthened with power through His Spirit in the inner man, so that Christ may dwell in your hearts through faith; and that you, being rooted and grounded in love, may be able to comprehend with all the saints what is the breadth and length and height and depth, and to know the love of Christ which surpasses knowledge, that you may be filled up to all the fullness of God.

EPHESIANS 3:16-19

Preface

As our Maker, God created each person with specific objectives in mind. Only He sees the overall picture of each of our lives. He knew what our circumstances would be and what our work would be, all within the framework of His intention for the kind of person we would be. We best fulfill our purpose when we see all of life from His viewpoint. Logically, we can know His joy (really co-joy with Him) when we are receiving divine direction from the One who created us with purpose.

As our redeemer, God has a role for us in His kingdom work, and that includes right now. Because we are partners together with Him in His work (1 Corinthians 3:9), we need direction in carrying out our responsibilities. Of course, we are very junior partners and God is the divine Master in His work. God does not need us at all. In His omnipotence, no task is large or small, but His beneficent love includes us even in our small portion of His work. We can work with God only when we perceive His perspective on what we are doing.

Most of us will have to shift gears for our outlook to be heavenly rather than worldly (see the sidebars in chapter 1). We can either continue our lifelong habits that are shaped by the world around us or choose to learn to think in a new mode, but it will not be easy. Thinking Heaven's thoughts requires a continuous effort. Real intercessory prayer is hard work. Do not be discouraged if you find yourself slipping into old, familiar ways of thinking. God works in us in process (Mark 4:26-29; see also chapter 4). An infinite God is patient with us in our struggles (2 Peter 3:9). We can learn patience with ourselves only by keeping our attention focused on Jesus (Hebrews 12:1-2).

He thought His Father's thoughts 24/7 (John 5:30), a daunting task for us. Yet Paul, according to his letters, very nearly thought God's thoughts during all his waking hours: in church, in prison, in shipwreck, in a walk through the streets of Athens. Our model is Jesus, but Paul and most of the writers of the New Testament proved that a finite human can come close to imitating our Lord.

We wrote this book to help you see all of life from God's perspective—that is, from Heaven's view. All twelve chapters treat life in general from Heaven's view; two of the twelve discuss Heaven's view of all kinds of suffering. As you will see, many of the insights in these pages were forged when my (T. W.'s) wife, Laverne, and my daughter, Melana, were diagnosed with cancer. When this book was first published, both were cancer survivors and doing well. However, in 2001 Laverne's cancer came back and she died in 2009. While the pain of losing Laverne was severe, the truths and insights in this book brought comfort and helped give meaning to our grief.

We will be praying that you, the reader, take seriously the biblical injunctions to conform to the image of Christ and diligently apply these insights to your daily walk.

Note to the Reader: Some of the ideas in this book differ from the usual approach to the Christian life, and we struggled with the simplest and most useful means of communicating difficult concepts. By "Heaven's view," we usually mean how God sees our circumstances and us. Daniel referred to God as "Heaven" in Daniel 4:26. To keep our meaning of "heaven" clear, we chose to capitalize it because it usually refers to divinity. We capitalized God's pronouns throughout, mainly to help you keep track of the antecedents in our sentences. When "heaven" refers to a place, we did not capitalize it in the hope that you can distinguish our destination from the main idea of the book: learning to look at ourselves through God's eyes.

At times it became necessary to use "Heaven's view" to refer to how God's angels and the redeemed with Him in heaven see Him, as in the sections on His attributes. Even there, the occupants of heaven see Him, in kind, as He knows Himself. Context indicates whether we are looking at God's viewpoint or that of all of Heaven.

To make our point, we often had to repeat key passages of Scripture, so we had to choose whether to write them out every time or refer to a previous citation. Those earlier citations often occurred far from the current passage, possibly several chapters back. To keep the ideas moving, we felt it would be helpful to repeat them fully in the various new contexts. Therefore, certain significant Scriptures are repeated frequently, especially in the Corinthian letters, Romans, and Hebrews. We hope it facilitates your understanding and the flow of your reading.

In the same way, it was impossible to cover all aspects of a given subject in one place. For example, context demanded that we provide certain insights into humility in chapter 4, but then others in chapter 7. Developing the difference between angels and humans required that we mention their fall in chapter 2 but develop the Fall more fully in chapter 8, on evil. We hope the particular flow we developed will help you grasp Heaven's view in a way you can apply practically to your life.

Part I

LEARNING TO SEE FROM HEAVEN'S VIEW

CHAPTER 1

The Advantages of Seeing from Heaven's View

Let him who boasts boast of this, that
he understands and knows Me.

JEREMIAH 9:24

What would it be like to live each hour of my day seeing my thousands of words, choices, reactions, prayers, temptations, thoughts, views, and feelings from the perspective of Heaven? What would it be like to see the Father as Jesus does or view Jesus from the perspective of the Holy Spirit (not in degree but in kind)? How would it be to worship His glory in the same way that He respects His own glory? What would it be like to see the beauty of holiness?

Would it make a difference to be able to see Satan from the perspective that Heaven sees him? If I could see the vileness of even "mild" sin in the way the saints and angels and Holy Spirit do, how would I be different? How would I counter temptation? If I could see from God's perspective, wouldn't His promises become solid reality rather than tenuous prospects because I would know His integrity intimately?

GOD WANTS US TO SEE FROM HIS VIEW

Most Christian books, sermons, and personal studies begin with a "me-ward" perspective: how *I* can please God, how *I* should pray, how *I* must treat my spouse, how *I* can be organized or lose weight. We are predisposed to tune our perspective from that of the world (me, here and now) and look upward, inward, or outward from ourselves. Would it be possible to see from His point of view? Could we learn to see His ways that are so much higher than ours?

Seeing from Heaven's view means recognizing each big and little detail of my life — my relationships, dreams, frustrations, hurts, ambitions, secrets, fears, lusts, and loves — from God's perspective and ultimately with His understanding of their value.

Seeing from Heaven's view means understanding His specific reason for creating me and, therefore, my ultimate purpose in life.

Seeing from Heaven's view means knowing God in the way He designed me to know Him. With this perspective, my prayer and worship begin to mirror the beauty of holiness continuous in heaven.

Seeing from Heaven's view means that God's loves and griefs become my own and, therefore, my own priority.

Seeing from Heaven's view gives me God's value on and purpose for the thousands of minutes and hours that make up the long process of bringing me to glory.

Seeing from Heaven's view helps me seize with fervency the importance of every person in my sphere and makes me realize my personal need for each one. Holy humility is inevitable when we see others from Heaven's view.

Seeing from Heaven's view allows me to perceive suffering from inside His heart. As I grow to understand what endurance accomplishes within my spirit, I eventually treasure trials because of what they produce within me.

Seeing from Heaven's view enables me to view Satan, sin, and temptation in the way God sees them and gives me tremendous motivation to hate wickedness. This results in much greater faith and greater ability to flee from or withstand temptation.

Seeing from Heaven's view enables me to regard death with the same joyful anticipation He has in contemplating our Graduation Day. Death can become precious to us as the pathway to glory in the same way that our death is precious to Him (Psalm 116:15).

———————————

Months of suffering in our family caused us to search and yearn earnestly for God Himself and His glory in us. We slowly realized that He was revealing to us His viewpoint of our pain.

As we began searching in the Bible for ways to see our lives from His perspective, God revealed new paradigms in every passage we studied. We learned to see not only suffering from Heaven's view but also (1) God Himself, His nature and attributes, (2) worship and prayer, (3) God's use of process in bringing His children to glory, and (4) His perspective of temptation and evil. In fact, we realized that the Bible, God's written Word, is really an explanation of how to see from His view. Jesus, the incarnate Word, is the model of how to *live* with eyes fixed on Heaven's view. God's revelation, both through the Bible and the life of Christ, shows that, from Heaven's view, bringing His children to glory is the heart of His ultimate purpose and the reason for His continuing work on earth.

THE WORLD'S VIEW VERSUS HEAVEN'S VIEW

Our points of view (that is, the perspective most Christians have; this is the sense of "we" in the rest of this book except where context or designation indicates otherwise) usually originate from the perspective of "the here and now" in our world. However, our "here and now" view limits us; we do not realize how far short of God's view this perspective falls. We cannot see through others' eyes; we cannot perceive all the factors in our situation, and we have no control or influence over time. Seen in this light, our points of view often become untrustworthy. If we could perceive from Heaven's view, we would have the perspective of God's vantage point.

Scripture makes a distinction between the "earth" and the "world." When the Bible refers to the *earth* (especially in the Old Testament), it is clear that God's glory reigns here. On the other hand, the *world* is the domain of Satan, and Scripture says he is the prince of this world. (Note that the distinctions are most clearly drawn between the two testaments, after Jesus came and clarified many aspects of God's nature and work.) Scripture reveals an enormous difference between God's view and the world's view.

The earth is the LORD's, and all it contains. The pillars of the earth are the LORD's. All the earth will be filled with the glory of the LORD. May the whole earth be filled with His glory. Do I not

G○○D

fill*the heavens and the earth? (Psalm 24:1; 1 Samuel 2:8; Numbers 14:21; Psalm 72:19; Jeremiah 23:24).

Do not love the world nor the things in the world. If anyone loves the world, the love of the Father is not in him. If the world hates you, you know that it has hated Me before it hated you (1 John 2:15; John 15:18; see also John 12:31; 14:30; for a New Testament distinction, see 1 Corinthians 15:48).

To begin with, God is truth and the Author of truth. Whatever He says in His Word defines the *realities* creation intended. His truth is pure; He never mixes any selfish motive, mistake, error, or "white lie" in anything He says (Numbers 23:19; Psalm 57:3; 119:160; John 14:6; 15:26; 17:17). If we seek to see our circumstances and relationships from His view, we will have the incredible advantage of seeing what God regards as authentic and true. In His Word, God shows what is real and what is false.

Satan controverts reality. Not being a creator, he cannot offer anything but convoluted, obscured, disoriented, and deceptive facts, even if he uses an apparently true statement to accomplish his end. Therefore, Satan can offer *no reality*.

In the following comparisons, watch how Satan's view (the world's view) is a distortion of Heaven's view, a view of universal and absolute reality.

Throughout this book, the world's view and Heaven's view will come in conflict. The world gets its view from its immediate society, and too often the church does also. At other times, the world misrepresents or skews the genuine biblical view, even among believers.

From the World's View	From Heaven's View
I interpret God's goodness in light of myself: When something good happens, I think He is good; when something bad happens, I want to ask why a good God would "allow this to happen."	His tender mercies are over *all* His works.
"Right" is whatever is best for me.	All "right" originates in the nature of the Creator. "Right" describes His judgment of every moral and ethical issue. It is the same for all people in all ages and will remain the same in eternity.
Circumstances loom bigger than God's control.	Satan's malevolent power is limited; God's benevolent power is infinite. If God is for us, who can be against us? Nothing can separate us from the love and providence of God.
Judgment comes from my opinion and perspective.	I would not dare judge because of so many factors I cannot be aware of.
Heaven is in the distant future.	Christ is working within me right now, hourly developing the glory that will finally be mature at the moment I reach Graduation Day.
Under certain circumstances, obeying God may seem unreasonable.	Obedience always results in personal contentment for me and is an acceptable sacrifice for God. Obeying because I believe in His goodness makes disobedience unreasonable.
I must know why.	God does not necessarily explain to our finite minds His understanding of the best process for us. He does, however, reveal Himself.
Spirituality seems distant and mysterious.	I am being conformed to the image of Christ; therefore, my spirit images His Spirit. I seek a spiritual lifestyle.

From the World's View	From Heaven's View
I view each event with finality.	God focuses on the process of bringing me to glory. Single events get their importance from their place in that process.
Immediate needs or desires are urgent.	I perceive immediate needs in the light of learning to think and respond from Heaven's view.
I believe I understand others' feelings or reasons for behavior and therefore can conclude what is wrong.	God considers multitudes of factors; He knows all sides.
I choose my prejudices and loyalties from the background of my culture.	At Jesus' feet, I love all that He loves. My love does not derive from my culture.
I naturally resent interference in achieving goals I have set.	I stay on the right road to achieve complete spiritual maturity without being stopped by obstructions or passing events.

HEAVEN'S VIEW AND OUR EARTHLY EXISTENCE

Our Creation

Incredibly, we humans sometimes act as if it were Satan who created us and understands our real needs. As a race, we identify with his failings and have accepted his warping of our nature in a nonchalant, "nobody's perfect" way. From Heaven's view, that attitude is an unspeakable horror! Satan has no comprehension of the ultimate needs of humanity nor any ability to meet those needs.

Satan's original sin was obsessive, with intense desire for self-promotion. Since that sin, he has demanded or "needed" immediate satisfaction. His influence overwhelms us when we are willing to believe that our desires are really needs. Like him, we tingle with craving.

Moreover, Satan believed that he had found a better purpose for himself than that for which God had created him. The father of lies offers this same self-determination to each of us. We, too, think we know better than God. As a created being, Satan will face judgment before his Creator for disdaining the purpose of his existence. If we choose his orientation to self, then his rejection and sentence to hell before the throne of God must also be ours.

Heaven condemns our autonomy. Yet, knowing our determination to rebel, God planned beforehand to exercise His justice in the light of His compassion and mercy for us. His intention to have a family with whom to share His glory triumphed over the painful grief He had to endure to secure our rescue — our release from Satan's way of thinking. The definitive nature of God's purpose (sharing some of His glory with us) will be clarified in the next chapter.

Our Time on Earth

God gives us time on earth so that we may grow in spiritual maturity. This does not mean that a long life guarantees maturity; it does not mean that people who die young do not reach God's goal. It does mean that we are to use our time for intentional growth through the choices we make each hour. God helps us through it all. He fashioned us in such a way that the Christian life should continue in upward growth.

If we mature spiritually, we also will be increasingly transformed into Christ's image (Romans 8:29). Jesus shared His glory with His own as He walked on earth. He shares it with us now so that we will become like Him. We share His loathing of evil, His earnest passion that not one person be lost, His desire for continuous, unbroken fellowship. We rejoice in the growth and righteousness of others. Having His perspective grows out of a multitude of big and little choices. We are maturing, and God leaves us on earth to become more conformed to Christ.

The goal of spiritual maturity is higher and more difficult than we would expect. The Bible often emphasizes concepts such as completion (Ephesians 2:10), maturity (Ephesians 4:13), finishing (Hebrews 12:2), and perfection (Matthew 5:48). Long-suffering, endurance, and patience through this process equip us to become perfect and complete, lacking nothing (James 1:4). For this reason, we are able, if we see from Heaven's view, to welcome trials; they *do* perfect our faith as we struggle through the process of testing.

Nothing Satan or the world can do changes God's intention in our creation. God's intention will give us lasting satisfaction, peace, and purpose. This book will examine how we cooperate with Him to reach the maturity that will show forth His glory.

HEAVEN'S VIEW OF OUR IDENTITY
Our Worth

God places more value on humanity than on anything else in His creation. Although Scripture exhausts the words and phrases of human language to describe the love God has for us, we super-impose our prior understanding of love (derived from our culture) and fashion a diminutive model of His unselfish love.

After the Fall, we were worth redeeming; He had made us that way. From Heaven's view, the redeemed belong to Him as His own family. He promised that He will never relinquish His familial relationship with us, regardless of our ignorance, mistakes, and sin.

Loving us so greatly, He does not love us blindly. Heaven sees our abysmal ignorance and our awkwardness in handling the majesty and attributes of God. Ignorance is not sin, but remaining in *neglectful* ignorance is. Ignoring His majesty and glory as well as His revealed purpose for us stops the process of growing toward full stature. Remaining unaware of His purposes wastes our time for learning Christlikeness.

Yet love anticipated every possible obstacle we could encounter in becoming like Jesus. God helps constantly and immeasurably as He looks within us for signs of growing Christlikeness. Self-worth cannot be defined in terms of intelligence, looks, wealth, or accomplishment. The only worth available to us is His likeness in us, God's love for His Holy Son and His love for us combine to work with us unceasingly, conforming us to Him as our model.

Our worth derives from God's love for us, His choice of us, His image in us (as humans), and, supremely, the realization in us of the image of Christ explicitly demonstrated to those around us and to our Creator. Believers rarely realize the only valid concept of self-worth: Christ in us, and us in His image. Paul expressed this view rather clearly (Ephesians 1:3-19; 4:13). It is Heaven's view.

Our Need

Heaven sees only weakness anytime we attempt a gesture independent of Him (John 15:5). When we recognize our dependence as a *need*, the Holy Spirit breaks our pride, our humility matures, and He can lift us up compassionately. Few believers recognize how desperate our need for dependence is.

The difference between the disciples and the Pharisees was that Jesus' friends *needed* Him. Nothing in the Pharisees' behavior demonstrated felt need. The disciples, though, recognized Jesus' authority. They constantly asked questions or begged favors; they behaved as though they needed Him, in spite of their many mistakes and wrong directions. When He told them how dependent they were (John 15:5), they understood Him. The book of Acts proves that they learned this lesson.

Most of us today learn dependence through brokenness, manifested in pain or in a broken heart. Brokenness makes us tractable or teachable and then dependent. Brokenness can come from identifying with God's love and concern for this world (this rarely happens) and from grief over our sin (also too uncommon). More often it comes from difficult circumstances. Cancer, debt, a serious mistake, or death can make us cry out to God. Broken people need the Holy Comforter, who is ready to teach us our need of the Lord and His work in us. Once we discover His readiness to help, in our dependence, gratitude grasps the unexpected hand lifting us up.

If we are willing for the Holy Spirit to work in and through us, we discover His use of our brokenness to be preferable to the deceptive joys of the world. In learning dependence, we are learning a different kind of joy. The path may be unanticipated, but the joys are greater than what the world offers. Heaven rejoices constantly.

HEAVEN'S VIEW OF OUR RELATION TO GOD
We Know God Through Prayer

Our family had always had times of prayer, individually and collectively, but an urgent crisis brought us up sharp against the urgency of an even more continuous, constant contact with God. Before, we would have claimed a healthy, regular prayer life. In our new desperation, pain and urgency made us realize that our prayer life had been at times sporadic (although we prayed every day), at times inattentive and distracted, and often inept or even embarrassed. Occasionally, we contented ourselves with surface-level praying ("God bless the missionaries," "bless this food," "be with so-and-so").

Now our family needed to know how God felt about us while we were in the act of praying—all the time. From that need itself, God led us to a new level of prayer—a level that constitutes one of the most challenging aspects of Heaven's view: God pays unremitting, close attention to each of us, not only when we are aware of Him or need Him but also when we do not even realize how dependent we are on Him.

The former ineptness and discomfort we both felt in prayer usually expressed itself after we failed to "stay with Him" and sin or worldly attitudes crept in without our conscious awareness. Our desperation made us realize that regardless of circumstances, God keeps His word that He will never leave us (Hebrews 13:5). Once we became conscious of that, we could not ignore His helping presence. Heaven concentrates on us, and we learned that we can also be instant with God continually. We do not return to God—we never leave Him!

This unexpected aspect of Heaven's view was difficult to handle at first, but time and the new process of growth God had instituted began to make us crave the comfort of God's unceasing attention. That comfort was to become the joy of His steadying presence with us. Jesus called this unceasing prayer "abiding." Heaven does it, and Christians can too.

Living in the perpetual company of God led to understanding an attitude we had not fully comprehended: the unremitting, unselfish nature of His love. Love demonstrates itself in compassion, and the compassion was always there for us when we needed it, far above any measure we had known before. The compassion expressed itself by giving us appropriate insight into our journey at precisely the right time.

Much in our current culture tells us that we must earn the love of God, confusing approval with love. Most of us do not really know that our greatest need is not endorsement but unconditional love—love that always reassures us regardless of our actions or condition.

Love is a need, and now we knew that we had always needed that kind of love, aware of it or not. God does not love His children because of our attractiveness, our service for Him, or our gifts to Him; He loves us because that is who He is! A new father loves his infant because of his identity as father, not because the baby has earned any love.

Somehow the men and women around Jesus knew He loved them. They knew it by being around Him continually, over time. At last we were learning the same thing: When anyone stays around God, he or she experiences His love and involuntarily responds with love for Him. Heaven is about love.

To be consistent with His nature, God must sometimes (in sorrow) chasten those He loves, but it is always with respect, dignity, and nobility—never in derision or ridicule. Satan confuses us with feelings of rejection. He loves derision and ridicule. God never rejects us when we appeal to Him (John 6:37). We are not outsiders; we are family, and only the family of God actually learns the depth of unconditional love.

Heaven always has a warm welcome for us as God's children, whether in repentance, gratitude, desperation, or the joy of His company. God wants our focus on Him, for He is unceasingly attending to us. No more "surface praying" for even an instant.

Sometimes our family had intense, deep prayers, but we were never without a prayerful attitude; we were abiding in Christ at every moment. Finally, talking to the Father on all occasions became the most natural and joyful activity we could pursue. That is the way Heaven works. Heaven's view cannot be temporary or passing; it is forever—and forever includes "right now."

We Become Like God in His Intention and Passion

Most of us carry on our daily activities casually and even thoughtlessly. Nothing Heaven does is routine or superficial. God never becomes casual about His work even though it is ceaseless. Neither do the inhabitants of heaven sing their psalms and praises carelessly. Every note, every syllable of praise, emanates from a joy that is fully and continuously conscious. If we had Heaven's view, our present service would be filled with intention and our songs would be passionate.

Creation was certainly not perfunctory. The enormity of the cosmos and the fine-tuning of this solar system and of our wondrous earth indicate an attention to detail that has to be infinite. Yet even creation—grand as it is—falls far short of the greater grandeur (assiduously prepared) that will be ours when creation's purpose is consummated.

Redemption was not accomplished in an offhand manner. Our salvation was carefully worked out before the creation of the universe. In eternity, when we finally understand how enormous and designed this work was, we will fling ourselves in delight at the feet of Him who died for us.

We cannot take the glory of God casually. His glory is unique (Isaiah 42:8), undiminished by our modest participation in it. As we grow in glory, understanding the distinctive nature of God's glory, we must persevere with attention to what He is and what He is making of us. Heaven's view is single-minded.

We maintain our attention on God's purposes, gradually

becoming aware of His continuing help. Nothing Heaven does and therefore nothing we do can be perfunctory.

Only God Can Give Us His Own View

If God is God, how final is His word? If God is God, how thorough is His work? If God does anything, how "done" is it? If God were to decide to make a universe, how big could He make it? If God were to make a human brain, what kind of perfection would scientists marvel at? If God redeems us, how much has He accomplished? If God gives us glory, how great will that glory really be?

At present our family is not even able to appreciate the questions, much less the cosmic extent of their answers. This is why we are so excited about death, or "Graduation Day." True, we waste no time in this current life's process, but we also yearn for that knowledge that will finally be complete in the free and unrestricted presence of Christ.

Seeing from Heaven's view is a way of life, a different orientation from the one most of us exercise. The circumstances of cancer were painful, but reorienting ourselves was joyous. We pray that this book will enable you to orient yourselves as "seated . . . in the heavenly places" (Ephesians 2:6) regardless of the struggle. Glory costs more than we expected, but the price was far below the new kinds of joys we experienced.

The struggle continues; we have much growing yet to do. As long as God leaves us on the earth, we are not "finished." In our case, God has pointed out many areas yet to conquer. We approach them with an eager openness in the face of the challenge and new wonder at how far we will be going.

Heaven's view of our life is the view that realizes God's purpose in our existence. It is the only view that keeps the beginning

and ending of creation—and of our own lives—in mind. After
Graduation Day, we will spend all of eternity with no mixture of
the world's view in us, so God gives us the advantage of learning
His outlook now. Heaven's view transforms cooking, earning a
living, reading a book, raising our children—all of life—into
daily glory. And that glory will never fade.

CHAPTER 2

Heaven's View Establishes Heavenly Priorities

The path of the righteous is like the light of dawn, that
shines brighter and brighter until the full day.
PROVERBS 4:18

Throughout history, most Christians have preferred to look at the immediate and proximate in their lives. This is the way nearly all of us work. To hear us talk, one would think God went to a tremendous amount of trouble in creating and redeeming us simply to keep a few people out of hell or (the same thing) to get a certain set of people into heaven, as important as that is. Indeed, as the cornerstone of a larger process, redemption does demand fervent attention, as God does not want anyone to perish.

However, in always concentrating on the immediate, we fall short of grasping the grand culmination God planned for us from the beginning. Certainly, the vastness of creation and the terrifying cost of redemption ought to make it obvious that He intended some unexpected splendor for us.

In His larger works, God always had in mind a much broader and nobler ending than most of us have suspected. No one can comprehend the sheer size of the works of God. The psalmist cried, "O Lord, how many are Your works! In wisdom You have made them all" (Psalm 104:24). Modern believing scientists would call that an understatement! Even David exclaimed, "Many, O Lord my God, are the wonders which You have done, and Your thoughts toward us; there is none to compare with You. If I would declare and speak of them, they would be too numerous to count" (40:5).

THE THREE GREAT FRAMEWORKS OF GOD'S DESIGN

For our purposes, the issue to uncover is not the detailing of God's enormously complex works but rather the ultimate purpose He had in mind from the beginning in creating us. We may therefore structure all those "many wonders" into three enormous frameworks. All the manifold works of God may be cataloged under one of three broad structures in order to perceive God's greater purpose from the beginning. They are first, *creation* (Genesis 1); second, *redemption* (Romans 3–8); and finally, the most important, *bringing His children to glory* (Hebrews 2:10).

Each of these three grand works provides a context for other divine actions. For example, all the works throughout the New Testament after the Cross are secondary to the Cross itself. The subsidiary works in the Bible and in our lives are important because they originate in God Himself, but each of the lesser actions originates in a context of one of these three wide-ranging main frameworks.

Before He made the universe, God's great plan was to orchestrate centuries-long works that would in the end give Him a people with whom He could share the glory that has been His always throughout eternity. God carried out the first two broad works, creation and redemption, as necessary foundations for the final framework and eventual product: a family of persons made like Himself to share His greatness, love, and glory. Jesus asked to return to this glory in His last long prayer (John 17:1-5), indicating the preeminence of that glory from Heaven's view.

The First Framework: Creation

God began His work with *creation*, but He has not given us many details about it, compared to His other revelations. The Bible always gives us the information we need and no more, although sometimes we can uncover hints at greater truths than those on the surface. Science is discovering many things for us about physical creation, and, astonishingly, its discoveries agree completely with the biblical account. However, the Bible only hints at the spiritual motives of creation, which have most to do with God's sharing His glory with us.

The creation of angels. Although we know little about the creation of angels — for example, whether they were created before the universe itself — we do know they sang at the foundation of the earth (Job 38:7). God created them as *spirits* (Hebrews 1:14) and equipped them to work as messengers and servants of God. Being pure spirits, they seem removed from us, yet they help us in many tangible ways (Psalm 34:7; 91:11).

The Bible indicates that they have *intelligence* and can make authoritative decisions. Gabriel could decide to strike Zacharias dumb (Luke 1:20). However, God would not create intelligence without also giving it *free will*. Intelligence without freedom to act would be useless. Because his will was truly free, Lucifer was able to rebel against God (Isaiah 14:12-15). Obviously, the angels have intelligence and, consequently, free will.

Angels also have tremendous *power and energy.* A single angel destroyed the entire Assyrian army — 185,000 soldiers — according to 2 Kings 19:35. Another angel ascended in the flame of Manoah's altar (Judges 13:20; see also Psalm 103:20). Intelligence coupled with the power of the angels always made them able to execute decisions and carry out God's orders. In fact, had we been given more information about their power and intelligence, we might regard them as higher than we ought.

Angels also apparently have *no conscience* in the sense that humans have. In their (normal) faultlessness, they have no need for that particular guide. When the angel killed 185,000 Assyrians (2 Kings 19:35), he evidently felt no compunction, no "conscience." A human could not have performed such a feat without qualms because God built into us a delicacy about moral matters. (This is not to evaluate the "morality" of killing the army; it is only to describe a peculiar sensitivity in humans.) For the good angels, obedience is enough. A sensitive conscience is not a factor; they serve out of their nature.

The Bible only records angelic emotions *at the extremes of the emotional range* we know about. Both good and bad angels are pictured only as "one-ended" in their emotions. The angels in heaven rejoiced when the earth was created (Job 38:7). They have joy when a sinner repents (Luke 15:7), and they praise God continually (Isaiah 6:3; the book of Revelation, *passim*). The good angels express only positive emotions.

The fallen angels, on the other hand, seem to experience only trembling (James 2:19), fear (Matthew 8:29), and, evidently, from all the trials they manufacture, extreme malevolence (John 3:20). No demon is ever recorded as experiencing regret or shame (it seems likely that they will know this at judgment and then ever after). Their lack of conscience may relate to God's restricting them to a narrow emotional range. They are never recorded as being repentant.

From Scripture, unfallen angels know only joy, love, and bliss on the affirmative, encouraging side. Evil angels express negative, discouraging thoughts. All the angels we know about exhibit only extreme emotions.

What we might call "middle" emotions — that is, not extreme emotions (such as pity, dislike, and even the ability to enjoy a chuckle) — are missing from the biblical record. Moreover, emotions coming from both ends of the spectrum by a single angel (hatred *and* love) are not recorded. The angel apparently destroyed the Assyrian army dispassionately; he felt no pity. The angels, therefore, express a narrow emotional range, so far as the record shows, in one extreme or the other. The human makeup seems to be closer to God's than that of angels. Our emotional resemblance to God is a rare gift, one that makes us more like Him in our ability to enjoy what He enjoys.

The angels were created *perfect*. God apparently "finished" them at the time of their making. The Bible exalts them. They are holy (Matthew 25:31) and wise (2 Samuel 14:20). They minister ceaselessly for God (Psalm 68:17; Luke 16:22). No mistake is ever recorded by a good angel. Those who did not fall have continued without sin; the Bible reveals unquestioning obedience and flawless behavior.

Volumes have been written about the strange origin of evil springing from perfect angels. The greatest minds for centuries have puzzled over their rebellion against God. Einstein came to believe in God but spent a lifetime rejecting Christianity because he could not solve the problem of evil. In this life, we are not likely to understand that incredible rebellion.

The creation of human beings. Human beings, on the other hand, were not created perfect or finished. They were created *inno-cent*. Innocence is a wondrous quality, but it is not the final perfection God had in mind. Yet, although not created perfect, humans were created in *the image of God*. The Bible records that they also fell, as did some of the perfect angels. Therefore, existing in the very image of God does not secure humans against sin. We know from this that being in the image of God is not the perfection God wants of us—yet.

What, then, does the Bible mean when it says we are created in the image of God? The angels, not in the image of God, still have certain of His attributes, such as intelligence and power. God also gave these qualities to humans, albeit in a degree inferior to that of angels (we will see later why we have so much yet to learn). God demonstrated that His image is valid in us by His becoming human Himself (Philippians 2:7).

The most important and distinctive aspect of God's image in humans is His gift to them of a spirit. God is Spirit; the angels are spirits, and we can spend eternity with them because we, too, have a spirit-nature. From Heaven's view, our spirit-nature is more substantial than our physical nature.

Being in the image of God gives us a hint of the importance of our particular creation. Furthermore, Genesis 9:6 provides the disconcerting information that even after the fall of man, humans still had the image of God! We have to admit reluctantly that Judas, Hitler, and Mao Tse-tung were made in the image of God.

We mar the gift of the splendid image of God. The Garden of Eden proves that man, too, had *free will* from the beginning. Adam, like Satan, had the freedom to exercise his own free will. History and experience bear out the extent to which we can desecrate the image of God.

Considering what humankind has been able to accomplish in

our arts and sciences, God patently also gave human beings power and energy, as He did the angels. The Lord Himself is "great . . . abundant in strength [energy]; His understanding is infinite" (Psalm 147:5). This part of Himself (power and intelligence) He shared with angels and with men. Men vary greatly, however, in their intelligence and strength. What matters is not the quantity but the use of our gifts.

Humans have one gift that seems distinctive to us: a conscience. Conscience is the ability to distinguish between right and wrong with emotional attachment to the right. When we violate that unusual awareness, we experience shame or guilt (and also sometimes, tragically, pride). After their sin, Adam and Eve immediately felt shame; they knew to hide from God. They instinctively wanted to please Him.

The discomfort of shame would have no moral significance to an animal or, apparently, a fallen angel at the present, at least not to the degree that it creates repentance. Their shame at judgment will be more profound and irremediable than the shame that produces our repentance. Our present dictionaries probably could not define their eternal shame.

The conscience functions both cognitively and emotionally. It understands the reasonableness of the right—an operation of the mind. When it is clean, it enjoys God's rightness—an emotion. The conscience unites the mind and heart.

As we grow more like God, our emotional attachment to the right (the desire to please God) becomes firmer and stronger. It begins to reflect God's immutability. God can never know shame because He will not contravene His knowledge of right. His "knowledge of good and evil" does not allow Him "freedom" to do evil; He cannot violate His own perfection.

God has shared with us the unique gift of a conscience—an

understanding of the right! He does not need this as a guide; in us, having a conscience is the nearest we can come to His eternal *rightness*. God knew that it would enable us to become more and more like Him if we would allow it to function in the way He intended. We instinctively desire rightness (Ecclesiastes 3:11).

God also made humans with *the full gamut of emotions He Himself has*, along with the possibility of their perversions. People can hate, detest, pity, love, rejoice, have aversions, and have compassion, just as God can. God bestows on humans an extraordinary emotional capacity. This generous gift comes out of God's unstinting attention to every aspect of our development in becoming like Him.

God also shared a part of Himself by bestowing on us *creativity*. God's creativity brought a universe out of nothing, and the Bible records His inventiveness in bringing *newness* throughout history: the mark of creativity. Our Rembrandts, Shakespeares, and Bachs show an affinity to divinity in the magnificence of their works. The Handel oratorios have a *newness* that has remained fresh. All humans, Christian and pagan, have some degree of this gift. Even little children concoct stories that are often inventive.

The angels do not seem to exhibit creativity. Although they have immeasurable intelligence, they have written no novels or symphonies that we know of. Satan has created no universes. Although he is subtle, his intelligence expresses itself by perverting what God has already created.

The devils apparently lost neither their power nor their intelligence when they fell; they retained the qualities they were originally given for service. History, Hollywood, and the enormous presence of evil in all art forms prove that such high gifts can be hideously perverted. Satan's "creativity" consists in driving evil persons (who retain their gift of creativity) to invent distortions of God's intentions.

Humans could not be creative unless they had flexibility (the ability to change) and imagination. Jesus could always be interrupted (Matthew 9:20-22; Mark 1:36-38); He often seized the opportunity of the moment, regardless of circumstances. He was flexible. He was also imaginative in His awe-inspiring use of creative stories to make a point.

In summary, the fact that all of us humans have a spirit, intelligence, free will, power, energy, conscience (in God, perfect rightness), emotions, and creativity confirms that God made us in His image. The Bible shows His exhibiting these in their perfection, although none of us uses them as graciously as He does.

The differences between God's purposes for humans and angels. God made humans and angels with different purposes in mind. The angels were created (already) perfect; they had "nowhere to grow" and "nowhere to go." They had "arrived" at their finished form at their creation. They were to be God's messengers along with other service assignments, such as guarding His throne.

We do not know much about the creation of the angels, but we certainly know that they are not a race begotten by procreation (Matthew 22:30); He is the King of Hosts (Jeremiah 50:34). It appears that God created enormous hosts of angels (no problem for infinity). Had God wanted to redeem the *fallen* angels, He would have had to die a separate death for each individual *fallen* angel. Because our sin nature derives from Adam as the progenitor of all humans, Christ could die a single death for all people as the head of His new creation.

Humans, on the other hand, were created both flexible and imaginative. God did not make the ultimate destination of humans evident at their creation. He made them flexible and as such they could change for the better or for the worse.

Angels were created perfect; humans were created innocent. This allows humans room for growth and provides for the possibility of change after their fall. A fall from innocence differs greatly from a fall from perfection.

The angels have high responsibilities. The Bible indicates that they guard and praise the glory of God (over the ark and in the temple in Isaiah 6); it never states that they have the glory humans will have.

However, God's plans for humans were far more vast than His plans for angels. Of the three great frameworks—creation, redemption, and bringing His children to glory—the angels are only a part of the first: creation. God had two more huge steps for humans but no more steps for angels. The angels help us in these last steps, but only humans can become God's children and participate in His glory. The angels, of course, retain that glory given them in their creation.

The Second Framework: Redemption

Knowing that humans would fall, God planned their nature in such a way that *He could redeem them*, which is His second major framework and aims toward the final great work. All humans, unlike the angels, descended from a single couple bearing the image of God and are, therefore, redeemable even though fallen. Christ's death redeems all humans who will accept His atonement.

The Cross served an additional purpose beyond our redemption. It vindicated the glory of God in the light of our sin (Romans 3:25-26), and that vindication would be worth another book! However, we are presently concerned with what it also did for humans in that process. Knowing that we would fall, He *still chose* to create us. For His greater purpose, sharing His glory with a family transcended the cost.

Redemption rescues us from Adam's fall. In redemption, we gain a nature that God can "work with" even beyond the original malleability of Adam before he fell. If we were unable to change, God would not have given such elaborate instructions on how we can grow.

We had nothing to do with our own creation; we did not choose to be created. We also had little to do with our own redemption. The significant difference between our creation and our redemption is that we personally *choose* our own redemption. Our will steps in, and we can decide for or against the work of God in giving His Son for us.

In our new condition, we desire the salvation of all people just as God does. We know the dreadful fate of unredeemed humans. If we look at people from Heaven's view, we cannot neglect evangelism. We cannot redeem them, but we can give them the same choice we had when we accepted Christ.

The Third Framework: Bringing His Children to Glory

With those who accept the gift of redemption, God begins operating in the third main framework, present in His original purpose, present in His great mind from all eternity. *He can bring the redeemed into His personal glory and share it with them.*

When the Bible teaches our glory and nobility, it does not at all suggest that we will become gods. The Bible clearly establishes only one God (Exodus 34:14; Deuteronomy 6:4; 32:39).

Jesus reaffirmed this great truth in Mark 12:29-31. The Bible maintains the distinction between Creator and created. The tenor of the book of Revelation suggests that the created will eternally praise the Creator.

In bringing us to glory, He magnifies His own glory and at the same time gives expression to His infinite love. Redeemed humanity is headed toward participation in a plan we would never have invented, left to our own nature: We will share the indescribable glory of God with Him throughout all eternity. He will enjoy us, and we will enjoy Him.

If God were "efficient" (from the world's view), all redeemed human beings would die and join God as soon as they accepted His salvation through Christ. However, God had a much broader plan for humankind than He did for the angels. We are to *develop*. Even before salvation, we understand development as process in many parts of our unredeemed lives: in growing, in learning, and in teaching.

God is certainly the initiating agent, and it is His work to bring us to perfection. But at the same time, it is *we* who are His fellow workers (1 Corinthians 3:9). *We* are to work out our salvation with fear and trembling (Philippians 2:12), yet Paul immediately says that it is *God* who does the work (verse 13). Salvation is not a work; it is a *workout*. The workout both leads to and participates in God's glory. We are not saved by anything we do, and we do not accept Christ for mere security. Salvation is the first of many steps that will lead to the glory of God and our participation in His glory.

Jesus never sought His own glory; He sought only that of the Father (John 17:4). In the process of seeking the Father's glory, He Himself was glorified. We also do not seek our glory; we seek only the glory of God. In the process of seeking that glory, we will be stepping deeper into its light.

We can thank God that we do not seek the glory without help, nor can we receive glory apart from God's glory. Accomplishing our glory is a reciprocal work; we work together with God—the higher working with the lower, the greater working with the lesser. Reciprocity is the way God wants to work with us and bring His kingdom. Only in continuing reciprocity with God can we participate in His glory.

Therefore, *after* redemption begins the culmination of God's work, the third overarching framework—the work of perfecting us to share His glory with Him. His glory is ultimate; our glory is lesser and derived but nevertheless glory. The purpose of salvation is not safety but glory.

Adding the third great framework of bringing us to glory must not downplay the importance of evangelism. Although our only role in our personal redemption was choosing Christ, we have a major role in bringing others to Him. That, too, is a part of our glory.

Jesus commanded us to be perfect (Matthew 5:48). The fact that it is a command indicates that we assume a role in fulfilling that expectation as we finish (perfect) the process. He would not command us to do something we could not do.

"When Christ, who is our life, is revealed, then you also will be revealed with Him in glory" (Colossians 3:4). Although the Bible clearly indicates that we will have glory, our glory differs from God's in that His remains commensurate with His infinity and eternity. God cannot share infinity with us; we will always look upward to Him as above all in every aspect. He will not share the uniqueness of His glory (Isaiah 42:8). We remain subject to Him and worship Him only. Infinitely inferior to Him, we enjoy the lesser glory of conforming to the image of His Son in our lower being (Romans 8:29). God shares with us all He possibly can.

One of the primary meanings of both the Old Testament Hebrew word for *perfect* and the New Testament Greek word for *perfect* is "finished." We arrive at our (final) perfection through process—we have to be "finished." The word *perfect* can also mean "complete" and "without blemish." We will be complete (without blemish) when we are finished, and that will be a glory beyond anything we have known.

We had nothing to do with our creation, very little to do with our redemption, but everything to do with joining God in His glory. Most of the time, the Bible speaks of our arrival at God's glory through suffering:

> The Spirit Himself testifies with our spirit that we are children of God, and if children, heirs also, heirs of God and fellow heirs with Christ, if indeed we suffer with Him *so that we may also be glorified with Him.* (Romans 8:16-17, emphasis added)

GOD'S USE OF PROCESS IN PERFECTING US

Down through history, people have tended to emphasize *event* rather than *process*. Many of us can point to the day we accepted

Christ, had a birthday, were baptized, or were married. In fact, for most people, life moves around events, and we measure progress in terms of events: graduation, a new job, a promotion.

Events are, indeed, important. The angels rejoice when a sinner repents. A new pastorate or a recommitment to Christ can be important markers for our memory books. Christmas can be a joyful celebration of the Incarnation, and Easter is an event calling for thoughtful contemplation. This life, at least, calls for significant milestones along the way in the form of events.

Events may also be propitious or opportune for the process. This is why we are to pray "in a time when thou mayest be found" (Psalm 32:6, KJV) and seek Him at opportune moments that He provides (Isaiah 55:6). Still, events become significant as they relate to process. God takes much more interest in our *development* than in our milestones.

Creation and redemption are themselves events in the sense that they have specific beginnings or times. Their ramifications, however, are worked out in process. A birth must be preceded by gestation; the completion of creation required time; we are to "work out" our salvation (Philippians 2:12). In this process, we are not *earning* our glories; we are *choosing* them — thousands of times every day, in the big and little directions we take with our will.

Process theology emphasizes God's limiting Himself in our time. However, the two of us believe that the limitations are placed on us as humans. Although God involves Himself in our process and helps us within it, He also remains transcendent, immutable, and eternal. Only as we understand Him as both immanent and at the same time transcendent — seemingly contradictory concepts that cannot be fully understood in our present limitations (see chapters 7 and 12) — can we accept the reality of God's present help in and with us and, at the same time, His "beyondness." We cannot place limits of any kind on God or His work. Process theology sees God becoming like us. We are emphasizing that redeemed humans are becoming like God although eternally inferior to and subject to Him.

The word *doxai* (majesties) in 2 Peter 2:10 and Jude 8 refers to angels, possibly even fallen angels. The Bible leaves no doubt that they possess dignity and splendor beyond our comprehension. It behooves us to use great caution with such magnificent creatures. From these passages, we see that danger lurks in reviling "angelic majesties."

Obviously, our *development,* indeed our "finishing," can be accomplished only in process. From Heaven's view, our progress is much more important than the events of our lives. God providentially allows some events beyond our control: death, accidents, abuse. The glory for God emanates from our availing ourselves of unexpected training in nobility. Each event managed from Heaven's view yields an upward process "from glory to glory" (2 Corinthians 3:18).

As we grow in process, the kingdom of God grows along with us — in process. One of Jesus' most neglected parables spells this out:

> The kingdom of God is like a man who casts seed upon the soil; and he goes to bed at night and gets up by day, and the seed sprouts and grows — how, he himself does not know. The soil produces

crops by itself; first the blade, then the head, then the mature grain in the head. But when the crop permits, he immediately puts in the sickle, because the harvest has come. (Mark 4:26-29)

The parables of the mustard seed (Luke 13:18-19) and of the swelling yeast (Luke 13:20-21) reinforce this point, especially about the kingdom.

The individual Christian also grows slowly, little by little. The normal path progresses upward. "The path of the righteous is like the light of dawn, that shines brighter and brighter until the full day" (Proverbs 4:18). Our glory unfolds in ever-increasing measure as God leads us through our valleys, our smooth roads, and our high events.

As long as we are in process, we will remain inferior to the angels in every way. They are clearly superior in intelligence and power. (While the translation of Psalm 8:5 is equivocal, the New Testament version in Hebrews 2:7 of the same verse is not and indicates that we are presently lower than the angels.) The angels are "mighty in strength" and intellect and superior in rank. In our present weakness, we are grateful that God has equipped them to be a prodigious help (Hebrews 1:7). They require power and intelligence to be able to minister to us while we are learning.

The Biblical Pattern of Process

Growth in process will inevitably be incremental and, astonishingly, four verses in the Bible point to incremental progress. The first of these is Exodus 33:13. Moses asks, "I pray You, if I have found *favor* in Your sight, let me know Your ways that I may know You, so that I may find *favor* in Your sight" (emphasis added). Perceiving the favor of God, Moses dared ask for *more* favor. We obtain more favor by understanding the ways of God and hence

God Himself better. Moses understood this: Perceiving a little favor from God emboldened him to ask for more.

Every human being on earth at one time or another receives the favor of God. Even unreached people groups could perceive God in nature (Psalm 19:1-6; see also Romans 2:11-14). God bestows this universal favor on all peoples. Those of us in Christianized lands know thousands of (usually unacknowledged) favors from God. Favor leads to favor, if understood and grasped appropriately. "Whoever has, to him more shall be given" (Matthew 13:12).

God provides a second incremental increase in Psalm 84:5,7: "[Those] whose strength is in [God] . . . go *from strength to strength*" (emphasis added). Because the strength is "in God," this does not refer to physical stamina but spiritual vigor. We demonstrate spiritual strength especially by perseverance and endurance. Moses, Daniel, and Paul grew in ever-increasing strength.

The New Testament picks up the same idea of incremental growth. Paul tells us in Romans 1:17, "In [the gospel] the righteousness of God is revealed *from faith to faith,* [in those who believe, verse 16]" (emphasis added). Following the redemptive work of Christ, we must increase in faith, the foundation of our relationship with God. The book of Acts and all the Epistles show us men, women, and churches constantly increasing in faith.

God climaxes the idea of our growth toward greatness in 2 Corinthians 3:18: "We all, with unveiled face, beholding as in a mirror the glory of the Lord, are being transformed into the same image *from glory to glory*, just as from the Lord, the Spirit" (emphasis added). God's process began with His favor and ends with our glory. Our life in Christ consists not merely of a series of glories; it progresses toward ever *higher* glories!

The real climax, clearly, comes when we go to be with the Lord forever in never-dimming glory—our Graduation Day. At the funeral of my (T. W.'s) godly brother, I told the congregation, "Jim has finished all his hard tests. He has his diploma!" No more struggle from "glory to glory" for him! He enjoys the permanent glory above all: the never-fading splendor of the presence of Christ forever. (Incidentally, I added, "And here I am, still taking tests!")

We can diagram this progression in increments: favor to favor, strength to strength, faith to faith, and glory to glory as a constant progression upward:

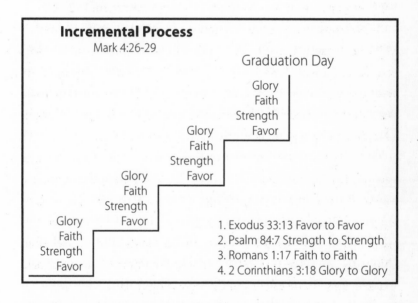

Incremental Process
Mark 4:26-29

Graduation Day

Glory
Faith
Strength
Favor

Glory
Faith
Strength
Favor

Glory
Faith
Strength
Favor

Glory
Faith
Strength
Favor

1. Exodus 33:13 Favor to Favor
2. Psalm 84:7 Strength to Strength
3. Romans 1:17 Faith to Faith
4. 2 Corinthians 3:18 Glory to Glory

Satan Can Subvert Process

The Enemy, of course, does not want any of our progression toward our final glory. He has a number of mistakes he can plant in our minds along the way. For example, when we reach the second step upward, we will be tempted to think that the faith we had back at the beginning was not real faith. If our beginning was not in faith, we could not take the second step. The father of lies deceives many with this trickery.

Another common lie emerges when we reach the third or fourth step: Simply because we really have made progress, we will be tempted to think, *I have more strength than all those other folks.* We must rejoice also in the growth of others; only a self-centered blindness fails to appreciate the growth of others. So we praise God for our progress and praise Him also that others around us are also progressing.

Still another tempting thought occurs on the higher steps when we think, *When I come to Graduation Day, I will really have glory.* In that delusion, we fail to recognize the genuine work of God at this time in our lives. God fills every day with His glory, even when it is hard to see. We see it in our brothers and sisters in Christ; we see it in the church; we see it in the expansion of the gospel to many previously unreached peoples; we see it in the endurance of Christians in persecuted lands. God manifests His glory on every side for those "who have eyes to see" (Ezekiel 12:2).

Each Increment of Process Has Unperceived "Perfection"

As we proceed through our process, God's definition of our "perfection"—at any given point in our lives—may be different from what we suppose. Laverne used to tell me (T. W.), "I'm going to make a cake" (to which I responded, "Hallelujah!"). She gathered the flour, sugar, and dry ingredients as well as the milk, eggs, and wet ingredients. When I saw all those items on the kitchen counter, they didn't look "perfect" to me. But was Laverne dissatisfied with what she had done *to that point*?

She mixed them all into a gooey batter. To me, that cake still didn't look like "a cake." But she knew her baking was in process. She was not angry with the batter because I couldn't see a cake. Then there came that terrible moment when, if a cake could talk, it would have cried out, "Oh no, not the oven!" Laverne, quite accustomed to the process, immediately put the cake into the awful heat of the oven.

At long last, she pulled the cake from the oven, and finally even I could see what she had been aiming for. The finished cake required process. That process has steps. To Laverne, perfection was finishing each step just right.

God, too, takes us through many steps. We cooperate with Him each step of the way and do not blame Him or ourselves if we haven't finished the oven part (or any other part). We are "successful" or "perfect" when we keep on working with God regardless of where the steps take us. The cake illustration breaks down in the fact that the ingredients do not have any choice about the next step. Unlike them, we have a will. We can balk at or we can cooperate with any step of the process.

We do not realize the awesome importance of our daily choices, because of the relativism of the world we live in. In the world's view, small choices are unimportant. Heaven views every choice as important because our choices have to do with absolutes. To understand absolutes properly and in balance requires great wisdom, and Christ Himself is our wisdom (1 Corinthians 1:24).

Jesus—our wisdom—had to pass through process. When He was twelve years old, He knew who He was, but the Father did not demand that He go immediately to the Cross—that is, to complete His purpose in coming to earth. The Father had another "finishing point" in mind, greater than His twelve-year-old perfection. Yet Jesus was "perfect" *at that point* from the perspective of Heaven's view.

At His baptism, not only *He* knew His identity but John the Baptist announced it publicly. Still, the Holy Father was not commanding Him to finish His work right then; He was pleased with where Jesus was at that time. He had to "work out" through process His own finishing—His perfection (being yet perfect in the sense of having no blemish)—until the fullness of time came for the Cross. This is why the Bible tells us, "It was fitting for Him, for whom are all things, and through whom are all things, in bringing many sons to glory, to perfect the author of their salvation through sufferings" (Hebrews 2:10).

Jesus' process of suffering is also described in Hebrews 5:7-9 and in the detailed narratives of the Gospels. We follow His example (1 Peter 2:21). As we follow Him, He becomes our wisdom to help us understand what God is accomplishing in each step of our process. Like my wife's cake, we are simply to be on the "step" where God wants us.

Adopting Heaven's View of Process Changes Our Thought Processes

If we are learning to measure by development rather than event, our thought processes will be marked by significant changes. Rather than consisting of alternating disappointments and "mountaintop experiences," life will become the joy of continuously obeying the Holy Spirit.

Crises lose their urgency as we keep our eyes on the goal of sharing Christ's glory. "Culminations" are no longer a gleeful climax with a fall back into the "valley" afterward. Rather than seeking the satisfaction of the moment, we become watchful at all times, "fixing our eyes on Jesus . . . who *for the joy set before Him* endured the cross" (Hebrews 12:2, emphasis added). Chemotherapy, radiation, and surgeries were for us a series of "crises and culminations," but during our third time through cancer, our family found itself in development, moving toward the high goal of becoming like Christ.

In fact, toward the end of the treatment, my (Melana's) daughter made an amazing observation. One evening as we were watching television together, a commercial about breast cancer came on the screen. The script began, "Breast cancer: the disease women fear most." Katie looked over at me with a puzzled expression. She queried, "Why do people say that? Breast cancer has been nothing but good for our family." Even our children understood what God was doing with us. They, too, were learning to enjoy the God of each step.

Rather than being irritated by interruptions, Christians understand them as either redirection or movement. If we are in process, we do not live for the moment but for the movement. Understanding the meaning of process rules out both pride and frustration. Instead of mood (temporary), we learn to express the permanent emotions of God as occasion dictates.

God created the angels in completed, instantaneous perfection. He planned our creation to follow a more arduous path. With us, God is carefully painstaking and meticulous because we are being ennobled. We will reign with Christ (Revelation 5:10). We will ultimately judge angels (1 Corinthians 6:3). Among the grand intentions God had in creating us, one was our ennoblement.

Our human condition does not impede glory. Jesus, eternally human as well as eternally God, is eternally glorious. Redeemed humanity, as royalty, will enjoy the glory of high nobility — even sharing the glory of the most high God!

Even the old prophets suspected that far more than redemption was in the mind of God as they wrote. First Peter 1:10-11 says of them,

> As to this salvation, the prophets who prophesied of the grace that would come to you made careful searches and inquiries, seeking to know what person or time the Spirit of Christ within them was

indicating as He predicted the sufferings of Christ and *the glories to follow.* (emphasis added)

The angels also yearned to understand these destined glories. The next verse tells us,

> It was revealed to [the prophets] that they were not serving them-selves, but you, in these things which now have been announced to you through those who preached the gospel to you by the Holy Spirit sent from heaven — *things into which angels long to look.* (verse 12, emphasis added)

Going Through the Process

Much of our entrapment in event-oriented thinking comes from the influence of our culture. Most Western cultures through history have centered on events. Today the idea of develop-ment in process has been hampered by our preoccupation with fads, the influence of the entertainment industry, and the technical means to hurry our various activities. We live in a "rush-oriented" culture that knows little of such ideas as waiting and watching.

Admittedly, the process may be long and difficult because of the enormous importance of the finished product. God's work with Peter could be called an "exhaustive" work, characterized by the prayer of Jesus Himself (Luke 22:32) and attention to detail (Luke 5:3-8). His work with Joseph turned out to be far more grand than Joseph had dreamed back in Canaan. Most of the great saints of the Bible actually had stories with many setbacks along the way. God's orchestration of each of our lives will never be careless. We are the nobility of His grand story. Ennobling us will demonstrate God's own ineffable nobility and glory.

Therefore, we do not concentrate on setbacks, departure, arrival, or success but on progress. We do not anticipate the "next town" (event) so much as we concentrate on the road. We keep our eyes on the highway that leads to the true destination. As the "towns" arrive, we may enjoy their distinctions and learn from them patience, faith, endurance, boldness, or whatever God intends. Both the road and the towns instruct us, but our daily goal is forward movement.

In this life, we do not seek attainment or achievement. Victory comes when we can recognize progress, which might not come at the moment of a "success." In fact, progress may happen in what seems to be a defeat. We can and should learn to enjoy the process when it is ever upward and even praise God for that process, especially when it is producing positive virtues (patience or endurance) regardless of circumstances.

We do not limit our praise of God to the times when we "succeed," because God never changes. His worth becomes clearer as we progress along the road, even though the road may be "bumpy." We always look to Him, not the good or bad events.

We need not concentrate on the apparent rapidity of our development; we focus on only the *direction* of our process. The speed of our progress is God's business; some arrive more quickly than others. God has a different path for every individual. But we have to make choices about the direction as we work with God. Our minds no longer dwell on the temporary; we concentrate on the eternal—every day, moment by moment. This is Heaven's view.

CHAPTER 3

Heaven's View Begins with Relationships

[I ask] that they may all be one; even as You, Father, are in Me and I in You, that they also may be in Us.

JOHN 17:21

The Christian's process through life, described in the previous chapter, cannot progress unless it begins and continues on the right basis. All religions have certain distinguishing bases. The basis of Christianity is *personal* relationship, expressed in personal love. The whole of God's work in us has at its heart that *centrality of relationship*. God carries out His actions within the three general frameworks of His great plan only through a personal relationship to us.

We discovered for ourselves this paramount emphasis on personal relationship long after we became Christians. Over a period of years, I (T. W.) have traveled in many lands on many continents, teaching conferences for nationals and for missionaries. The missionaries always showed me the local religions they have to work with. Many times I have visited Hindu, Buddhist, and Taoist temples. Missionaries have shown me Shinto shrines. I have been around Muslim mosques and heard stories of working with Muslim people. Christians have taken me to animist emblems when they dominated a local area. The contrast between Christianity and all other religions slowly began to surface as I understood more of their bases.

PLACING THE PROCESS ON THE RIGHT BASIS

Relationship Distinguishes Christianity as a Religion

I gradually began to realize that the fundamental difference between Christianity and all other religions is that Christianity alone is based on personal relationship, especially expressed in personal love. In other religions, I discovered superstitions, stringent laws, sometimes multiple gods, and even manipulation of the gods, but not interaction with their gods or with other people on a consistent personal level. Nearly all the religions have some sort of emphasis on social obligations, which, of course, is healthy. They have some emphasis on social virtues such as pity and compassion, yet the element of personal love is emphasized strongly only in Christianity.

The Bases of the World Religions

Most of the Oriental religions try to negate pain or personality—to learn how not to suffer, how to become nothing, or how to be absorbed in a great realm of oblivion or, more rarely, depersonalized bliss. The Hindu must go through a series of painful reincarnations on the road to union with Brahma (who is impersonal). The Buddhist seeks to escape this world and its cravings. A bodhisattva achieves heroic stature by sacrificing his entrance into Nirvana in order to help others. Most religions have a number of noble persons.

Sometimes the Oriental religions pursue a poorly defined "way"; the "way" often leads to an illusively interpreted end.

Certain of them emphasize various *public* or *social* obligations, but not normally individual *personal* relationships in the sense that Jesus commanded. Most of them have many gods but without authentic personal relationships pervading their way of life unless a person becomes attached to one of the gods. Other Oriental religions worship ancestors but without emphasis on living associations. Patriarchal reverence differs from the relational love in Christianity practiced with contemporaries.

Islam is a religion of law—very rigid rules and regulations—but it does not single out the importance of individual *personal* relationships in the way they are emphasized in Christianity. The Quran deals with certain interpersonal relationships—such as how a man ought to treat all his wives or take care of his parents—but not the two love commands discussed later in this chapter.

In Muslim conversion, the convert states his or her profession as an avowal of belief. Conversion in Christianity differs radically: It begins as a personal relationship to Christ. Doctrine and theology follow the acceptance of Christ in a relational role.

Sin in Islam violates a code. Getting into "paradise" results as an attainment of works; virtue receives its reward at judgment. Christianity teaches sin primarily as a violation of personal relationship. Lying betrays our kinship with the Father of truth. Stealing, murder, and adultery violate the relationships of humans. Although a human can sin against himself (as in suicide), even that sin violates personhood. Drunkenness and foolishness debauch the nature of Christ in us and often rupture human relations as well.

Parenthetically, the paramount place assigned to personhood also distinguishes Christianity from other religions. Christianity does not merely value people as in the social strictures of most religions; Jesus valued individuals. Note Paul's references to large numbers of *persons* in the closings of his letters as well as in the context of the letters. Personhood gives identity, and God acquaints us with Himself specifically by many relational titles. A deep, profound relationship depends on personhood.

While Christian virtue reaps an eternal recompense (as also taught in Islam), personal relationship is itself a *present* reward of specific virtues, a peculiar aspect of New Testament teaching. As understood biblically, we cannot achieve Christian virtues on our own. Most of them are developed by interaction (humility, patience, kindness) or by a gifting or assistance from God (wisdom, love, joy, peace). The Muslim law on giving alms demands pity, although personal interaction may be missing; it is obligatory. Christianity declares its virtues for the purpose of establishing relationships with other humans or for deepening our relationship and likeness to God. The Christian often not only contributes money but also befriends the poor in many interactive ways.

Furthermore, the relationships in Christianity spring from *inner* qualities that are a part of the new nature the Christian receives from the Holy Spirit. Except for Allah's blessing on the marriage relationship (Quran 30.21), the relationships in Islam result from obedience to an *outer* code. Even the love that Allah has for people results from their performance or obedience (Quran 2:177, 195, 222; 3:31, 76, 146, 148, 159; 5:13, 42, 93; 9:4, 108; 19:96; 60:8).

Animism teaches a fearful dread of spirits occupying various objects or else it attempts to manipulate those spirits, but neither of these develops personal relationships. It locates power in totems rather than in God. Valid personal interactions are extremely limited in any kind of superstition.

Although all religions have healthy points, some of which benefit humankind, seldom do they build in accountability for loving relationship with God or with other people. In Christianity, however, the love relationship between God and His people is singular. It is basic to everything else in the faith.

THE TWO FUNDAMENTAL RELATIONSHIPS OF CHRISTIANITY

Jesus' Emphasis on Relationship Is Distinctive to Him

The entire fabric of Christianity grows out of two fundamental personal relationships. Without them, the whole edifice of church, the Bible, missions — Christianity — falls. The majority of Jesus' teaching has meaning only if these two relationships are understood, directly or indirectly, as the basis of His concepts.

When asked the greatest commandment, Jesus emphatically declared,

> The foremost is, "HEAR, O ISRAEL! THE LORD OUR GOD IS ONE LORD; AND YOU SHALL LOVE THE LORD YOUR GOD WITH ALL YOUR HEART, AND WITH ALL YOUR SOUL, AND WITH ALL YOUR MIND, AND WITH ALL YOUR STRENGTH." The second is this, "YOU SHALL LOVE YOUR NEIGHBOR AS YOURSELF." *There is no other commandment greater than these.* (Mark 12:29-31, emphasis added)

Jesus' wording made emphatic the basis of all His teaching. The first fundamental is that we are to love God above all and give ourselves to Him completely. That is the foundation of everything else in Christianity — our *personal* loving relationship to God. Having given that as the first commandment, Jesus then added the second fundamental: We are to love our neighbor as ourselves — a second *personal* relationship. In another reference giving the same two commandments — love God above all and love your neighbor as yourself—He emphasized, "On these two commandments depend the whole Law and the Prophets" (Matthew 22:40).

Christianity grew directly from Judaism, which also taught these two commandments, especially the first (in the *Shema*, the creed of Judaism; Deuteronomy 6:4-9). However, the Old Testament did not juxtapose them as Jesus did. In Christ's command, the first demands the second. Jesus highlighted these two commandments *in conjunction* more prominently than anyone else; all else depends on these two. God placed them in the Old Testament to build a foundation for the stronger emphasis throughout the New Testament.

Heaven's View of Love Differs from That of the World

The world knows love as an affair of the heart. To be sure, love springs from the heart; but according to the Bible, true love also involves the will. We are to love God with all our minds. Love is cognitive (this aspect of the heart is discussed in chapter 8) but does not require superior intelligence. Rather, love involves two kinds of mental effort: (1) exercising the will by proper choice and (2) acquiring knowledge of God. Loving God with our minds does not mean trying to "act cerebral" or "be intelligent"; it requires a conscious choice of Christ followed by going on to know God in His attributes, His actions, and His Word. To know God is to love Him.

We know the visible easily and therefore love it without willful effort. The invisible usually does not merit our attention. Yet God is Spirit, and we are to worship Him in spirit (John 4:24). We *can* love the invisible because God reveals Himself perceptibly and particularly in His dealings with us and in His Word. God does not hide Himself in nebulosity; the invisible is not intangible.

Those who "get to know" Him learn *specific* attributes in His Word and respond to *specific* leadings of His Spirit.

Love cannot be merely a response or God would never have loved us. "While we were yet sinners, Christ died for us" (Romans 5:8). The original love is an *attribute*, a quality inherent in God from all eternity. Because love begins in God, the initiative lies with Him. When He comes to us, we respond first by believing Him and then continue by seeking Him. In one way or another, God manifests Himself to all humans (Psalm 19:1-4; Romans 2:12-16). The fact that we seek Him does not spring from our inherent nature but from the wooing of God. In seeking, we learn, and then, knowing Him, we absorb His attribute of love. We become like what we know.

Love is not merely a relationship. Again, in the Bible it is an *attribute*. Relationships result from the attribute. Because of its strength as an inherent trait, it takes action. It reaches to the beloved and performs specific operations on behalf of the loved person. God's attribute of love acted in history, and it still acts today.

We can love our enemies because love is not tenderness or affection. The fact that Jesus commanded us to love shows that love (agape) does not come from chemistry (like some of our "loves"). Most chemistry happens involuntarily or carelessly. Godly love expresses itself by cognitively taking deliberate action, even with the least likely candidates: our enemies.

By its nature, love draws forth reciprocity, and this involves exchange. The reciprocity we have with God and with others must have *voluntary* actions; genuine reciprocity cannot give unwillingly. God initiates actively; we respond freely and start a chain of reciprocity with God and with others. "Give, and it will be given to you" (Luke 6:38). When we bless God, He blesses us. Our mutuality (God's directing Himself and His gifts toward us, and our directing ourselves and our gifts toward Him in return) expresses itself in His sustenance and our dependence, in His giving and our returning what He has given us.

Moreover, forgiveness also originates in reciprocity. We forgive because God in Christ forgave us (Ephesians 4:32). Our forgiving comes from what God has done. The mutual interchange at times becomes stern: "If you forgive others for their transgressions, your heavenly Father will also forgive you. But if you do not forgive others, then your Father will not forgive your transgressions" (Matthew 6:14–15). Infinite mercy forgives infinitely only where we magnify our cooperation with it.

Reciprocity characterizes the original attribute of love within the persons of the Holy Trinity. God's attribute seeks humans who will respond and develop the same kind of love that the Father, Son, and Spirit have for one another. It is the nature of love to extend itself, and it does this by actions that become complementary.

Reciprocity involves interaction in which one person returns in kind what he or she has received from another. God gives to us; we give back to Him and to others what He has given us. Reciprocity indicates mutual interchange between persons but does not indicate equality of rank.

In the sense of initiative-response, humans can be reciprocal with God whereas angels cannot because only humans are made in the image of God. Apparently, angels are not expected to forgive or love their enemies (or at least the Bible doesn't record it). Being made in the image of God requires of us more severe strictures than an earthly "love" would have chosen.

Each human being represents a desire of God's heart. God never creates accidentally. He made each of us to love Him and, in the process, to love what He loves. We are made that way; we are made to love.

LOVING IN THE RIGHT PRIORITY
God's Reason for Placing Love for Himself First

Many of our earthly "loves" originate in glands or good looks or position. Some are rooted in wealth, fame, or even prejudice. The intensity of our passions deceives us into thinking they are permanent and perhaps even godly. Heaven views many of our "loves" as sensuality, bigotry, gluttony, or selfishness. In Heaven's view, these "loves" depersonalize their objects, and Christianity is about persons.

In these worldly senses of the word, we can "love" our neighbor without loving God or anyone beyond our neighbor. However, if we understand the biblical emphasis, we cannot love God without loving our neighbor. Our love for our neighbor and everyone else is "spillage" from the proper kind of love for God.

The book of Deuteronomy emphasizes loving God above all because only that will produce godly love in other parts of our lives, a befitting "spillage." The Old Testament had to start there, and Jesus deliberately planted it at the head of all love. Love starting anywhere else perverts Heaven's view of the nature of love.

The principle of "spillage" even applies to earthly loves. A boy in love loves all that his girl loves. He loves everyone who loves his girl. "Love," whatever it may be (good or bad), spreads infectiously. The Creator knows what love is and what is best for the created.

Therefore, the *Shema* and Jesus placed the right kind of love first. The ensuing loves then result from the appropriate quality.

God's love differs from ours both in degree and in kind. In degree, He demonstrated the enormity of His love by giving Himself in a merciless, cruel Roman death. In kind, His love is selfless. Love gives itself totally (John 3:16) and keeps on giving ceaselessly, unremittingly. The biblical command to give all has a generosity more grand than the petty nature of our "loves." Few Christians grasp the significance of Jesus' example of love. Only godly love will achieve total, uninterrupted, continual giving of self.

The kind of love Christ showed on earth utterly opposed worldly obsessions and infatuations. The love He expressed never sprang from self-satisfaction or any kind of selfish desire. "We know love by this, that He laid down His life for us" (1 John 3:16). Love manifests itself primarily in sacrificial self-giving. "Greater love has no one than this, that one lay down his life for his friends" (John 15:13).

Both testaments clearly tell us what kind of love God is and what God's love practices. God's kind of love will not manipulate the beloved. We cannot manipulate God, so we love Him not for what He can do for us, and, recognizing that God's love is selfless and total, we enter into His attribute of love within the confines of its nature. God does not force our love; He appeals to it. The choice is ours.

Although God rewards our love lavishly, we do not love Him just to get the rewards. In His mercy, God accepts almost any awkward move toward Him, even for wrong motives. Nevertheless, we must not remain in infancy. If we ever grasp the cosmic wonder of God, we (or at least these two authors) cannot aim toward the rewards; we aim toward God Himself and His kingdom and glory.

Love distinguishes itself by acting. Only cognitive love has the wisdom to choose legitimate actions. Love delivered Israel, instructed Joshua, touched Ruth, answered Hannah, and called Jeremiah. God forgave David and restored Jonah, totally and selflessly. The supreme Love assumed human flesh and gave His all for our redemption.

Among the redeemed on their path to glory, all loves derive from a pure, selfless love of God. Starting anywhere else mixes in foreign elements, inordinate desires, and self-centered "needs." Jesus never indulged extraneous wishes for Himself or for others (Matthew 20:20-28). He stuck straight to the essential every time; He put His Father first and related everyone else to God (John 17:4). The "spillage" of our love for our neighbor, our faraway brother, and our separated sister—as important as they are—will please Heaven when it derives from Heaven.

Loving God First and Above All

Our love for God must be defined biblically. The clear declaration of both testaments leaves no doubt that we *can* love God intensely and above every earthly love. That high love usually lies outside our experience and our observation. Nevertheless, we are able to do anything God commands; God commands only the feasible.

Joseph's love for God (in this paragraph, love for God is marked by placing Him above circumstances) enabled him to surmount a long series of obstacles. David's love for God produced the superb psalms that have inspired countless generations. Elijah confronted Baal worship with a love for God that enabled him to stand alone. Love emboldened Daniel in the lions' den. The apostles remained faithful under pressure through self-sacrificing love for Christ. Only love for God could produce the courage of centuries of martyrs. The Bible and history prove that ordinary people can put God first.

Love for another person above God almost always slips into self-interest. Putting a human, worldly love first can result in a "love" that is selfish, jealous, and demanding. That kind of love is not permanent and often yields disastrous consequences. David's "love" (lust) for Bathsheba produced years of agony for him. Loving a person because of his or her position, wealth, or popularity becomes self-serving.

Any love for another human—even a normal familial love—above love for God violates the commandment (Matthew 10:37). By definition, love for God can hardly be self-serving. No one can claim God "just for himself," as we sometimes claim people. The right quality of love rules out self-centeredness. Godly love is totally "unself-conscious"; it concentrates on others.

Genuine love for God has to be *pure* and it has to be *single*. God loves us "just as we are"; therefore, we love God "just as He is." We cannot remake God to suit our tastes. From Heaven's view, all love starts with what God is and how He loves. Once we orient ourselves primarily vertically—that is, heavenward—our horizontal loves are authenticated.

Three Frames of Reference That Help Us Love God Above All Else

To help us return God's love, Scripture provides three ways we can view our relationship to Him. These three frames of reference help us orient ourselves to God. He tells us that (1) He will be in us and we will be in Him (*mutually occupy* each other), (2) we can have a number of personal *relationships* with Him, and (3) He will remain in close *proximity* to us. All three help us love God in the way He commands.

(1) **Mutual occupying.** The first frame of reference, mutually occupying one another, begins with God's being *in* us or occupying us. Jesus set the stage for understanding this by promising that

the coming Spirit would be *in* the disciples (John 14:17). Paul commanded the Ephesians to be *filled with* the Spirit (Ephesians 5:18; a command for all Christians). We are the temple of God because the Holy Spirit dwells *in* us (1 Corinthians 3:16). Christ *in* us is the hope of glory (Colossians 1:27).

We may ask, "If God is omnipresent, isn't He already present in all beings?" Indeed He is, but He manifests His presence in us *personally*. We usually express ourselves impersonally in our business but personally to someone we love. Until we accept Christ, God remains an abstraction to us. God reveals Himself primarily through Christ. When Christ comes "into our heart," He becomes a specific person whom we *know* as we know our most intimate family member.

The other side of this first frame of reference shows *us* being in God. Ephesians refers constantly to a person *in* Christ. "If anyone is *in* Christ, he is a new creature" (2 Corinthians 5:17, emphasis added). Christ lives *in* us (Galatians 2:20) and *dwells in us* (Ephesians 3:17). Paul declares that we are "hidden with Christ *in* God" (Colossians 3:3, emphasis added).

It may seem a contradiction that God occupies us and we simultaneously occupy Him. If I submerge a cup in an aquarium upside down, no water can pass into the cup. The cup is in the water, but the water is not in the cup. However, if I turn the cup right side up, the air in it bubbles out and water fills the cup. Now the water is *in the cup* and the cup is also *in the water*. It is not a contradiction for both to be in the other. (We might add a moral: If you want to be filled with the Spirit, you have to be upright, like the cup!)

In His omnipresence, God occupies all places. He is around us at all times. When we accept Christ, God manifests a *personal* occupation both within us and around us, as the previous

Scriptures make clear. We are in Him, and He is in us. He knows our thoughts not only because He is omniscient but also because He is right there where the thoughts take place. This makes our silent prayers more powerful than we realize. When we and God mutually occupy each other, we are able to love with all our heart, soul, mind, and strength.

Relationships. God laid out a second frame of reference to Himself by planning a number of *relations* we can have with Him. Consanguineous relations make us bond together and function in unison. He planned for our basic relationship with Him to be that of a child to his or her Father (Matthew 6:8-9), one of the most important love relationships even among humans. Father and child love each other not because of merit or worth; their love derives from the nature of who they are in the relationship. Jesus emphasized this relationship more than any other.

The Bible also spells out many other relationships with God: He is our Brother (Hebrews 2:11), Master (Matthew 6:24), King (21:5), Potter (Isaiah 64:8), Friend (John 15:14), and Shepherd (Psalm 23:1), to mention only a few. For each of these, we complement Him in significant ways that require interaction with Him: We are brother or sister, servant, subject, clay, friend, and sheep.

One of the most helpful prayer techniques we can learn is to appeal to Jesus in these various relationships. The two of us have appealed to Him in all the ways previously listed as well as Judge (Acts 10:42), Creator (Genesis 1:27), and Savior (1 Timothy 4:10). For example, when you concentrate on serving Him, call Him "Master." When you need to remold a part of your life, pray to Him as "Potter." Praying in a given relationship should be suitable for the particular moment and the particular need.

Proximity. Our third frame of reference to God is His *proximity*.

David claimed that God was *at his right hand* (Psalm 16:8,11). The Old Testament repeatedly asserted the nearness of God (Exodus 33:14; Joshua 3:10; Psalm 73:23; 145:18; Isaiah 43:2; 50:8). In his repentance, David pleaded, "Do not cast me away from Your presence" (Psalm 51:11), indicating his awareness that God dwelt with him. Regular contact assumes great importance with those to whom we are close. Breaking the contact is painful.

The New Testament also asserts the presence of God with us. Jesus promised that He would be *with us* always (Matthew 28:20). "Always" cannot mean "occasionally" or "conditionally." The writer of Hebrews saw God's promise of remaining with us as a basis for trusting only in God:

> Make sure that your character is free from the love of money, being content with what you have; for He Himself has said, "*I WILL NEVER DESERT YOU, NOR WILL I EVER FORSAKE YOU,*" so that we confidently say, "THE LORD IS MY HELPER, I WILL NOT BE AFRAID. WHAT WILL MAN DO TO ME?" (Hebrews 13:5-6, emphasis added)

Loving God above all else was so basic that loving our neighbor did not occur in the *Shema*. Jesus emphasized the primacy of putting God first with such sternness that He instructed a multitude, "If anyone comes to Me, and does not hate his own father and mother and wife and children and brothers and sisters . . . he cannot be My disciple" (Luke 14:26). These are strong and terrifying words, but they leave no doubt about Heaven's view.

Many of us already utilize these frames of reference unconsciously. In prayer meetings, we constantly hear, "Lord, fill that sanctuary with Your presence" (mutual occupying), "Master, I need to know Your will" (relational), or "Lord, manifest Yourself to Joe" (proximity). Once we understand that God wants us to know His availability and how He manifests that accessibility, the more likely we are to call on Him in one of the three frames of reference. We always turn first to God; our principal relationship is to our Father, and our first love is vertical.

Much Christian teaching today focuses either on horizontal relationships (family, marriage, social obligations, church) or personal self-improvement (how to succeed, lose weight, get a promotion). These often help or prove useful and even necessary. However, the Bible puts the vertical first. Heaven's view makes our love and relationship to God paramount; the command is an absolute. Everything else gets right when that gets right.

LOVING OTHER HUMAN BEINGS

Our Love for God Defines What All Our Other Loves Must Be

All true love originates in God. Genuine love is derivative and resembles God's love in its unique ways. The Bible distinguishes occasionally between divine love and friend love, yet it even uses these two kinds of love interchangeably. The differences in various "loves" that our earthly languages attempt (lust, affection, sentimentality) fail to grasp the importance of the Creator, the origin of all things in heaven and earth. Even Jesus' love for His friends is *agape* (divine) love (John 13:1). Heaven's view of marital love, with all it entails, places it in the category of Christ's love: "Husbands, love your wives, just as Christ also loved the church and gave Himself up for her" (Ephesians 5:25; both verbs derive from *agapao*).

"Middle" emotions, such as pity and affection, are legitimate. God pities His children. Normal people develop affection for a pet or a house or a group, and the Bible does not condemn normality. Still, our everyday life is rooted in God, and His nature defines our emotions. He has the right to define hatred, fondness, and routine.

Whenever the Bible talks about love, it invariably categorizes it as an extreme. Love is fierce; affection is gentle. Love is compassionate; fondness is sympathetic. True, gentleness and sympathy characterize God and we also are blessed with them, but love accomplishes great works that fondness never could.

Jesus offered no halfway love. We are to love God with all our heart, soul, mind, and strength. Jesus instructed us to love our neighbor *as ourselves*. Normal people usually give all for their personal self-interest; Heaven's kind of love gives all. Every Christian is to love other human beings with God's kind of love.

One evening, Steve and I (Melana) sat in a meeting with a trusted family friend. As minutes slid into hours, we slowly realized that this friend was not the loyal soul mate we had supposed but had willingly believed hurtful lies about us.

She seemed cruelly happy to "take us down" and gave no inkling of grief, compassion, or desire for restoration. As the meeting ended, we both were in stunned grief, as much from the realization that she did not love us as from the false accusation itself.

As the next few mornings arrived and I tried to pray for the woman and our situation, I realized that my love for her was dying. In fact, intense dislike was taking hold and consuming my attention. How could I claim to be a follower of the King of love and have such passionate feelings against a fellow (

Each morning before God, I began to unders\
my life I had never loved someone I did not trust. I fo

not do it. To me, love and trust were interdependent. I loved those I trusted, and I trusted those I loved. How could I love a Christian I knew could betray our friendship?

God's love for us does not have anything to do with His "trust" in us, and I came to realize that my way of loving was fundamentally different from His. Loving someone does not require that we trust him or her; in fact, that is irrelevant. I can be kind and patient toward a person without trusting him or her at all. The qualities of love listed in 1 Corinthians 13 describe the way God is in His essence, and they also describe the cognitive choices He makes concerning His response to our thoughts and actions. For the first time, I saw that I must love a person because of what I am (because of my reborn nature made in God's image), not because of what he or she is. This emotion did not feel like the "love" I had known in the past. This new, different emotion was born out of a desire to please the God I do love. God provided me with an "acceptable sacrifice" that pleased Him and helped me.

Love from "Spillage" Will Involve Thoughtful Interaction

Using an analogy with music theory, we can understand how relational interaction functions. Two kinds of music dominate the modern public arena. These two types of music are found in all countries but are dominant in Western music. Where the styles are not Western, the music still tends to fall into one of these two categories in varying degrees of sophistication.

The most familiar music to most peoples of the world is *homophony*. In homophony, a single melody dominates and all the other notes or parts support that main tune with harmonies and ⌐rds that suit the course of the melody. Popular songs might have an orchestral, guitar, or keyboard accompaniment that enhances the one prominent tune. Hymns might have a familiar soprano melody with the other parts helping it. A soloist singing with a choir or orchestra sings the lead while the other parts shore it up.

Polyphony, on the other hand, is made up of several melodies sounding at once, with each melody helping all the others. The melodies might intertwine or they might maintain a restricted note range, but each retains its identity as a true melody on its own. (Monophony, or a solo melody without accompaniment, no longer has the prominence it once had, except in Gregorian chant and other specialized kinds of music.) Three hundred years ago, most music was polyphonic. Today only composers of serious music write polyphony; we rarely hear it in the popular arena.

Polyphony is composed in such a manner that the melodies, although able to stand alone, contribute to one another when played or sung together. They create harmonies in interaction. The musical pleasure originates in the weaving of the fabric. Attending to several melodies at once requires intelligence and concentration. Composing polyphony involves even more careful attention to detail.

In creating us, God never intended that we be "soloists," with all others at our disposal. Among His people, especially, God is writing polyphony. This is not to say that each individual "melody" (person) may not be a strikingly beautiful "tune." Neither does it imply that the "tunes" could not stand alone in their individual perfection. God's writing of all of us in polyphony means that all the "melodies" contribute to a grander music, a totality not possible without thoughtful interaction.

God intended not only that each "melody" be beautiful in

itself but that it contribute to other "melodies" He writes. This may mean that if He wants a certain "chord" to help the alto, the tenor or soprano will need to fit into that "chord." It may signify that if He wants one person's "melody" to go up temporarily, another's melody will help it by temporarily going down. If all our purposes suit only our desire for our own "melody" (our life-course), then we are not paying attention to how our "melody" will, in God's design, help another's "tune" or His purpose for that person's life.

Our purpose in life cannot exclude the larger purpose God has for all His people. More important, God's purposes for His people will include our contribution in the light of a bigger plan than we can perceive on our own. While the church and the kingdom will have leaders, God loves (and uses) those fulfilling the lower positions just as much as He does the prominent members.

The members stand in two dangers. The leaders may come to feel that they really are "soloists" and that others do not have their own peculiar usefulness. A true leader under God understands how much he or she needs the other "melodies." In polyphony, the soprano *needs* the bass. Alone, she sings only a solitary tune; in God's design, she makes up part of a grander fabric than she is able to hear alone. The grandeur of God's design cannot come from the soprano but from the soprano's function among the interweaving melodies. The glory shows forth from the texture of the total.

The second danger is that those in inferior positions sometimes denigrate their own role in the polyphony. This attitude arises from our inability to appreciate the importance of the larger picture. In an Oriental rug, every thread is important. No thread can boast above another thread. The weaving of effective polyphony depends on many *important* individual parts. God attends to each part of the picture making up a whole. Each part helps Him achieve a larger purpose than one part can comprehend.

Our part, therefore, is not to design our life but to cooperate. We feel neither pride nor shame in our position. We respond to God's call and leading, always bearing in mind that His larger design may seem incomprehensible from our present situation. None of us will abandon his or her "soloist" mentality unless he or she trusts the great Designer completely. Vertical trust also comes before horizontal trust.

We will love our neighbors when we understand their value to God. If we love them, we enhance their work, glorify God's purpose for them, and give ourselves to them unselfishly. Unselfishness becomes reasonable when we understand the greatness of God's plan for all of us. Heaven's view of His people does not mean that we understand how they function in the polyphony; Heaven's view means we joyfully help each of them achieve God's purpose.

THE CONTEXTS OF OUR EARTHLY LOVE FOR ONE ANOTHER

Just as our love for God manifests itself in reciprocity, our love for our brothers and sisters in Christ inevitably shows itself in interaction. Both vertical and horizontal mutuality demand a context in which relationships can be exercised. The reciprocity of the relationship will mean nothing outside of context.

The oldest *earthly* context in which these relationships exist is the family. Family development has been treated widely in many books and conferences. The marriage context also was instituted at the creation of humans. Abraham's friendship with God shows that the friendship context can be vertical. David and Jonathan demonstrated a horizontal friendship with godly qualities. In all these contexts, the earthly pleasures of companionship are enhanced by godly love.

God created the family, marriage, and friendship, and these relationships require reciprocity. However, they retain certain joys peculiar to earth. The earthly contexts are not immortal in themselves, but we will carry certain contexts into eternity as they related to the kingdom and the church.

Because the two of us are not eschatologists, we cannot treat the coming kingdom (Revelation 11:15), although we anticipate it joyfully. Here we speak of the kingdom in terms of God's sovereignty over His own creation and, especially, of His reign in the hearts of His people. We concern ourselves with how His rule functions among His own at present.

The Bible appoints two contexts of relationship that are divine and eternal. We will exercise relationship forever in these two God-ordained affiliations: the kingdom and the church. In both the kingdom and the church, we express the vertical and the horizontal relationships.

The Context of the Kingdom

The kingdom of God existed from the foundation of the earth and is eternal (Psalm 10:16; 145:13; Hebrews 1:8). It exhibits the sovereignty of God (1 Chronicles 29:11) and is glorious (Psalm 145:12). Jesus manifested the kingdom in His coming (Matthew 4:17). The kingdom is where the King is: among us. He declared that it was not of this world (John 18:36) and we are now immortal. Although it will come in its supremacy later, it also exists at the present time (Mark 10:14; Colossians 1:12-13). Currently, it continues growing inexorably (Luke 13:19).

Only in the *kingdom* can nobility arise. Heavenly nobility differs radically from earthly peerage, which depends on rank or station. Nobility in Christ's kingdom does not derive from position but from character. Becoming common, acting cheaply, or speaking vulgarly does not befit the nobility of heaven. We exhibit all His regal forgiveness, all His kingly beneficence, all His majestic view of life—Heaven's view. As royalty within that kingdom, we pray and work assiduously for the lordship of Christ (His ultimate nobility) on this earth.

Earthly kingdoms function by laws; Christ's kingdom functions by principles. We begin here by examining three neglected but pertinent principles. (Two principles that are far more important will be introduced in chapter 12.) These principles are given at this point because they will recur repeatedly throughout this book and will need to be applied in a number of contexts.

The kingdom principle of compounding. Both sin and virtue compound or increase themselves (James 3:16). We grow and the kingdom grows by this principle. When Moses was shown favor, he asked for more favor (Exodus 33:13). In the kingdom parable of the minas, Jesus said, "I tell you that *to everyone who has, more shall be given*, but from the one who does not have, even what he does have shall be taken away" (Luke 19:26, emphasis added). The thinking Christian seizes every advantage God gives him or her. "Seek the LORD while He may be found; call upon Him while He is near" (Isaiah 55:6). Kingdom growth by compounding or personal growth in nobility cannot happen in a vacuum. Compounding requires the help of others in God's kingdom. Paul's letters to the churches and individuals facilitated their growth (and many others since).

The kingdom principle of potential. We can do far more than we think we can. God told Jeremiah not to call himself a child (Jeremiah 1:7). Jesus expected Nicodemus to understand more than he did (John 3:10-12). He rebuked the disciples for not understanding His reference to the leaven of the Pharisees (Mark 8:14-21). He expected Philip to understand more than he expressed (John 14:9). Jesus chided Cleopas for being slow of heart to believe what the prophets had spoken (Luke 24:25). The Lord is pleased when we learn, "Blessed are you, Simon Barjona, because flesh and blood did not reveal this to you, but My Father who is in heaven" (Matthew 16:17). The kingdom does not advance but is retarded by our timidity in using God's gifts and help. Again and again, God and His people help us realize our gifts. We need vertical and horizontal prodding and assistance — relationship again.

The kingdom principle of forward movement. Paul grasped this thoroughly: "Not that I have already obtained it or have already become perfect, but I press on so that I may lay hold of that for which also I was laid hold of by Christ Jesus" (Philippians 3:12). People in process cannot look back (verse 13). They cannot even pause at success. All sin is retrogression. If we fall, God will pick us up (Psalm 145:14); once should be enough for any sin if we are sensitive to God's Spirit. The kingdom must move in only one direction: ahead. But we do not progress alone. Our song is "Onward, Christian Soldiers." An army functions only with relationships acting in concert.

The Context of the Church

The church, unlike the kingdom in existence from eternity, began at Pentecost. She holds the lofty position of the bride of Christ (2 Corinthians 11:2; see also Ephesians 5:25-32). Any normal bride anticipates her wedding joyfully and carefully plans for it. She desires to be chaste and to be lovely for her bridegroom. She longs for more intimacy with the beloved. If Christ is important to us, His bride matters too. We execute our role in her preparation for her wedding by means of our wills and our choices within the context of the church.

The church is universal (Matthew 16:18; Ephesians 1:22-23) with a local expression (Revelation 1–3). Paul called the universal church the "body" of Christ (Colossians 1:18) and the local Corinthian church "the temple of God" (1 Corinthians 3:17). The majority of us work most effectively in the local expression but, like Paul, we may exert ourselves for the larger body as well.

The church forms an assembly at work; the kingdom consists of individuals ruled by God. In the church, we are members of a body; in the kingdom, we are citizens of a government. The church is a bride; the kingdom is a domain. Mutuality characterizes both.

The church was immediate, though it grows; God completes the kingdom in process. We are to pray for its coming (Matthew 6:10). The church is an outer expression; the kingdom is realized inwardly. The church is visible; the kingdom is invisible. The church performs assigned actions; its emphasis is *doing* (Ephesians 3:10). The kingdom exists in a certain kind of *being*. The church has a role in bringing the kingdom. The kingdom helps the growth of the church and helps define its nature. Even the church and the kingdom function in mutuality with each other.

The locally manifested church can fall (Sardis, Revelation 3:1; Laodicea, Revelation 3:14-19). The kingdom cannot fall (Psalm 145:13; Hebrews 1:8). Many churches try to get into the world, and the world in turn infiltrates the church. The world cannot penetrate the kingdom. One way of helping the church remain chaste and virginal is to apply the three kingdom principles on pages 81–82 and the two in chapter 12.

Churches also relate to one another (Acts 15:22; Romans 16:5,16) just as persons within the church relate. The latter relationship has order: God designates specific offices for the church (1 Corinthians 12:28; Ephesians 4:11-12). Kingdom nobility, on the other hand, will not be declared until judgment (Revelation 22:12).

In Heaven's view, we cannot exclude any person from the church except on rare scriptural grounds of unrepented, active sin. Exclusion is the enemy of reciprocity by the nature of what godly reciprocity is. Heaven's view includes all races, cultures, intellects, and stations in life. Heaven loves all human beings made in the image of God.

God places eternal relationships for us within the context of the church and of the kingdom. In the church, we love one another, work together, and spread the gospel. In the kingdom, we adore our king and gratefully appreciate all those who are trying to establish His lordship. Heaven's view puts godly love into the context of *every* human relationship, but of all these, we will treasure only the kinship within the church and the kingdom forever.

CHAPTER 4

Seeing Glory from a New Viewpoint

We are no longer to be children, tossed here and there by waves and carried about by every wind of doctrine . . . but speaking the truth in love, we are to grow up in all aspects into Him who is the head, even Christ.

EPHESIANS 4:14-15

The two of us are not mystics and are not usually inclined to unusual experiences. Our daily prayers are normally somewhat arduous, if joyful, and we concentrate intensely to pray for those things that will bring Christ's kingdom. However, I (T. W.) once had a dream so different from any other experience of my life that, although it happened in October of 1973, I did not share publicly about it for twenty-five years. I have felt reluctant to share such a private experience but believe that now God has released me to describe parts of it.

THE OUTER GLORIES OF HEAVEN
God's Gift of Our Bodily Senses
Sometimes while I dream, I become so aware of the fantastic nature of the events that I inform myself even in the dream, "This

is a dream. It is not real." Most of my dreams do not have color and I am unaware of bodily senses such as sound or touch. However, the 1973 dream had the flavor of reality; the memory of it is far more vivid than any other dream of my life. In fact, no conscious memory stands out like the events of that dream. In it, my body's senses were more acute than they are when I am awake. Sight, sound, and touch were more vivid than any other memory. The sensations from the senses in the dream remain sharper than anything else I can recollect except where I note below.

In the dream, the Lord Jesus came to me and announced, "I am going to take you to deep space." He did not say He was taking me to heaven, but, although I did not understand, I dared not question Him because of who He was. He took me to a place vastly different from anything I had ever seen on earth. It seemed to be a definite locale with a specific environment and identifiable entities, such as flowers. I do not remember the mode of transportation, but I remember the arrival.

For years I have struggled to find words to articulate the indescribable. The beauty there surpassed any beauty I had ever seen. I had never seen this kind of magnificence; I had never imagined what splendor could be. It somehow touched every sense in my body in a strange interworking between my faculties. I have not yet found words to convey the mere *physical* aspects of the dream.

Every detail in that place was a masterpiece and surrounded me.

No Rubens, Bach, or Shakespeare could have possibly approximated what, all around me, had to be glory that no human could create. If I had had breath *consciously* (I don't think I was aware of breath, but I had some kind of definite bodily senses), I would have held that breath suspended among these inexpressible wonders. No earthly light could match that kind of light. I do not know how, but I seemed to see as though I had never seen before and also to take in most of it.

The most physically unusual aspect of the experience consisted of the colors—colors that did not exist on earth. I saw flowers in colors far more dazzling than any crimson I had ever seen in this world. Others were pastels more delicate than any pink or violet we see here. In spite of the wide range of color, the ensemble blended into works of art unlike any I have seen in the Louvre or the Prado. In some strange way, my entire body participated in the sublime details of those masterworks. My senses cooperated to engulf me in sheer pleasure.

However, the strongest impression of the dream came through the eyes of the Lord Jesus. The expression in His eyes overwhelmed me. They emitted an unsurpassable beauty, to be sure, but that was not the root of the impression. The power of His eyes surpassed the strength of any force I had seen on earth. Still, even that inexorable strength did not strike me like one other quality I had ever seen or encountered before. His eyes poured forth the mightiest and yet most tender love I had ever imagined.

Somehow Jesus' eyes fulfilled every need I had ever experienced in my life. All my previous needs would never again be as essential as I thought they were. I realized that I had never wanted anything but Him, and I have never wanted anything else since. At that moment, He seemed to be fulfilling every ambition, every desire, every need I had ever had—just *Him* in His incomparable, transcendent love.

Other events happened in the dream that I do not feel free to share, but the Lord has now allowed me to tell you as much as I have just described. Apparently, the time has come for those beauties and splendors to have meaning for my brothers and sisters in

Christ, and He now wants me to share them. I do not know all His purposes in giving me that experience, but I hope to share the little that I understand.

When I awoke, it was the middle of the night. I realized it had been a dream, but it did not smack of the phantasmal to me. I am not accustomed to dreaming in color, but the realities of those incredible colors clung to me. I was able to recall them and "see" them in my mind's eye for about half an hour. Awake, I still reveled in their glory. Then they began to fade. I struggled in my bed to get them back, but the fading continued. For all these years, I have longed to see those colors again, but no amount of effort will summon them back. I have wondered not only if I saw a situation different from any earthly place but also if God temporarily *gifted* me with unusual senses to "take in" what natural endowments cannot assimilate. My current perceptual apparatus and my mental equipment cannot handle what I briefly saw.

However, I can recall those penetrating eyes. If I had grasped the meaning of beauty or strength before, I certainly never had imagined the degree of love I saw in Jesus' indescribable eyes. That love overwhelmed me, captured me, and changed my life forever. I knew when I perceived that love that He would "do anything for me" (like going to a Roman cross) and I would do whatever He asked.

The Super Senses of Coming Outer Glories

Our eyes see a remarkably tiny portion of the enormous spectrum of light (or electromagnetic radiation) that instruments can register. Color results from the length of the light wave, which can be extremely long or almost immeasurably short. Of all those waves, the longest light wave we can perceive in the visible spectrum is red. After the red, in order of decreasing length, our eyes can distinguish orange, yellow, green, blue, and indigo, and then our faculties stop functioning after violet.

Below the red, the next longer group of waves is infrared, invisible to our eyes. Below the infrared waves come microwaves and then, the longest of all, radio waves. Modern instruments can utilize all these long waves, but our eyes are not designed to see them.

Above the violet, the next shortest waves are ultraviolet. Ultraviolet waves burn the skin; if we could see them, we might avoid many an uncomfortable sunburn. Shorter than ultraviolet are the X-rays, so potent that they will penetrate most matter except extremely dense materials, such as heavy metals. Even shorter than X-rays are the extremely powerful gamma rays.

All these waves exist on our planet in some degree; some are generated naturally on earth, but they originate mainly in the sun. However, they are produced in great profusion best in deep space—in neutron stars, gamma-ray bursts, supernovae, quasars, and other phenomenal sources of energy. Even if we were close to them, our present eyes could not see light waves in those spectra. God made us with limited perceptual tools to use in this life.

However, God has promised us a new body (1 Corinthians 15:35-44). In our present bodies, we cannot see the radio waves below our visible spectrum or the gamma rays above it. But who knows what unimaginable new equipment we might have in our new bodies? Who can imagine what kind of luminous colors might regale our new eyes if we could *see* the entire spectrum? For that matter, what if God were to create new laws of nature and physics even more wondrous than our present ones?

God limited our present range of hearing also. We are able to perceive sound waves only in a narrow spectrum. Elephants and whales are able to hear long waves below our capacity to hear.

Bats and dogs can hear short sound waves above our hearing range. Imagine a new hearing mechanism that could allow our brain to register sound waves far beyond our present capacity! What kind of music might lie in our future? What if music did not even rely on sound waves in order to be communicated? The possibilities stagger the imagination.

God did not have to give us taste buds. Some animals do not have them; earthworms have no sense organs except the sense of touch. God could have so made us that we would eat instinctively in order to preserve life. But because God also wanted us to *enjoy* the act of eating, He created our extraordinarily sensitive taste buds. Not only that, God gave us bananas! And nutmeg, salt, peaches, and lemons! When Jesus ate in His resurrection body (Luke 24:42-43), He probably enjoyed the fish more than He did in His natural body. Our senses enable us to relate to our environment—to danger, gravity, heat, and many factors around us. Scientists have been able to isolate approximately twenty senses, yet the senses' extraordinary usefulness does not spell the end of their utility: They also make our environment pleasurable and even exciting. God wants us to enjoy surviving.

We are treating at this point the glories we appropriate when we attain the final goal of our life process. Some arrive at it in death, in heaven. Some will reach it at the second coming of Christ. In this chapter, all these terms—*heaven, eternity, Graduation Day*—refer to our final arrival at all we have aspired for, however we reach it. What we are talking about is arrival at the goal, using various terms in this chapter.

Our present senses and present environment hint strongly at future physical perfections beyond conception. Now we have gardenias, sunsets, lakes, and cinnamon. We have Mozart, Goethe, Rembrandt, Michelangelo, and the human brain. If *these* wonders pass description, in eternity surely we will need some kind of mind and perceptual equipment presently impossible to envisage. God plans for us super senses, probably more of them, and possibly an interworking of the senses not now imaginable. The world around us and the stars beyond us whisper that anticipating our new senses, our new mind, and the different environment should bless every waking moment. Yet the physical features are only the outer glories.

THE INNER, GREATER GLORIES
The Image of Christ
Although all humans are made in the image of God, most of us do not act like it. We have already mentioned the ugly perversions current in our world. From Heaven's view, most of us in this world become repulsive while passing through our life course. We came into the world in God's *general* image and very early spoiled it. However, that undeveloped image was transformed into a being more delightful to Heaven when we accepted Christ. Heaven *wants* to view us growing in the image of Christ.

In receiving Him, we took the first giant step toward the glory God made us for. Christ now lives within us, and when the heavenly Father looks at us, He primarily sees His magnificent Son. God no doubt enjoys the physical beauties He created, but far more beautiful to Him is the glory of Christ within us. We follow a radically different road once Christ begins living His life in us. Now we are not merely in the image of God, universal among humans, but we are being further conformed to that image in the revealed specifics demonstrated by His Son.

We are *created* in the image of God and then *conformed* to the image of Christ (Romans 8:29). In this image, we begin with glory and then ascend from glory to glory. Even if we do not appreciate inner beauties, the image of Christ in us is far more glorious from Heaven's view than any outer, physical perfection.

The ultimate glory we are moving toward was intended for humans only, not for angels. The angels carry messages and serve God authoritatively, but they do not bear the image of Christ. The Bible does not speak of angels as being partakers of Christ nor as sharing kinship with Him. Hebrews 2:10-13 puts the redeemed into close kinship with the second person of the Trinity:

> It was fitting for Him, for whom are all things, and through whom are all things, in bringing many sons to glory, to perfect the author of their salvation through sufferings. For both He who sanctifies and those who are sanctified *[being* sanctified — process again] are all from one Father; for which reason He is not ashamed to call them brethren, saying, "I WILL PROCLAIM YOUR NAME TO MY BRETHREN, IN THE MIDST OF THE CONGREGATION I WILL SING YOUR PRAISE." And again, "I WILL PUT MY TRUST IN HIM." And again, "BEHOLD, I AND THE CHILDREN WHOM GOD HAS GIVEN ME."

Once we accept Christ, we become sons and daughters of God. "As many as received Him, to them He gave the right to become children of God, even to those who believe in His name" (John 1:12). This does not mean we are on a par with Christ. He remains eternally divine, and we live under His lordship. But it does mean that we have the privileges of children and regard God as our true Father. We can ask for what an offspring would ask for. We express love for Him explicitly in these new kinships. We conform to Christ's image because family members do that. Their "genes" dictate resemblance.

Being in Christ's image tells us that we are to go far beyond the image of God we were born with. First of all, now we are becoming purely spiritual beings. Prior to our new life, we were dominated by the physical world. We had appetites and urges that originated in our old nature or in our body. Now new wants and longings delight our spirits. As we seek fulfillment of these new hungers, God feeds them with His Son, the Bread of Life. Christ's spirituality dominates more and more of our nature.

Parenthetically, we receive help from Christ because He took our nature into His being in the Incarnation. When Jesus came, a human body was born, killed, resurrected, and ascended. "There is one . . . mediator also between God and men, the man Christ Jesus" (1 Timothy 2:5). Jesus' eternal humanity indicates to us God's original intention for humanity. We make His humanity-spirituality the goal of our process.

Second, that process will require continuing and constant renewal. "Glory to glory" cannot be progression unless we are sloughing off the old (that is, the old man) and adding new (to us) aspects of Christ. "Glory to glory" becomes more and more of Him.

Finally, being conformed to the image of Christ means that our moral character becomes increasingly like His. Everybody has some kind of morality, even Catherine the Great and Hitler. Morality consists of a standard of righteousness. Christ's nature establishes our permanent standard of right and wrong.

The Greater Glories Are Within Us

The character of Christ defines the greater glories God wants within us. The traits of His character developing within us thrill Heaven far more than the possible outer splendors I described in my dream. These greater glories develop us into the nobility we will enjoy when we reign with Him. Heaven concentrates on the inner qualities.

All these qualities are embryonic in us as a result of the new birth. We had certain latent qualities in our natural birth: our IQ, talents, and natural bents. As we grew, we had to develop all our innate abilities by a process of education. We had to learn to speak, read, handle arithmetic, and understand the meaning of history. In the same way, our dormant infant spiritual faculties grow with education and proper exposure.

We can have and develop these inner qualities now, before Graduation Day. The outer glories of new colors and senses (not defined in Scripture) await us, but the greater character traits are available to us now. We do not merely earn them for later reward; we grow them now through the choices we make. They glorify God even in this life.

We may divide these optimal inner qualities into two groups: (1) those God takes primary responsibility for and (2) those we are responsible for learning and developing with His help. Because God's work comes first, we base the latter, our responsibilities, on the perfections that God is responsible for. The qualities God puts into us by means of our new inner Christ are either attributes or a result of the attributes. An attribute is inherent, permanent, and not likely to shift with circumstances.

God gives us two attributes in Christ: righteousness and holiness. We inevitably also radiate glory from these two gifts. They stay a permanent part of us because Jesus is in us. These attributes of Christ remain our permanent birthright.

Satan cannot diminish them or inhibit them, but we can refuse to grow in them. Satan can influence us, but he cannot touch our birthright. We guard against his influence on our behavior or thoughts, not against the threat of losing our birthright.

God's intention is that every believer in Christ remain inherently righteous, holy, and glorious forever. Whether we show it or not, we retain 100 percent of these qualities every step of the way. However, a baby's 100 percent is less than a mature person's 100 percent. As our spiritual stature grows, Christ has more of us to fill.

Yet we can hinder our growth. We inhibit our growth in these attributes by failing to define them and understand them. The world defines them negatively, and therefore we often follow suit. The world views these attributes in the light of what they are not. We define righteousness in terms of behavior; it is abstaining from sin. Holiness is separation from the world. Heaven views these attributes so positively that their definiteness is more solid than platinum.

We can grasp the nature of these attributes by looking at how they operate in God. Most people talk about righteousness as though it were an autonomous standard of "right and wrong." If so, God has to adhere to a standard independent of Himself. Righteousness is the rightness of God's essential, original nature.

Obviously, God does not strain to abstain from sin — the negative definition. God's positive righteousness is not defined by His behavior but by His being. God's righteousness is His unmitigated freedom to be Himself. He has never changed His essential nature. Behavior results from His being; He can act only in concord with His perfect nature.

Whatever God does, He does freely with no constraint except

human will. He acts out of the wholeness of absolute, ultimate wisdom. Every divine work in the Bible manifested right-minded holiness that was unstoppable (Psalm 145:17). Nothing could hinder Him from delivering the Israelites from Egypt or returning them from Babylon. He voluntarily became man and died for our sins. The Cross demonstrated at once His liberty, sovereignty, and righteousness.

When we *try* to adhere to an autonomous standard, we fail. Our righteousness results from a new freedom to conform to the character of God — to the Christ now within us. We engross our minds in Him (Hebrews 12:1-2). We become like what we admire. The better we know Him, the more we become like Him.

Most of us think of Christ in one of two places: in Israel two thousand years ago, or on a throne high in heaven distant from us. We find Him easy to admire there. We need to pray that God will reveal to us and make us fully understand the Christ presently within us. He is knowable here.

Three translations of Psalm 29:2 are possible. The Amplified Bible compromises with the two most frequently used translations of this passage: "in the beauty of holiness or in holy array." The NIV has "in the splendor of his holiness." The Spanish Bible agrees with the KJV: "in the beauty of holiness" ("en la hermosura de la santidad," *Santa Biblia* [Buenos Aires, Sociedades Bíblicas en America Latina], 1960). The French Bible has the third possibility: "in His magnificent sanctuary" ("dans son sanctuaire magnifique," *La Sainte Bible*, revue sur les originaux par David Martin, Brussels, Societé Biblique Britannique et Étrangére, 1866). Harris, Archer, and Waltke affirm the definitive

idea: "The major emphasis is on the Lord and His appearance"
(R. Laird Harris, Gleason L. Archer Jr., and Bruce K. Waltke, eds.,
Theological Wordbook of the Old Testament, vol. 1 [Chicago:
Moody, 1980], 208).

God's holiness cannot come negatively by separating Himself
from the world. He was holy before the world was unholy. God's
holiness is the perfection of beauty. When we "give unto the
LORD . . . in the beauty of holiness" (Psalm 29:2, KJV), we are
adoring the original holiness before all time.

Our holiness grows as we are freed from this world to conform
increasingly to God's otherness. God meant for all of life to be
sacred; the spiritual Christian sees it that way—indeed, in the
midst of distracting ignobility. Many of us taint our everyday
activities with perversion; we corrupt our talk with superfluity or
exaggeration, our food with gluttony, our cravings with satiety,
our appearance with pride or shame. But God meant for our conversation, food, appetites, and looks to be holy. *love Him*

However, our holiness goes beyond mere separation. In
heaven, there will be no evil from which to sever ourselves. There
God will see our holiness as our beauty, the beauty of Christ in
us. But if our beauty will be our holiness there, it has to be our
holiness here. Therefore, every detail of life—parking our cars,
disciplining our children, sitting down to a meal—is sacred here
and consequently beautiful to God. We cannot be pure while
we pray and impure while we drive down the highway.

Jesus' everyday life was utterly pure. Every thought was clean,
every talk fruitful, every meal enjoyable without indulgence. If
God and His purposes permeate every activity and if self-centeredness does not violate the goodness of God's gifts, our lives

will be wholesome and satisfying. Life that flows unceasingly from God blesses, refreshes, helps others, and glorifies its giver. It is beautiful.

God's glory shows as the bright splendor of His majesty. It is the aura radiating from the sum total of all that He is. Three disciples saw it in the transfiguration (Matthew 17:2). Our perception depends on the proper light (Psalm 36:9). No shadow can darken anything in the light that is Christ. Commoners will shun such revealing illumination, such stately regality (John 3:19-20), but we are not commoners (John 3:21). God has designated us the nobility of His creation. We rejoice only in the light of His glory (Revelation 19:7).

Our glory shows when the Christ within radiates outwardly. The older artists depicted this as a halo around the heads of saints. The aura of Christ should be the main emanation from all His followers. Jesus designated us "the light of the world" (Matthew 5:14). After this startling announcement, He warned us not to cloak the light (verse 15) and declared that if we exhibit the light, we would glorify the Father in heaven (verse 16).

We fail when we appropriate the glory for ourselves. We possess it more when we direct it to its source—that is, when we have the wisdom and technique to deflect all glory to God. Only He stays forever worthy of that attribution.

How We Acquire the Attributes

The attributes of righteousness, holiness, and the resulting glory are bestowed on us in the new birth. God imputes them to us (Romans 4:6,23-24; 5:19); He puts them in us. We do not earn or develop them. We do not do anything at all other than accept the Christ in whom they are whole. Imputation cannot be a human work; it can be only a divine work.

God gives us righteousness, holiness, and glory in the same way that He gives us our IQ and our natural talents. The latter were determined in conception, and the former were determined in our spiritual conception. Like our natural aptitudes, our spiritual attributes can grow and develop. We are responsible for at least part of their progress.

Our first job is to reckon the work God has done (Romans 6:11). The term *reckon* is a mathematical term; we calculate or consider as certain the work God says is His. Satan can affect mood; he suggests doubt. He cannot argue with reckoning, a cognitive act. Cognition can ignore mood.

A fiat is a command that is executed instantly and cannot be contravened. The attributes arrive as the fiat of God. They do not develop gradually; they come in fullness, although they can grow. The authority for the fiat is almighty God.

Satan cannot quarrel with the legal fact of God's work in us. In the deepest valleys of our various cancers, the two of us relied heavily on the judicial declaration of God that current moods had nothing to do with our righteousness or holiness or glory in the Lord. Our birthright is just that: a lawful right.

These qualities are ours by virtue of our position. Not only are we positioned in the family of God but He has "seated us with Him in the heavenly places in Christ Jesus" (Ephesians 2:6). Therefore, we must have Heaven's view. Any other perspective is out of place.

These attributes are indwelt and are basic to all God will do with the rest of our lives. The Father first and primarily sees in us His gift to us of the indwelling Christ. Our Father will proceed with our development only on the basis of Jesus' righteousness, holiness, and glory.

The Virtues We Are Responsible for Developing

As opposed to gifting us with inherent attributes, God places in our hands other virtues that we are responsible for emphasizing and learning. We can raise these to whatever level we please and are willing to pay the price for. God holds us accountable for their stature as we grow and as we arrive at Graduation Day. We are daily choosing the glories we will carry into eternity.

These virtues arrive not full-fledged like the attributes but rather in such infant stature that growing them intimidates most Christians. We do not start at ground zero; we are developing the Christ Jesus who is in us from the time of our acceptance of Christ. Still, the New Testament injunctions about these qualities place their manifestation squarely on our shoulders.

We are responsible for magnifying these virtues as opposed to the bestowed attributes. We acquire the attributes directly from God for eternity; they endure into our next life in the same essence that they have now. The virtues, on the other hand, earn huge interest as we cultivate them.

Humility. None of these virtues is easy. We begin with the most rare and perhaps difficult. Jesus said the following words two thousand years ago; they have been the least believed and practiced of all His teaching. Even today, they are ignored more than anything else He said. Jesus asserted, "Many who are first will be last; and the last, first" (Matthew 19:30). Later, after their quarrel about kingdom rank, Jesus told the disciples, "Whoever wishes to become great among you shall be your servant, and whoever wishes to be first among you shall be your slave" (20:26-27).

Humility goes against the grain of our old nature more than any other virtue. Few of us see the value of this quality. It doesn't get you anywhere—except with God. Only Heaven's view can supply any worth to lowliness. God's perspective, in the light of

worldly opinion, startles us: "I dwell on a high and holy p
and also with the contrite and lowly of spirit in order to reviv
the spirit of the lowly and to revive the heart of the contrite"
(Isaiah 57:15).

We once knew a young man who was quite limited intel-
lectually. Unable to support himself, he lived meagerly, from
hand to mouth. But he loved our Lord as totally as anyone we
had ever known. He could not teach in the church or take the
offering. But he voluntarily went from room to room, gathering
trash and cleaning without salary. Suddenly one day we understood his incredible heart and saw the purity in his eyes. From
that day forward, we tried with all our hearts to honor that
"majestic one" of God.

Each of us is a single part of a large polyphony (many melodies
helping each other). Only in our humility can God orchestrate
His polyphony. Pride demands that its own "melody" be paramount, or at least important. The church cannot function without leadership, but leadership is only one role in the polyphony.
When one "melody" must have its own arrogant way, the music
becomes homophony (all notes help one main melody), the Devil's
way. In good polyphony, the melodies do not simply submit to one
another; they cooperate and enhance one another.

As we have struggled with this important issue, the two of us
have found help in deliberately appreciating the roles of the other
"melodies" in God's polyphony. We have even learned to enjoy
elevating them to their proper roles. At judgment, we will be
shocked to discover (finally) what God considers great.

...understood clearly the importance of the two
...nts:

- ...nandment (love God above all else): "I said to
  ...'You are my Lord; I have no good besides You'"
  (Psalm 16:2).
- Second Commandment (love your neighbor as yourself):
  "As for the saints who are in the earth, they are the
  majestic ones in whom is all my delight" (verse 3).

"The majestic ones" includes every one of God's children,
even those whose station in life appears to be very lowly. Choosing
the humble shows greatness. David's choices indicate his deference
to the down-and-out. He befriended Mephibosheth and Abner
and married Abigail. Jesus went even further by choosing the
twelve disciples, Mary Magdalene, Zacchaeus, and many more.
Jesus chose humility graciously; we can achieve it only with effort.

Faith. Humility is the *condition* of our relationship with God;
faith is the *basis*. Actually, any genuine relationship is based on
faith. Those coming to God must believe in His reality and His
availability (Hebrews 11:6). God will clearly reveal Himself to
anyone willing to believe. In our experience, unbelief has usually
been willful. The refusal to believe usually grows out of resolute sin.

The Christian who wants to believe should prove God for
himself or herself. The Quran strictly forbids questioning Allah
under painful warnings of harsh punishment (Quran 2:1-10;
3:19-74; 4:114-124; 6:15-30; 14:88-99), but the God of Christ
invites us to test Him (Joshua 24:15; Malachi 3:10; Matthew 9:28;
John 9:35-38). Jesus repeatedly invited faith (John 10:38; 14:1,14).
Because He created and redeemed us, He Himself wants His
creation to act on His promises.

Three other virtues we are reluctant to ask God for are endurance, patience, and long-suffering. In truth, we do not need to pray for them! If we are willing, God Himself will provide the opportunities to grow in such difficult challenges, and then God assists us in realizing their fullness in our lives.

Dozens of times, the New Testament enjoins virtues we can demonstrate by an act of the will: joy, peace, power, knowledge, goodness, self-control, and sobriety, to name a few. Each is within our reach, and each requires thoughtful effort. Jesus had all of them wholly and perfectly, and we are realizing His person in our daily walk.

Temporal and Eternal Virtues

We will not carry some of the virtues past Graduation Day in their present form. Some of the virtues occupy us mainly within the present life, in time. When we take them into eternity, they will be ennobled in forms not available to us now. God had to spell them out in terms of our confinement in time so they could be transmuted into eternal graces when we sit on our thrones and wear our crowns. The world cannot see the virtues' final, transmuted form, so we demonstrate Christ to the world in their temporal form.

Within time, we need *faith*. We need it now because it is the present "assurance of things hoped for, the conviction of things not *seen*" —*yet* (Hebrews 11:1, emphasis added). The reality exists in our spiritual minds, not in our physical eyes. Every decision, every action, every thought at present must be based in that certainty that faith gives.

We will carry faith into eternity, but there it will transcend its present shortcomings when God provides a wondrous new estate: Faith becomes magnificent *realization*. We will need no "conviction of things not seen." Our present faith needs to be as solid as the grand facts still lying in our future. In Melana's cancer, God provided a solid choice for us. When one goes through critical testing, the spiritual looms large and the material seems inconsequential. It may require struggle, but spiritual reality can be more concrete than physical reality for the truly willing mind.

Also confined to time, we need *hope*. Hope will take a different form in eternity: *joy*. After our arrival in heaven, if we are waiting for the appearance of the King, the anticipation will itself be pure delight, with no tinge of uncertainty. (We doubt that we will "wait" much in heaven.) We will later take hope with us into a higher form, but its mode there cannot be compared to the present insubstantial wish that most Christians call "hope." All qualities in heaven will be so potent that our earthly vocabulary falls short of describing them.

Endurance, patience, and *longsuffering* are temporal virtues. Who or what will frazzle our nerves in eternity? We need these virtues now because they develop in us the lasting attributes of *immutability* and *faithfulness*. (Parenthetically, immutability might not have the exact meaning it does in this life. Its primary meaning in eternity may include the dynamism described in chapter 12. Certainly, it will include an inability to fall or sin.) The testing that produces these three virtues results in eternal attributes.

Gentleness will assume a higher form in eternity than it has now. At this point, gentleness is a kind of courtesy, but that courtesy will go into eternity as a grace we are not equipped to exercise on earth. If you were to have an audience with the queen of England, you would have to be trained in the proper protocol. Can most of us imagine what kind of etiquette would be observed if the queen of Spain were to visit the queen of England? In heaven, meeting another king or queen will be delightful in the indescribable sensitivity we will then have for our fellows under Christ. Earthly gentleness will become *heavenly courtesy*, full of joy in one another.

We will not need *self-control* in heaven as a deterrent to sin. What temptation could we have to resist there? What discipline would be necessary for perfected saints? In our present milieu, we can deal with setbacks and worldly enticements only by practicing self-control. But all the temporal virtues are immortalized in higher form at the climax of our journey. Self-control will become sheer *goodness*.

Courage will not be a necessity for heaven's environment. There, God will reward courage by a *rest* that is a positive celebration, not a negative quiescence (Hebrews 6:11). All the people of God will enjoy a heavenly rest (4:1-10), but the welcome Jesus gives His martyrs goes beyond mere repose (Acts 7:56). Our earthly courage will become a new regal bearing.

Most of the other virtues available to us we will carry into eternity in their present temporal form. These include such obvious graces as humility, joy, peace, diligence, knowledge, and truth. These will not be transformed in kind but magnified in degree.

We realize the virtues in this chapter by consciously applying the three kingdom principles of the previous chapter: We compound them within time; the potential exists as glories even in our infancy; and we advance upward, never backward, with our eyes looking to Jesus for the next glories. We carry out these principles as an act of the will. They do not occur spontaneously; we are responsible. The glories require effort, and we practice them with intention. We must *choose* to be like Christ and show Him to the world. The world watches us. Only through us can they catch a glimpse of Heaven's view.

CHAPTER 5

Heaven's View Sees Christ in Us

*God willed to make known what is the riches of
the glory of this mystery among the Gentiles, which
is Christ in you, the hope of glory.*

COLOSSIANS 1:27

When God the Father looks at us, His first perception is His glorious Son within us (the *you* in Colossians 1:27 is plural), living out the vine life within the confines of time. Heaven views us as "little Christs," bringing the kingdom of God and demonstrating the glory of God to all our fellow humans. Most Christians see themselves as representatives of Christ with an occasional duty to show Him to others in whatever way Heaven makes available. Few of us see ourselves primarily in the light of Christ within us, not simply helping us but actually showing Himself to our world through us. Christ realizes His own person and intentions directly through us.

"As He is, so also are we in this world" (1 John 4:17). The Father sent the Son so we would grasp explicitly that part of God's nature that we can realize in ourselves. As Jesus incarnated God, we are to incarnate Jesus on our limited scale. Furthermore, we will bear His clear-cut likeness in eternity: "It has not appeared as yet what we will be. We know that when He appears, we will be like Him, because we will see Him just as He is" (3:2).

OUR STATURE DERIVES FROM THE INDWELLING CHRIST
The Manifestation of Christ in Us

We can have two reactions to such a promise. His great stature can cause us to ask, "How can a mortal become immortal? How can weakness participate in omnipotence? What about omnipresence?" and many similar ponderings. These misgivings are the most common and the most reasonable. We are so preoccupied with our present frailties and our sinful nature that 1 John 3:2 sounds like presumption. Our reservations here are sensible. They seem to suggest an irrational equality with Christ.

The second reaction is rare, but it has led to the gross false doctrine that we can be *equal* with Christ. The surprising number of adherents this interpretation engenders tells us how attractive this rank is to our old nature.

Likeness to Christ does not imply equality with Him. That conclusion is patently false. If I (T. W.) were to tell you how much like the president of the United States I am, that would not make me equal with him. It simply means that I happen to have some of his qualities. It does not even mean that I have his qualities in the same degree he has.

The first error leads many Christians not to labor for the realization of Christ in us. We commit grave error in that unwarranted reluctance. The second error brings in suppositions that destroy the proper perspective of creature to sovereign.

Obviously, no creature will become omnipotent. We share none of God's attributes in the degree He has them. But we can "receive power when the Holy Spirit has come upon [us]" (Acts 1:8). We never have *all* power, but we should have *some* power.

We receive from God portions of His attributes by prayerfully realizing the intention of Christ being in us in our smaller measure. Because God is *omnipresent*, we give some manifestation of His *presence* to our peers. Being omniscient, He shares portions of His *knowledge* with those who are willing to learn. Christ in us is the *wisdom* of God (1 Corinthians 1:24), and our lesser insight reflects a share of His ultimate wisdom. We derive our *holiness* from Absolute Holiness. Becoming like Him in small measure does not bestow on us His stature or position.

He is the original; we are the copies. We partake of His nature (2 Peter 1:4). Our calling in this life, within the church, is to "attain to the unity of the faith, and of the knowledge of the Son of God, to a mature man, to the measure of the stature which belongs to the fullness of Christ" (Ephesians 4:13). Taking on His personality, we journey from glory to glory—we can "handle" more and more of Christ—until God determines that we move on to Graduation Day.

Christ's Attributes We Can Show to the World

We must begin with exceptions. Because He is God, three of Christ's qualities can never be "in" us, and we would pursue them fruitlessly: His infinity, His transcendence, and His immanence. Infinity removes all limits from Him; He has no limits in time or space. Being creatures, we will always have limits. His transcendence (or His "beyondness") means that He exceeds us in every way and every measure that exists. We cannot surpass the ultimate. His immanence means that He pervades all of His creation. We cannot be at the center of the sun or within any cosmic activity. We cannot enter the body processes of our friends. We do not need to. Because

He is maintaining all of creation (Colossians 1:17), He has to be present in all of it.

It seems likely that we will learn new attributes of God at Graduation Day as well as the attributes of God that are most prominently emphasized in the Bible: omnipotence, eternity, immortality, omnipresence, immutability, holiness, omniscience, and wisdom.

Omnipotence. God is omnipotent (all-powerful) because the spirit is greater than the physical and controls the physical. A spiritual God created the physical universe. The spiritual preceded the physical, and therefore the physical is dependent on the spiritual. God intends that we use some of His power, especially to witness and pray.

Eternity. Some will object to our defining eternity as an "attribute" of Christ, although most of us do not object to using it as an adjective ("eternal life"). Because "eternity" is neither an emotion nor a disposition, the most convenient treatment here is simply to call it an "attribute," a quality in God.

Our problem is that the Bible uses the word in a number of different senses. One sense refers to the fact that God never had a beginning and will never have an ending; He exists eternally. We, obviously, cannot claim that for ourselves; we had a beginning. We can claim "everlasting" life, but not "eternity" without beginning.

A second sense refers to the state in which God is absolute source. Ecclesiastes 3:11 describes us as having "eternity" in the heart. Context indicates that this refers to "the sons of men" (verse 10). In the deepest part of our hearts, we know that all things come from God and that our truest satisfaction can come from only Him — from eternity. Jesus may have included eternity as a quality of life (as well as endlessness) when He prayed, "This is eternal life, that they may know You, the only true God, and Jesus Christ whom You have sent" (John 17:3).

In this second meaning, we can legitimately regard ourselves as being in "eternity present" — that is, living with God as our only source even in this life. "Eternity past" would include the life of God before creation, and "eternity future" will be the lives we live with God after Graduation Day or after the second coming of Christ.

A third sense enters when the Bible refers to *us* as having "eternal life," or life that can never end (John 3:16). Obviously, this meaning differs from that of our Creator, where His "eternity" indicates that He is uncreated.

In the second meaning (God is absolute source), we share the mind of Christ with our fellows who are seeking the fullest meaning of life. They already have "eternity in the heart," and we can help them realize God's intention for life itself — a life grounded totally in Him. Only "Christ in us" satisfies a longing that many people do not realize they have.

The third meaning (life that can never end) gives us assurance. Also, in sharing Christ with others, we are offering them the privilege God has given us of knowing Him forever. We grow and develop by sharing Christ in both the second and third meanings.

Immortality. Immortality has a meaning similar to the third meaning of "eternity." That we are immortal indicates that we will never die the second death. This immortality is a gift of God. That we are eternal means that we cannot die the second death. This eternity means we are participating directly in the life of Christ. Jesus promised of "those who are considered worthy to attain to that age and the resurrection from the dead" (Luke 20:35), "for they cannot even die anymore, because they are like angels, and are sons of God, being sons of the resurrection" (verse 36).

Omnipresence. God's omnipresence means He is everywhere, in all places. Our prayer for a missionary in a distant place is effective because God is as much with him or her there as He is with us here. His omnipresence indicates that He is *personally* with each of us and with His creatures: "You open Your hand and satisfy the desire of every living thing" (Psalm 145:16). His *immanence* describes His control from within of His own creation: "[He] covers the heavens with clouds" (147:8). We grow by manifesting His presence to our fellow creatures; we cannot (and need not) manifest His immanence.

Immutability. Immutability signifies that our essential nature will remain stable once we "graduate." It is an eternal quality of God, but we develop it only through process, as indicated in the previous chapter. In Christ, it does not indicate that He acts in a static manner but rather that His essence never changes. Our trials help us develop this quality. We are manifesting Him when we remain solid in our faith and witness. Steadfastness has to be intentional.

Holiness. The previous chapter showed that holiness is a gift we receive at salvation. Although God gives it to us, we are responsible to grow in holiness. We can abet the process of growing in holiness (sanctification) by our *dedicating* or setting aside our life, or parts of it, for God alone. Only God can sanctify. We can dedicate, but God sanctifies what we dedicate! The two of us have dedicated our bodies, our houses, our possessions, even this book, to the glory of God.

Omniscience. God is omniscient (all-knowing) because He is everywhere and nothing escapes His divine attention. He could not maintain the universe if He were not omniscient. Though we can study and learn faithfully, we cannot become omniscient. We are privileged to acquire such knowledge of God and His ways as He reveals in order to have Heaven's view.

Wisdom. God considers wisdom important because He emphasized that Christ in us is the wisdom of God (1 Corinthians 1:24). In a day when some of the media and politicians dictate a kind of "wisdom," we must know how to make choices that present Christ to His world as wisdom. Wisdom is the "know-how" that keeps Christ at the forefront. Omniscience is the knowing, and wisdom is the "knowing-how."

These qualities are "supernal"; they come from above and indicate God in His cosmic greatness. Supernal attributes are majestic and therefore imposing, even somewhat frightening, to average people. But at the same time, they indicate God's high ambition for each of us. Heaven's view lifts us above the crowd.

WE IMITATE CHRIST'S VIEW OF HIMSELF

Jesus closed His final prayer in the Garden of Gethsemane with this statement: "The love with which You loved Me may be *in them*, and *I in them*" (John 17:26, emphasis added). Just before, He had told His disciples, "He who abides *in Me* and *I in him*, he bears much fruit, for apart from Me you can do nothing" (15:5, emphasis added). Jesus emphasized the mutual occupying explained in chapter 3.

Paul consistently amplified Jesus' intention: "To me, to live *is* Christ"; "Christ may *dwell in your hearts* through faith" (Philippians 1:21; Ephesians 3:17, emphasis added). He stated it most positively in Galatians 2:20: "It is no longer I who live, but *Christ lives in me*" (emphasis added).

From Heaven's view, "the life of Jesus also may be

manifested"—uncovered, revealed, and laid bare—"in our mortal flesh" (2 Corinthians 4:11). No wonder the Father loves us so! The same Holy Spirit who worked in the person of Christ (Matthew 12:28) continues carrying out His work in our mortal bodies (John 14:16-17).

If we are to manifest Christ, He must have preeminence in our lives. John the Baptist deferred to Jesus: "He must increase, but I must decrease" (3:30). Paul, too, regarded himself with humility (1 Corinthians 3:5) and asserted that Christ must "have first place in everything" (Colossians 1:18). Only this humble perspective allows Jesus to manifest His presence to everyone in our sphere of influence.

Therefore, what Jesus was two thousand years ago to those around Him, we manifest to those around us today. We show Christ to the world. In order to do this, the Bible assigns us a responsibility to maintain purity and transparency: "I beseech you therefore, brethren, by the mercies of God, that you present your bodies a living sacrifice, holy, acceptable to God, which is your reasonable service" (Romans 12:1, NKJV). By rendering Christ this service, He will become explicit to those around us.

The gospel of John records more than thirty instances when Jesus said, "I am." Jesus clearly asserted who He was. He is immutable: He does not change, so He is still these qualities or aspects of life *within us*. We embody what He said He was long ago in our lower position and status.

John	Jesus said . . .
6:35	I am the bread of life (*working within you*).
6:51	I am the living bread that came down out of heaven (*working within you*).

John	Jesus said . . .
8:12	I am the Light of the world (*working within you*).
9:5	I am the Light of the world (*working within you*).
10:7	I am the door of the sheep (*working within you*).
10:9	I am the door (*working within you*).
10:11	I am the good shepherd (*working within you*).
10:14	I am the good shepherd (*working within you*).
11:25	I am the resurrection and the life (*working within you*).
14:6	I am the way, and the truth, and the life (*working within you*).
15:1	I am the true vine (*working within you*).
15:5	I am the vine (*working within you*).

(Note that He repeats each identification two times.)

This first list of "I am" verses pictures some of Jesus' roles and responsibilities. His roles and responsibilities remain the same, now manifested in us also. We have the responsibility to allow those in our presence to see Him as He is. A friend in the grief of conviction once exclaimed, "No one would want to become a Christian from looking at my life. Why would they want what they see in me—anger, criticism, anxiety?" Her concern is easy to understand. The world knows that they should see Jesus in Christians; they hate hypocrites. This is why 1 John puts so much emphasis on avoiding sin: "By this we know that we are in Him: the one who says he abides in Him ought himself to walk in the same manner as He walked" (2:5-6).

Several of these verses contain complementary identities: He is the vine and we are the branches. Because He is the vine (within us) and we are the branches (within Him), the mutual occupying pictures unity between Jesus and us. He claimed, "I am the door; if anyone enters through Me, he will be saved, and will go in and out and find pasture" (John 10:9). He is the door; we are the "enterers." God chooses that we offer people entrance into His kingdom through the door who works within us.

John, more than any other gospel writer, quotes Jesus denoting who He is by saying "I am." In the following list, Jesus explained His origin and His position. Christ is now in us, yet His orientation is still to the Father and not to this world. These positional verses have become easier for us to understand today through the letters of Paul than they were for the people of Galilee. Jesus' life manifested in us today retains these bearings:

John	Jesus said . . .
7:29	I am from Him.
8:23	I am from above.
8:23	I am not of this world.
14:3	Where I am, there you may be also.
14:10	I am in the Father.
14:11	I am in the Father.
14:20	I am in My Father.
17:11	I am no longer in the world.
17:14	I am not of the world.
17:16	I am not of the world.

(The repetitions, again, are important.)

The following "I am" verses clarify Jesus' *personal* identification. His presence within our spirit negates neither His identity nor our own. In fact, recognizing His unique manifestation within our spirit enables us to perceive how we complement Him: He is teacher, we are learners; He is king, we are His subjects. Moreover, as teacher, He teaches through us, and as king, He manifests nobility through us. We are not the begotten Son of God, but we demonstrate Him.

John	Jesus said . . .
8:18	I am He who testifies about Myself.
8:28	I am [the Son of Man].
10:36	I am the Son of God.
13:13	[I am] Teacher and Lord.
18:5	I am He [Jesus the Nazarene].
18:6	I am He.
18:8	I am He.
18:37	I am a king.

A number of "I am" verses illuminate Jesus' dependence on His Father or His relationship with His Father: "I am [the Son of Man], . . . I speak these things as the Father taught Me" (John 8:28). "I am no longer in the world . . . I come to You" (17:11). "I am the true vine, and My Father is the vinedresser" (15:1). These complementary relationships again picture unity. In the last discourse chapters (14–17), the identity-unity principle is even more amplified. A multicomplementary picture of Jesus, us, and the Father emerges: "I am in the Father, and the Father is in Me" (14:10-11); "I am in My Father, and you in Me, and I in you" (verse 20; see also chapter 17).

The gospel of John also cites what Jesus said He is *not*. The negatives He emphasized should be negatives that He displays in our lives as well.

John	Jesus said . . .
7:28	I have not come of Myself.
8:16	I am not alone.
8:23	I am not of this world.
16:32	I am not alone.
17:11	I am no longer in the world.
17:14	I am not of the world.
17:16	I am not of the world.

(Again, note how often Jesus reemphasizes important points.)

First Corinthians 6:17 informs us that "the one who joins himself to the Lord is one spirit with Him." He is in us, we are in Him; we are a union in singleness of spirit. To develop Heaven's view, we learn to see the world through Jesus' eyes.

The Bible contains two "I ams" that are more significant than all the others. When Moses asked God's name, "God said unto Moses, I AM THAT I AM: and [God] said, Thus shalt thou say unto the children of Israel, I AM hath sent me unto you" (Exodus 3:14, KJV). This singular identification—God's telling us who He is—gives Heaven's view of His own essence. The name implies self-existence, infinity, transcendence, and eternity—all that the uniqueness of His attributes contain.

For this reason, the Jews were scandalized when Jesus claimed that name for Himself:

"Your father Abraham rejoiced to see My day, and he saw it and was glad." So the Jews said to Him, "You are not yet fifty years old,

and have You seen Abraham?" Jesus said to them, "Truly, truly,
I say to you, before Abraham was born, I am." (John 8:56-58)

Jesus claimed identity with the Yahweh of Exodus 3:14, and
the Jews understood His intention clearly (verse 59).

This one statement elevates every "I am" of Jesus to varied
expressions we must embrace if we seek Heaven's view. His view *is*
Heaven's view. The great "I AM THAT I AM" in us is our hope
of glory!

THE HOPE OF CHRIST WITHIN US
ENLIVENS THE PRESENT

For two millennia, Christians have hoped that Christ would come
in their lifetime. Each century has seen numbers of predictions of
dates of His return and emphasis on readiness for it. Jesus predicted that perennial expectation throughout His Olivet discourse
(Matthew 24:4-41) and repeatedly emphasized the importance of
watchfulness (Matthew 24:42; Luke 12:37,40), the mark of those
with unceasing hope. Hope for His return is inevitable when we
know Him who dwells within us. We are to "fix [our] hope completely on the grace to be brought to you at the revelation of Jesus
Christ" (1 Peter 1:13).

We are also to hope for our own resurrection. "If we have
hoped in Christ in this life only, we are of all men most to be
pitied" (1 Corinthians 15:19). At our resurrection, "DEATH IS SWAL-
LOWED UP in victory" (verse 54). Hope is the present enjoyment
of a future blessing. It brings the future into the present. We can
enjoy our future privileges even now. In the afterword, I (Melana)
explain, "Hope is the peaceful anticipation gained through a relationship with someone who is trustworthy."

Hope seems natural to all who love Christ. The reason He is our hope of glory (Colossians 1:27) is that His very person (in us) is hope itself (1 Timothy 1:1), and that hope will endure. Hope is one of the three factors that will abide even if in a higher form (1 Corinthians 13:13).

Elements of Hope

Hope is not wishing; it relishes what it knows is coming. Language has limited us here (as in many places) because the hope in the Bible had a *certainty* missing from our usual senses of the word *hope* in modern usage. We can extract the elements in genuine hope from examples given in the Bible.

Anticipation. Hope is filled with expectancy. We are anticipating the coming of the Lord with excitement, "awaiting eagerly the revelation of our Lord Jesus Christ" (1 Corinthians 1:7). Creation itself longs for *our* revelation: "The anxious longing of the creation waits eagerly for the revealing of the sons of God" (Romans 8:19). The expectancy in waiting enables our endurance in verse 25: "If we hope for what we do not see, with perseverance we wait *eagerly* [with anticipation] for it" (emphasis added).

Waiting expectantly provides vibrancy to our walk. Even in the darkest days of her suffering, Melana had more zest for God's ultimate purposes than all the rest of us. Isaiah explains this unexpected vitality: "Those who wait for [hope in] the LORD will gain new strength; they will mount up with wings like eagles, they will run and not get tired, they will walk and not become weary" (Isaiah 40:31).

Steadfastness. Paul thanked the Lord for the Thessalonian church, "constantly bearing in mind [their] work of faith and labor of love and *steadfastness of hope* in our Lord Jesus Christ in the presence of our God and Father" (1 Thessalonians 1:3, emphasis added). His hope for the Corinthians was "firmly grounded, knowing that as you are sharers of our sufferings, so also you are sharers of our comfort" (2 Corinthians 1:7). Hope remains firm, not because of the inherent skill or mastery of the Christian but because of the God we place our hope *in*.

The afterword states that one of my (Melana's) earliest e-mails during my treatments explained to my prayer warriors the difference in hoping *that* something might occur (our usual usage) and in hoping *in* God as He carried me through my ordeal. We often miss out on things that we hope for. We can never miss out on the ultimate intentions of God, infinitely grander than we can imagine, when we hope in Him. The New Testament saints had hope in God during their persecution.

Joy and peace. Small wonder that joy and peace accompany biblical hope! Paul prayed for the Romans, "May the God of hope fill you with all joy and peace in believing, so that you will abound in hope by the power of the Holy Spirit" (Romans 15:13). Too many Christians think of hope resulting from a coming event, but in the Bible, the joy accompanied their daily work and comradeship (see also discussions of joy and peace in the next chapter).

Reliance on the Lord. When Sennacherib invaded Judah, Hezekiah encouraged his people: "With him is only an arm of flesh, but with us is the LORD our God to help us and to fight our battles" (2 Chronicles 32:8). Friends may desert us, our health may fail us, but the great martyrs of history somehow learned to cling to hope *in* God alone.

The Nature of Hope

If we ever comprehend the glory of Christ in us, our hope becomes one of the most solid aspects of our Christian walk. The writer of Hebrews called hope "an anchor of the soul, a hope both sure and steadfast" (6:19). Paul described Abraham as hoping "against hope" in his faith in God's promise to him (Romans 4:18). The psalmist turned to this granite in his perplexity: "Why are you in despair, O my soul? And why have you become disturbed within me? Hope in God, for I shall yet praise Him, the help of my countenance and my God" (Psalm 42:11).

Paul elaborates on the nature of hope by what he couples it with: "I pray that the eyes of your heart may be enlightened, so that you may know (1) what is the hope of His calling, (2) what are the riches of the glory of His inheritance in the saints, and (3) what is the surpassing greatness of His power toward us who believe" (Ephesians 1:18-19, numerals added). Hope, then, is a solid rock coupled with riches of glory and greatness of power.

The New Testament examples show us that we require hope not only in our need or in our affliction but also as a constant accompaniment to our ordinary daily life. It is a "living hope" (1 Peter 1:3). Perhaps if our lives exhibited the positive attitude of hope, we might draw more people to our Lord.

It is Christ (with all that He is) in us who is our hope (with all that hope is) of glory (with all that glory is). We cannot have Heaven's view without representing Christ to the world. Most of the world does not consciously realize the enormous value of the eternity God has planted in the heart. Paul felt deeply about those who knew no hope at all: "Remember that you were at that time [before they had hope] separate from Christ, excluded from the commonwealth of Israel, and strangers to the covenants of promise, *having no hope and without God in the world*" (Ephesians 2:12, emphasis added).

Our view from Heaven can become their hope if we are willing to share what we know.

CHAPTER 6

Heaven's View Sees Us Realizing God's Attributes in Our Lives

We know that when He appears, we will be like Him, because we will see Him just as He is. And everyone who has this hope fixed on Him purifies himself, just as He is pure.

1 JOHN 3:2-3

Heaven's view of us is that of redeemed creatures growing more and more like Christ. Accomplishing that purpose, we become like what we know. Therefore, we study God's attributes in order to become like Christ.

GOD'S PERSONAL AND SUPERNAL ATTRIBUTES ARE RELATED

Functions of God's Attributes

God uses the supernal attributes (heavenly or coming from above, described in chapter 5) for *governance*. His omnipotence ignites the supernovae; His infinity reaches to the microscopic reproduction of our cells. His omniscience enables the polyphonic interweaving of the melodies of willing and stubborn persons. His wisdom determines the best method of rescuing us from our sin. Nature could not proceed without God's immanence holding everything together. In our lack of knowledge, we cannot fully grasp the enormous work of His attributes in terms of governance.

On the other hand, God employs personal attributes to *exercise His relationship to us.* Our pity, joy, and disgust (personal attributes) are usually arbitrary: Most of us do not know which individual quality or emotion will take control next. We fluctuate because we are not single-minded in seeking relationship. But God's primary purpose is to have a relationship with each of us. His determination has at its bidding many personal attributes that He can use at any time; God does not fluctuate.

The supernal attributes of the previous chapter are at the disposal of the personal ones in this chapter. Jesus' *power* enabled Him to still the storm and feed the five thousand (showing the personal quality of compassion). His *omniscience* drew out the faith of the Syrophoenician woman (Matthew 15:21-28), encouraging her growth and the faith of the disciples. The *immutability* of Christ showed in His composure (His personal endurance) during His agonizing trial (Matthew 27:14; Mark 15:5).

In the same way, those smaller supernal attributes we develop are useful in knowing how and when to apply discipline. The supernal attributes were placed first, in the previous chapter, because the personal attributes *need* them in order to function.

We learn the supernal and the personal attributes of God in order to reproduce His life on earth. God could show His nature in huge letters in the sky; His mighty forces could compel universal obedience. Strangely, however, His intention is to show the world what He is *through us.* This may seem an inefficient way of communicating in view of His power and wisdom — what He could do if He wanted to. To our way of thinking, if God made His pronouncements more spectacular, people would believe them more readily.

But God will not force belief. The reciprocity He prefers depends on *voluntary* mutuality. The only way people will see Christ in us is to see love among us. Jesus prayed for this rare reciprocity among us: "That they may all be one; even as You, Father, are in Me and I in You, that they also may be in Us, so *that the world may believe that You sent Me*" (John 17:21, emphasis added).

As we demonstrate God's attributes in our lives, God through time imprints them even more deeply into our character. Becoming like Christ is not an instantaneous event; we learn through process. A virtuoso pianist does not become skilled without many hours of practice. That practice must be disciplined with intense attention to the composer's intention.

Our Maker intends that we be "virtuoso" Christians, and He goes to great lengths to help us in our "practice." When God shows us kindness, it springs not merely from His nature but from His desire that *we* learn to show kindness just like His. To His personal attributes, we respond in kind by sharing them with our fellow creatures. God wants to demonstrate His personal love, compassion, and empathy through us.

Even though God reveals His grace to all humans in various ways, He does not continue lavishing an attribute on someone who will not respond. He did not squander mercy on Pharaoh because Pharaoh continually hardened his heart (Exodus 8:15,32). God showed mercy to Nebuchadnezzar when he praised God after he learned not to take God's glory (Daniel 4:30-37).

God will not indulge any person, high or low. He did not show mercy for Pharaoh, Esau, King Saul, or Ananias and Sapphira. Yet His wisdom granted mercy for scheming Jacob, sinning David, and bumbling Peter. No one can presume to censure God in any of these cases. All we know is that Jacob ended as a God-fearing patriarch, David finished as the greatest of all Israel's kings, and Peter wrote the best book on persecution in the Bible. Wisdom knows where the line of divine mercy must be drawn.

Nor will God waste a gift on someone who will abuse it. Some spiritual gifts seem to engender pride, a serious danger (Proverbs 29:23; Daniel 5:20). God's great gift of the law produced self-righteousness in the Pharisees (Luke 18:10-14). God employs pragmatism in the use and bestowal of His attributes.

Our use of the attributes can be perverted. The most serious perversion is limiting God because we do not understand the greatness of His attributes. The Jews in the wilderness skeptically asked, "Can God prepare a table in the wilderness?" (Psalm 78:19). The same psalm informs us, "Again and again they tempted God, and pained the Holy One of Israel. They did not remember His power" (verses 41-42). Most of us do not trust God for all He wants to do.

We also can mix self into the attributes. With all his wisdom, Solomon increasingly satisfied his personal desire for houses, power, and women (Ecclesiastes 2:4-11). Bragging or displaying our spiritual gifts may attract attention, but self-display is far from the Spirit of Christ, for "even Christ did not please Himself" (Romans 15:3).

For God, a painful perversion of our attributes happens when we do not conform to the kingdom principle of forward movement (see chapter 3). Heaven's view is that of a generous Father who wants His children to grow in grace and knowledge of Christ (2 Peter 3:18). Paul was grieved at the retrogression of the Galatians: "You were running well; who hindered you from obeying the truth?" (Galatians 5:7). We do not need to wait for eternity future to become Christlike.

Determining the Surprising, Proper Sources of God's Attributes and Actions

We tend to link jealousy with love, but God's jealousy does not derive from the intensity of His love; it comes from His nature as truth. When He states the way for us unmistakably, our deviation from His word pains God. It is truth that does not want us to follow a lie. Heaven's view is jealous for ultimate truth.

God's firmness with us does not come from His immutability; rather, it is love that resolutely resists our tendency to sin. Tragically, our freedom of will can contravene the kindest desires of God. God prefers that we not have our own way, though He allows us freedom of choice.

We assume that God's benevolence is gentle with us, but only strength can truly be gentle. Gentleness from any other source would be weakness. Gentleness has no meaning if it does not originate in a strength that can be moderated by wisdom.

It is not mercy that forgives; it is holiness. Sin offends holiness, not mercy. Mercy is an aspect of grace that enables holiness to forgive.

Our sources must become like God's. We are jealous for the one true reality. Our firmness must come from love. Going from strength to strength gives meaning to our gentleness. Our holiness, properly understood, drives us to forgive those who mistreat us. We are seeking ways to help them become holy.

HEAVEN'S VIEW REALIZES THE EMOTIONS OF GOD IN US

The Difference Between Mood and Emotion

The Bible indicates that God has emotions: love, compassion, anger, and hatred. God's immutability reminds us that He never changes in any aspect. Therefore, His emotions cannot go "up and down" as ours do. God's love and hatred are permanent, unvarying aspects of His nature. God never "falls in love"; God *is* love. God never "gets mad"; He remains forever angry with unrighteousness and injustice.

There are two major differences between our personal attributes and those of God. First, every quality in God remains uncompromisingly holy. Most of our displeasure and much of our humor is unholy. God's loathing of falsehood and His disapproval of injustice come from absolute holiness. Our personal attributes, also, must likewise demonstrate holiness if we are to continue progress in our process. That we have to learn.

Throughout this book, we have emphasized the importance of acting cognitively. The importance of this derives from the fact that our *will* is the one aspect of our being over which we have control. We have little control of circumstances. The actions of love and pity can be dictated by our will, like God's. When we love and pity, we become more like Him.

Second, we undergo moods, but God never has moods. Satan, not being a creator, can only pervert the good, and he is very crafty (Genesis 3:1). His perversion of emotion is *mood*. He concerns himself less with our emotions than with our moods, which is where he can trip us up with his chicanery. He can use a physical condition or circumstances to induce a foul or doubting mood. Using the fallen part of our nature, Satan has mastered the art of inducing a mood to lead to a sinful emotion.

Mood differs from emotion significantly. God's emotions are

inherent, but He has no moods at all. God's emotions do not "happen"; He effects them according to our place in our process. Because His emotions never result from mood, His emotions are exercised cognitively (that is, He chooses with His mind) from the wisdom that recognizes our current need.

Although God involves Himself in our times and affairs, He remains outside time, in eternity. He cannot change because He works for us from His standpoint in eternity rather than from our perspective within time (Isaiah 57:15). We cannot have Heaven's view from the position of His eternity, but we can trust His leadership because of His knowledge. Seeing the past and the future, His wisdom dictates what is to us the *present*, existing work that will most effectively facilitate our growth.

For example, at times for our own sakes, we need to perceive His love. In a different time, other needs may occasion a beneficent displeasure. If our sin is serious enough from His perspective, God wisely acts out of anger, but that anger never causes Him to forsake us. Even in His anger, God's cognition also remembers His pity and compassion. The whole history of Israel illustrates this over and over. His actions stem from His wisdom, unaffected by mood. His wisdom releases one of His emotions appropriately (but never a mood).

Satan affects our moods without our awareness. Our moods are temporary and unstable. Sometimes they come on us quickly, resulting in precipitous action. They have little to do with our will. Foolishly, we may mistake changes in our mood to be changes in God. In us, mood can induce an emotion. The Christian should learn to dismiss mood as a tool of the Adversary.

If we overcome mood, God can mold our emotions to be like His. They become resident in us, ready to be called on when Christ in us needs to surface. Even if we have a weak disposition, prone to anger or self-satisfaction, Christ in us can overcome our natural tendencies. With practice, we can learn to control our emotions.

Although we spoke in chapter 2 of "extreme" and "middle" emotions, this does not mean they have "size" in God. Human emotions vary from day to day; we can have pity one day and less pity the next day for the same person. Some of us even vacillate between pity and disgust for the same person. God's immutability does not allow any change in His attitude toward us. The words *middle* and *extreme* are only conveniences to help us understand within our limitations what God is like.

By giving us the full gamut of emotions He has, God makes us more like Himself, with an ability to enjoy a gamut of life that even the angels do not have. We are able to enjoy such a wide range as high praise, a sunset, or a pear. Our mistake comes when we think our little pleasure or our little pity is trifling.

The "size" of God's pity is 100 percent; the size of His love is 100 percent. We cannot attain His degree in any attribute or emotion, but we can commit to sharing the mind of Christ in our limited degree with everyone in our path.

God's Personal Emotions

God's emotions are never negative. Because He realizes them cognitively, He can never be irritated, annoyed, or bothered. His "size" (the infinite generosity of His nobility) cannot allow the entrance of anything petty. Nothing will frustrate or exasperate Him. Because His plans cannot be ultimately controverted, God never gets anxious. When we fail, we can consider the next best step in the light of His positive attributes rather than sink in anxiety.

God's positive emotions are always active. They include such constructive emotions as love and compassion. However, His emotions also include purifying ones such as anger and hatred. Even in these, God will destroy only the unholy and unhealthy. We can legitimately imitate God in His constructive and destructive emotions, provided we act in the same holiness that He has. (Usually when we judge, we are not holy.)

Love. God cannot be creative without creating. He cannot be just unless He dispenses justice. Any attribute of God will manifest itself in deeds. Love is not love until it takes action.

The fifteen marks of love in 1 Corinthians 13:4-7 are all actions. The Incarnation showed God in operation. Loving the Twelve, Jesus taught them and fed them. No enterprise in history accomplished as much as the action of love on the cross. Real love is not for lazy people. What we do for our beloved discloses the size of our love.

The *agape* love of God does not depend on the qualities of its object. Love is inherent in God. We are to love our enemies because we are to think about them exactly as God does: from Heaven's view. His perspective of us did not derive from our repulsive sins; He saw far more than a current condition. Our perspective of our enemies does not derive from what they do to us; it comes from what we are.

We do not understand the meaning of true love if we think it seeks our comfort. Absolute love wants the ultimate good for its object. A true parent desires for his or her child honesty, truthfulness, and diligence more than a good television or popularity at school. Jesus wants purity for His bride more than bigness. What we want for our beloved reveals the character of our love.

Earth has many kinds of "loves." The wrong kind of love restricts the beloved with jealousy and possessiveness. The right kind of love is expansive and freeing. This partly explains why God leaves our wills free. Gladly proffered love thrills anyone.

When we grasp this, we can only fall in humble gratitude that God chose to give Himself.

"Greater love has no one than this, that one lay down his life for his friends" (John 15:13). The supreme self-sacrifice of all time happened when immortality assumed temporary (physical) mortality in order to bestow immortality on us. Our love for God and for our Christian family will show itself in action that is willing to pay any price.

Compassion. The Bible speaks often of God's pity and compassion for us. In most cases, God's compassion relates to a pitiable condition. "Seeing the people, He felt compassion for them, because they were distressed and dispirited like sheep without a shepherd" (Matthew 9:36). Astonishingly, God feels empathy with His people:

> They put away the foreign gods from among them and served the LORD; and He could bear the misery of Israel no longer. (Judges 10:16)

> In all [Israel's] affliction He was afflicted. (Isaiah 63:9)

> Truly I say to you, to the extent that you did it to one of these brothers of Mine, even the least of them, you did it to Me. (Matthew 25:40)

> Truly, I say to you, to the extent that you did not do it to one of the least of these, you did not do it to Me. (Matthew 25:45)

> "Saul, Saul, why are you persecuting *Me*?" (Acts 9:4, emphasis added)

Most of Jesus' miracles were acts of compassion. When He raised the widow's son from the dead at Nain, Luke specifically described His compassion for her (Luke 7:13). The leper coming to Jesus after the Sermon on the Mount appealed, "Lord, if You are willing, You can make me clean" (Matthew 8:2), and Jesus' response was, "I am willing; be cleansed" (verse 3). He was deeply touched at the lame, the blind, and the deaf. We cannot imitate Christ without sensitivity to the needy, and this will often mean personal involvement with them.

Tenderness. In view of His overwhelming power, God's tenderness surprises us. God's compassion comes from a tender heart. Isaiah's messianic prophecy stated, "A bruised reed He will not break and a dimly burning wick He will not extinguish" (Isaiah 42:3; fulfilled in Matthew 12:20).

Most of us need tenderness more than we realize. Every human has discouraging medical reports, fender benders, debts we can't pay this month, and dishwashers that break at the most inconvenient times. Days come for the toughest seasoned Christian in which his or her greatest need is tenderness. Our family had many days like that during my (Melana's) cancer treatments. We appreciated God's loving gentleness, sometimes expressed also through the quiet concern of the medical staff, who became friends.

Jesus was tender with a grieving Mary Magdalene when He granted her the first resurrection appearance (John 20:15-16). John sensed such tenderness that he felt set apart as special to Jesus (21:7). God knows our needs and remains constantly available at crucial points in our lives.

Joy. Jesus was a happy person. He cultivated many friendships, often enjoyed meals in various homes (Luke 5:29; 19:5-6), and blessed the wedding at Cana (John 2:5-10). On the return of the seventy from their mission, Jesus "rejoiced greatly in the Holy Spirit" (Luke 10:21).

Joy characterized the early church (Acts 2:46-47). Its infectiousness was one of the factors that drew thousands. As we progressed through cancer, the joy of the Lord became our strength on dark days (Nehemiah 8:10). Most of us wait for joy to "happen," but our family learned that even joy could become an act of the will. "In Your presence is fullness of joy" (Psalm 16:11); we *willed* to remain conscious of His presence. The joy of the early church did not depend on circumstance; they had found the fullness of God in redemption and in His Spirit.

Displeasure. "It was displeasing in His sight that there was no justice" (Isaiah 59:15). Even the "middle" emotions of God are intense. Jesus strongly disapproved of hypocrisy (Matthew 23:27) and pretense (6:16). God expresses displeasure when we are not genuine through and through. Jesus was also hard on unbelief (Luke 24:25). He rebuked the disciples when they were slow to understand—a violation of the second kingdom principle (see chapter 3). The displeasure of God indicates that we could do better than we do.

Grief. Jesus grieved over the rebelliousness of Jerusalem (Luke 13:34). He wept at Lazarus's grave (John 11:35). How appalling that Israel could grieve the Holy Spirit (Isaiah 63:10)! Paul cautions us not to grieve the Spirit (Ephesians 4:30). The grief of God, like all His emotions, measures 100 percent.

God's grief, unlike ours, stems not from circumstances but from our sin of rebellion against what is best for us. Jesus' grief at Lazarus's tomb (John 11:35) may have contained sympathy for Mary and Martha, but the primary factor was indignation at the horror that death had brought to the human race (verse 33). The context of Isaiah 63 and Ephesians 4 indicates that sin occasions God's grief. When our hearts beat with His, we will find how painful and wretched it is to deviate from His plan.

Jealousy. We have seen that God's jealousy stems from His truth, not His love. His jealousy, like His grief, shows His deep concern that we know Him and His way as the only right plan for our life (Exodus 20:5-6). Jesus summed this up in His declaration that only He is the way, the truth, and the life (John 14:6; see also Acts 4:12).

Hatred. The Bible speaks of God's hating sin or an individual who deflects another into sin (Proverbs 6:16-17; Isaiah 61:8; Amos 5:21; Romans 1:18). It never describes God as hating any person as such, not even Satan. God's anger is never malevolence. He directs it to accomplish a specific purpose.

Anger. The Bible notes that God is "slow to anger" (Psalm 103:8; see also Micah 7:18). Most of the time, His anger is directed against His own people in rebellion (Numbers 25:3; 2 Kings 22:13; Jeremiah 36:7). Anger is intense; we do well to avoid God's anger. The intensity of the previous emotions as they are described in the Word of God underlines His determination that His children ascend from glory to glory.

Applying This "Godliness" to the Routine of Life

As the work for this book was beginning, a young mother of four toddlers asked us, "But how can I develop the glories of heaven in my life right now? I live between dirty diapers and dirty dishes. I am not at a point in my life where great spiritual things happen, and I'm too tired to try very much. Right now I can do nothing of significance past my own kitchen."

The answer developed slowly for us, through our own process of humdrum daily living with typical irritations, boring tasks, and personal frustrations. We learned to remember intentionally that *every* word, thought, and reaction represents an exercise—a work-out, a training session—in realizing the emotions of God.

Sometimes even in our mundane "sufferings," God puts before us a prospect for deepening His emotions in us. When we waste a chance to take on His attributes, we squander an occasion for glory. Every moment we idly waste—when we glare, sigh sarcastically, or retort—we fritter away our prospects for growth. Seen in this light, the limited possibilities to develop our glories makes us value our emotional reactions as opportunities to become like Christ.

BECOMING LIKE GOD IN HIS PERSONAL QUALITIES

We are calling "personal qualities" those that fall below the supernal (majestic attributes used for governing) in human estimation, such as mercy and humility. Grace is actually an aspect of God's *disposition* rather than an attribute. We can learn these qualities from the Bible, but we can also discover them in our daily experience with God.

God's working in us does not depend on our consciousness of His presence. He never stops working, but our consciousness vacillates constantly between the spiritual and the physical. A prayer we learned early in my (Melana's) cancer treatments was, "Lord, make us aware of both worlds (the spiritual and the material) and how they work together." God rewarded that prayer with unceasing blessing on our talking, driving, cooking, fellowshipping, and worshipping. Every quality of God stays ready to manifest itself at any juncture; God remains eternally "on call."

Because God is infinite, only an infinite book could detail all His qualities. We will look at only two that affect humankind profoundly and that illustrate how His qualities function.

Mercy. What happened when God placed Himself at the mercy

of men made possible what happens when men put themselves at
the mercy of God. Mercy was what came to earth in the Incarnation. Men were merciless with God; He remains forever merciful
to any willing recipient.

Mercy implies a degree of reciprocity. To accept mercy from
God means you know how holy He is. Because of this, accepting
His forgiveness means you are accepting all that He is. We cannot
accept mercy with the intention of plunging back into sin. Mercy
is God welcoming us back into His holiness.

Grace precedes mercy because grace first calls us to repentance. When we repent, mercy forgives our sin (Psalm 32:1-7). If
David understood these facts, how much more should we who
have Calvary?

Peace. The fact that love, joy, and peace are *fruit* (Galatians
5:22) indicates that they begin as buds and ripen into mature
beauty. That they are fruit also indicates that their source is in
God; we work with Him only by receiving. All of God's qualities
grow in us by process.

Peace with God inevitably follows acceptance of His way.
That peace is God's business, deriving from His nature. We can
disturb it, just as we can offend anyone. When that happens,
we accept the glad reconciliation He offers. Our peace with
Him relates closely to our trust in Him. Anxiety says that God
is not worthy of trust. Peace declares that His trust cannot be
broken.

Peace with men is never a matter of deciding which member
of an injured party is right. It does not depend on the proof of
which is stronger. Being right or proving the right will not make
peace; it may create resentment. True peace cannot be accomplished by arbitration but by reconciliation. In reconciliation, the
one who is more mature shows love and a desire for reconciliation

to the less mature. Only humility will make peace.

The fullest peace will never be accomplished within the world system. Jesus made no effort to establish peace with His enemies: the scribes and the Pharisees. The way of peace is not compromise (Matthew 10:34-36). Jesus *gave* peace to His followers (John 14:27).

DESIRABLE ATTRIBUTES THAT GOD DOES NOT HAVE

This subhead might bewilder you after six chapters of emphasizing the Christ in us. Heaven's view, however, looks for two qualities in us that are indispensable to the achievement of our goals, yet they are qualities that do not exist in God.

Fear. Some would contend that our fear of the Most High corresponds to God's regard for the most lowly (Psalm 138:6) — in other words, that our fear derives from His regard, a quality that *does* exist in God. That correlation is valid but, more specifically, is an *exchange* rather than a *derivation*. We do not derive our fear of God from fear in Him, as we derive our love from His love. God has no fear, but the exchange is real: He respects the humble; in exchange we fear His greatness.

The only fear that is rational is fear of God. No other power equals His, but also no other kind intention equals His. All other fears are unfounded because no other haven is safe. Most often, the reason we do not fear God is because we have not proved Him.

We humans assign rank to the factors in our lives. What we fear tells God the rank we assign to the various features of our life. Many Christians fear money; their life commitment is to financial safety. Others "fear" (pay their highest respect to) position. These are the "important" factors in life. However, if we love God above all else, we fear offending *Him*; we fear deriving our maintenance and guidance from any other source. When we fear Him above all else, we are assigning to Him a rank higher than any other parts of our lives.

Fearing God acknowledges that all things are in His control. Heaven knows that and is pleased when we recognize it. Fear indicates real belief. Relationship with Him cannot exist without belief.

Shame. God cannot know this distressing emotion. Evil angels are incapable of shame (at present), and good angels have no need of it. In us, it occurs when we fail to confess sin. Adam's shame caused him to hide himself from God (Genesis 3:10). Ezra was ashamed of corporate sin (Ezra 9:6).

The embarrassment of social impropriety differs radically from the private, individual shame of betraying the high work of God in us. When we sin, we have double-crossed the purest love we have. Anticipating this treachery of our relationship with Him, God gifted us with conscience for the specific purpose of restoring our bond with Him as quickly as possible.

Therefore, any sin should be confessed as quickly as awareness permits. We asked God to give us grief rather than guilt when we sin; grief cannot wait and will confess without delay. Confession secures immediate forgiveness (1 John 1:9) and removes the shame. Shame is the opposite of glory (Hosea 4:7), and God purposes only glory for His redeemed.

THE SURPRISING ROAD TO GLORY

In the first half of this book, we have shown that God created us to share His glory with us. Our glory derives from a relationship with Him, the basis of Christianity itself. We heighten

the bond with God by *working* with Him (2 Corinthians 6:1).
Working together with God, we cannot help but cooperate with
the development of His attributes in us (Amos 3:3).

Our work may involve more than the usual idea of service. It
may involve steadfastness in difficult circumstances. Surely,
Stephen was working with God in His martyrdom! Paul worked
with God in His shipwreck. Suffering can become a "working
together with God."

People going through suffering (cancer, debt, loss) tend to ask
questions of God. Job asked many questions. God never answered
Job's questions: He revealed Himself. What Job needed was to
know the person of God, not an explanation of God's actions.
(We will understand this more thoroughly in chapter 10.)

God does not wait until the end of suffering to reveal Himself.
We begin by realizing that our suffering will somehow eventuate
in God's glory, so we seek Him rather than "answers." Seeking
God becomes one way of working with Him.

To be sure, we have pain and sorrow, but in seeking only God,
each hurt is met with further revelation of Him. The important
aspect of our learning is not the new insights God teaches us; our
highest reward is knowing God in a new depth.

The road to knowing Him introduces several surprising twists
and turns. The lower we place ourselves, the higher we perceive
God to be. Logically, that ought to make Him more distant from
us, but the "altitude" makes us closer to Him!

The more we submit to Him in humility, the greater the stature
we discover in Him. Astonishingly, surrendering our "stature" leads
to our growth in stature! Humbling oneself leads to an unexpected
ripening of the Christ within. A strangeness in God's working
begins to crystallize for us: Descending into lowliness leads to new
heights. We come to appreciate God's statement that "My thoughts

are not your thoughts, nor are your ways My ways. . . . For as the heavens are higher than the earth, so are My ways higher than your ways and My thoughts than your thoughts" (Isaiah 55:8-9).

The paradoxes multiply; we find that the better we know God, the more we realize how much we do not know. The closer we approach Him, the further into the distance His vastness stretches. The more we become full of Him, the more of us there is for Him to fill. The more we yearn for Him, the more intense our yearning becomes.

Most astonishing of all, we find that the more we work with God, the more He works with us! This compounding of service leads to deeper entrenchment in His kingdom. Serving Him, we want Him to rule. Our prayers for His lordship over His creation assume unimaginable intensity.

God's methods cannot be predicted by human logic. None of us asks for shame or suffering. We do not learn about God merely by study and investigation, although they do indeed help. The highest learning comes by working with Him to achieve His purposes. If we *cooperate* with Him as "fellow workers" (1 Corinthians 3:9) — not merely *submit* to Him (many regard shame and suffering as a demand to submit rather than cooperate) — we cannot avoid reciprocity. Working with Him even in grief and shame, we know Him more intimately. He seeks a *working* relationship to build His attributes into us. In the fullness of this growing bond, He carries us from glory to glory.

PART II

APPLYING
HEAVEN'S
VIEW IN
OUR LIVES

CHAPTER 7

From Heaven's View, Limitations Help Us Grow

Man's steps are ordained by the LORD, how then can man understand his way?

PROVERBS 20:24

God has made us so that discomfort can serve useful purposes. Pain can be a valuable signal to the body, and it also becomes useful in our spiritual growth. Another "discomfort"—discipline—develops our character. Overcoming builds muscles on an obstacle course, and overcoming in difficult life circumstances moves us from strength to strength (Psalm 84:7). God has so designed us that limitations force us to perform a work we might otherwise avoid. Divinely imposed limitations help us grow in the Lord.

FACING OUR LIMITATIONS
We Must Begin at the Beginning
We often ignore the fact that we begin at the beginning; it is such an obvious truism. Impatient new Christians often do not realize

that Paul instructed Timothy, "Do not lay hands upon anyone too hastily and thereby share responsibility for the sins of others" (1 Timothy 5:22). The assigning of responsibilities too early in the life of a new believer damages the lives of people trying to follow him or her.

A baby begins without developed abilities and without understanding and must depend on its parents for everything in life. The most important factor a new Christian ought to learn is how dependent he or she is on God. Prior to having Christ in us, we managed without God; following the old familiar pattern, we plunge into our new life in Christ, seldom realizing that every aspect of our new life depends on Him. If we start our Christian life relying totally on Him, we will be more likely to look to Him as the source for the rest of our lives. The growth, the process, can never be right unless each step of the process originates in God from beginning to end.

The disciples of Jesus began at the beginning. They were chosen, not because of their position, brilliance, or wealth but because they could recognize spiritual authority. They would remain dependent through their three-year training and hence into the spread of the New Testament church.

The record of their obedience amazes us today. Whatever Jesus commanded, they obeyed without question: "Follow Me," "Bring Me the five loaves and two fish," "Cross the lake," "Take up your cross," "Remain in Jerusalem until you are endued with power." In today's world, a disciple would need an explanation of the use of the little boy's lunch before going for it. The disciples often did not understand Jesus, but they never objected to or questioned any of His commands.

When God commands us to do something, we do not need to understand His directive; we need to understand His authority.

Obedience does not depend on the grasp of the larger plan; it depends on the relationship of the servant to the master or of the child to the parent. God cannot work through us unless we obey, but we need to be sure of the voice of the Shepherd, a recognition that grows with experience.

During our spiritual infancy, we can find plenty of commands in the Bible to obey while we are learning wisdom. To many young Christians, some of the Bible commands seem counterintuitive: "Love your enemies"; "Go the second mile." Obeying them, we learn their purpose: They help develop stature and nobility.

Little children must learn to obey early in life for their own safety. They learn obedience through discipline. (And, by the way, even the discipline has to wait until understanding grows in the infant; the earlier stages are given to diligent care by the parents.) Later the children arrive at a state where cooperation with their parents takes the place of the earlier discipline. Every one of us had to begin our physical lives by depending on others.

Any long-term job is the same way: We do things at the beginning that will not be necessary later. Beginnings always furnish important learning tools. Not beginning properly in our Christian lives leads to many failures later. At the beginning, we do not have patience; we haven't learned it yet. God does not abruptly give us patience and endurance at the beginning; they are mastered, like the piano. The music student needs a teacher, and the young Christian needs the Lord. The more important virtues — love, wisdom, and power, to name a few — may remain incipient or immature during our early stages. The Christian life requires skills, and developing skills requires process.

Few new believers realize they will still have to battle temptation and evil. They must learn to discern which desires originate from their fleshly nature and which are valid yearnings of the new nature. This important step again takes place in process, with some missteps but also encouraging successes.

Beginning at the beginning is not a disadvantage. New Christians have many traits God can use mightily. Such advantages as eagerness, joy, and excitement fit them for tasks befitting the new life. All kinds of prayer are available to the young Christian: In praying, they learn to pray. The infectious testimony of young believers captures the imagination of others: In witnessing, they learn to witness. The harder tests, trials, and disciplines may come later. These bring with them a lasting development of pain tolerance and the use of pain for growth.

At the beginning, we also lack knowledge and understanding. The angels were gifted with perfect knowledge. They made their decision to rebel from that standpoint, so they had no way back. We have to acquire our knowledge, and that is part of the process. It is hoped that young Christians will be careful before acting while they learn what they are dealing with in their life situations.

The limitation of knowledge has purpose; this particular constraint participates in moving us into ever-higher glory. The acquisition of knowledge is normally an act of the will. We often make our mistakes through ignorance, a drawback that can be overcome. The most helpful knowledge we can get is the knowledge of God through His Scriptures, which are available to most Christians in the Western world. We cannot become like Christ if we do not acquaint ourselves with Him, His ways, and His attributes, all of which require determined effort.

Bad Thought Patterns Within a Hostile Environment

Every Christian, young or old, labors under two disadvantages: an inherited twisted nature (Romans 3:23) and a hostile environment (Matthew 13:22). Although God gives us a new nature in Christ, we still keep the old body and many sinful thought patterns. These patterns include such resistant weaknesses as a disposition to anger; lust after sex, money, or position; fears from childhood; and ingrained self-centeredness. The good pleasure of God dictates that we learn how to overcome these.

The good angels have no such difficulties. God knew the stature we would acquire in surmounting difficulties. His beneficent will dictates that we participate in His work of growing us. We are not to become "self-made"; rather, we cooperate with God in the stern mutuality He desires while we grow.

Not only do we overcome our old nature but we also have to overcome extremely antagonistic surroundings. In our environment, we get Satan's education before we get God's. "All that is in the world, the lust of the flesh and the lust of the eyes and the boastful pride of life, is not from the Father, but is from the world" (1 John 2:16). We can expect no lasting help from business, society, or government. That is why we begin by learning to depend on God first. We learn accountability in our duties second.

God's strange arrangement that we retain our old nature in a hostile environment seems to suggest that He is being unfair to Himself and unfair to us. We worldlings demand that God be "fair," but God does not think in terms of "fairness"; He thinks in terms of greatness, nobility, and mastery. Terms such as *victory*, *overcome*, *reward*, and *dominion* are more native to Him than *efficiency*, *ease*, *comfort*, and *indulgence*. We are learning Heaven's view, so now we see that God's road may be challenging.

Jesus warned against persecution because He knew that the world could not grasp such concepts as self-sacrifice and humility. Jesus cautioned us, "If the world hates you, you know that it has hated Me before it hated you" (John 15:18). Insofar as we fail to understand Heaven's view, we also persecute. The world hates what it cannot understand. We must not make the same mistake.

The Constraints of Our Vocabulary

We have already mentioned this problem, and it will recur. Our vocabulary sets limits to our earthly framework. One of our difficulties in grasping eternity is our confinement to time words (*urgent, pressing, deadline*) that force us each day into captivity to the clock. Words such as *leisure* and *holiday* entrance us, and words like these will have no meaning in eternity. (We are not disparaging relaxation or rest, but these sometimes become more demanding on us than bringing Christ's kingdom.)

We have already stated that God words (*infinite, love*) can be expressed only in immeasurables that are difficult to grasp at present. The real problem presents itself in our assumption that we *do* understand these grand ideas. The little boxes we put God into are limited by culture and tradition.

At present we have to use many "good" words and concepts that will not be good in eternity. No one will consider "fairness" after Graduation Day. The kingdom of Christ will hardly be "democratic"; the more thoroughly we comprehend what God is, the more we appreciate this fact. The word *forgive* will disappear completely, and none of us will require *discipline*. These concepts are valuable in a fallen world; we function better where all of them work. Because they are so helpful now, we think we will carry them beyond graduation. We do not have the facility to imagine a world so much nobler than this that these ideas will not be necessary.

We could not function in today's world without "efficiency" as we know it. God, however, works from the standpoint of long-range goals that require modification of our natural desires. If God were "efficient" by our definition, the Bible would be a record of perfect men and women instead of bumbling, mean-spirited creations with whom God shows enormous patience. The Bible records how a perfect God deals with imperfect humans. If God were "efficient," the word *temporary* would have no meaning in this world. Conversion would destroy the flesh instead of leaving us with something to overcome. To us, "efficiency" describes how we would have designed the world and the universe from our present perspective. But this book is about Heaven's view.

Eternity will have no need of "efficiency." If we insist that God show efficiency *now*, we would be constantly seeking the ultimate purposes of our stubbed toes and bad colds (although God can use even these). Because we are yet within the fabric of time with limited wisdom, we do not need to *understand* every event; rather, we are to *glorify God* in every event (the earliest insight we learned in Melana's cancer). We fasten our eyes not on the momentary mishaps but on the direction and purpose of our process.

Mistakes We Make Within Our Limitations

We live in a world confused by the father of lies. Living in this situation, we adopt attitudes based on our culture and training. Historically, most of the cultures that started out Christian degenerated into a moral morass, in some cases rather quickly. Most of the advice we get from helpers comes from the same muddled life view. Therefore, in almost any culture, even seasoned believers occasionally take wrong directions.

Another misstep happens when we act rashly. This thoughtless world moves impetuously, and impulsiveness is "catching." Jesus never hesitated, yet He always knew what He was doing.

Our limitations tempt us to the dangerous blunder of judging others. Often we judge because we become impatient for God to take action. We assume too much. God waits to reveal all the factors until His timing fits into a larger picture. In other words, we judge in ignorance.

The most serious mistake we can make is sin of any kind: disobedience, disbelief, self-indulgence, lack of control, fixations, and the boundless like. Willful sin makes you "equal" with God. As if you know as much as He does!

PURPOSES OF LIMITATIONS

Satan can hinder the work of God, but he cannot pass the bounds God sets (Job 1:12). Through the Holy Spirit, we can overcome the work of Satan. God allows obstacles for the specific purpose of teaching us how to overcome.

God's limitations are more formidable than those of Satan. They require overcoming on a noble scale. They vary from person to person because God's limitations are tailor-made. He can allow illness, a difficult family situation, a physical restriction, a learning disability, financial distress, or an accusation in innocence — never for the sake of punishment, and often not even for discipline. Although God may not be the source of a particular distress, within it He can ennoble us on a far grander scale than we would have chosen.

When we were writing this book, we had a cousin who chose to glorify God in his terminal illness. The passing of time weakened his body but made his witness for Christ more incisive and convincing. Doctors and nurses were strongly influenced by his affirmations of God's goodness while he was suffering unbearable pain and struggle.

One purpose for limitations is to *teach us how to choose*. We live in a world of non-absolutes, and choices force us to consider final results. We are learning absolutes. The choices He imposes on us may be daily, as in a lingering disability. Continually preferring to glorify God in adverse conditions fast-forwards us into the highest glories.

The choice may come in the form of an event where, for example, we choose to believe God and His Word. We believe what we want to believe. The "belief problem" does not usually derive from lack of faith but from our lusts. Christians sometimes choose to escape hard choices by manipulation. They may lie to get a job or embezzle to procure some object. On the other hand, trusting the unchanging care of God, they can confess truth when truth has unpleasant consequences. Real choices have to be deliberate, an act of the will.

God may require situations that will force us *to see the right perspective*. He *is* the potter, and this potter has the power and wisdom to help us realize the pliancy of good clay. Many circumstances can introduce us to the rightful reference points of king-subject, creator-created, redeemer-redeemed, and master-servant.

The two of us have learned to devote a major part of our prayer time to confessing our desperate need for God. We found that the more desperately we presented our case to God, the closer He drew to us. Telling Him how urgently we need Him now takes a major part of the beginning of our prayer time. Suffering helped us learn that.

Another purpose of limitations may be *to procure the work of God in our lives.* One reason God's heart turns to the needy lies in their receptivity to His work. Jesus blessed the poor in spirit, those who mourn, the meek, and those who hunger and thirst for righteousness. Limitations make us more tractable.

Limitations *direct us to the path of life* (Psalm 16:11; this psalm has been vital to our prayer lives). If anyone on earth ought to understand the abundance of life Jesus described in John 10:10, it should be the experienced Christian. *Life* is that process in which the activity of the divine process is continuous. *Abundant life* moves from favor to favor, strength to strength, faith to faith, and, above all, glory to glory.

We can be sure of the presence of life when it reproduces itself. Reproduction may come by overt witness, teaching, example, or persistent kindness. God's divine process through the centuries has continued finding people who will multiply life by personal replication.

Limitations *develop character qualities* of endurance, stamina, and thirst for God, among others. At the beginning of this chapter, we noted that pain can stimulate spiritual growth. We become aware of something when it is in excess, such as pain or joy. Most of us do not give attention to minor particulars until they get out of order or else are blessed extraordinarily. God can use our heartbeat, an accident, a job loss, or a promotion to call attention to our prospects for growth. Both distresses and benefits heighten our consciousness. In full awareness (even in adversity), we can, with our will, move forward in the new strength God has prepared us for.

God's intention in limiting us is not to paralyze us but to expand us. He does not want pygmies ruling in the new creation; He prefers giants — princes of such stature that they can wear crowns and sit on thrones. Lives of ease hardly cultivate gianthood.

LIMITATIONS TEACH US THE NOBILITY OF HUMILITY

Our limitations are intended not to generate resentment but a special kind of humility. Although the Bible commands humility (Luke 14:10; Romans 12:16), many Christians, struggling to obey the Bible, apply the wrong kind of humility. Only our limitations force us to look to the nobility that true humility has. We understand genuine humility and nobility by looking at God.

Our humility must be like that within the Holy Trinity. Preachers and theologians require us to be humble because of our sinful condition, a condition that is absent within God Himself. Therefore, it may seem strange to speak of "humility" within the high station of the Trinity. That kind of humility transcends human understanding. We must grow before we can emulate it.

Philippians 2:8 specifically declares that Jesus "humbled Himself"; He did it deliberately, cognitively. The entire section, verses 5-11, describes the humility of Jesus as a quality we should emulate. Jesus cannot have a quality absent from the other two members of the Trinity, so the biblical concept must involve more meaning than merely lowering ourselves.

The New Testament describes each member of the Trinity as pointing to the other two in some way. The Father commands us to hear the Son (Matthew 17:5), and the Son glorifies the Father (John 17:4). It is the Spirit who relates us to the Father (Romans 8:16) and makes us cry, "Abba! Father!" (Galatians 4:6). The One who gives only perfect gifts (James 1:17), our heavenly Father, bestows on us the Spirit (John 14:16). The Spirit led Jesus into the wilderness (Luke 4:1), yet He glorifies the Son (John 16:14). Many scriptural passages describe this mutual deference within the Holy Trinity.

Humility is not a confession of inadequacy but of interdependence. In the polyphony described in chapter 2, each melody *needs* the other melodies in order to fulfill the composer's intention. One melody does not "yield" to another melody; it "yields" to the composer, who may choose to emphasize one and then another. God is the composer; and when we cooperate with Him, the polyphony strikes the outside world enough to draw some wanderers to Christ.

Obviously, our sinful condition requires lowliness when we stand before the perfection of God. Humility before God recognizes the enormous but not unbridgeable gulf between His being and our being. Christians make a serious mistake when they begin trying to be lowly before others instead of before God. A basic premise of this book has been that every aspect of the Christian life begins in God.

Chapter 2 of Philippians goes on to require lowliness before other humans. The implication of the divine "humility" for us is that our lowliness comes not from belittling ourselves but from esteeming others. Only this kind of deference will demonstrate the nobility we see within the Godhead. In eternity, we will probably get a stronger word for the amazing interaction within the three persons that are God, but in limited human language, the most accessible concept we can presently understand is "humility."

Paul uses the entire second chapter of Philippians to describe the humility we are to have. The first four verses appeal to us to be humble. Verses 5-11 describe the divine humility. Paul reinforces his point by describing his personal self-sacrifice (verses 17-18) and then the unselfishness of Timothy (verses 19-24) and of Epaphroditus (verses 25-30). Biblical humility for us, therefore, involves deference for others, self-sacrifice, and unselfishness — all of which we find in God.

From our strictly human side, faith and humility are complementary; each is necessary for the other to function properly. Faith is the *basis* of our relationship with God; humility is the *condition* of that relationship. Faith begins the connection; humility begins our character development on the right track. Only our limitations put us on that track.

Faith and humility have to go together because faith is perceptive. To be perceptive at all is to recognize the magnitude of God's glory. From that standpoint, we can proceed to a humility that is properly ennobled according to the divine "humility."

Humility is "unself-conscious" and totally God-conscious. If faith *perceives* God, humility *understands* God. It bows before the greatness it has comprehended. Again and again, God reassures us that He dwells with the lowly (Psalm 138:6; Isaiah 57:15). This is because the two elements of faith and humility are properly apprehending His nature; we are becoming fit for His company.

Only humility knows what to be bold about and what to have reverence for. This insight into propriety couples humility with wisdom, another complement. Humility is the one quality that will be reverent around absolute holiness. With the wisdom of humility, we begin to see that our qualities, like those of God, must work together (as faith, humility, and wisdom do). It turns out that Heaven's view emerges from an integrated personality (a wholeness explained in chapter 12), a prescription coming straight from the attributes of God.

Humility also couples with dependence, still another significant complement. Dependence presents us with an unexpected advantage: the help God alone gives. Jesus confessed dependence on His Father (Luke 2:49; John 14:10), and He also depended on the Holy Spirit (Matthew 12:28). If Jesus declared, "I can do nothing on My own initiative" (John 5:30), surely we can understand our helplessness when we override God. Dependence calls on God's mutuality with us.

Pride carries the grim disadvantage of independence. Uzziah "became strong, [and] his heart was so proud that he acted corruptly, and he was unfaithful to the LORD his God" (2 Chronicles 26:16). Uzziah had to face the consequences of his independence (leprosy), and so do we if we do not follow Jesus' model of humility and dependence. Our penalty may come in a more subtle form than Uzziah's, but the highest price any Christian can pay is separation in independence from the ceaseless work of God. All evil is arrogant and self-sufficient; all virtue is humble and dependent (again, the virtues working together).

Satan tricks us into thinking *we* are doing the work. Our confidence lies not in our ability but in the faithfulness of God's working with us (1 Corinthians 1:9). Humility is not an inferiority complex; it is a superiority complex about the greatness of God.

If birds could think, they would ask, *What are birds that You are mindful of them?* God is mindful of the birds (Matthew 6:26)! If lilies could talk, they would ask, "What are lilies, that You should bother about them?" God cares for the lilies (Matthew 6:28-29)! Small wonder, then, that David, so overwhelmed by immensity, asked the same question about people (Psalm 8:4). We humans—gifted with intelligence, perception, and insight—remain woefully ignorant of our high destiny described in chapter 2. A New Testament Christian already enjoys the glory, and much more lies ahead.

We are extremely valuable to God and indispensable to His purposes. That marvel does not contradict the role of humility as we have seen it in the Godhead, where each member values the others. Our limitations, properly understood, make us interactive with God and with humans. They help create a beautiful polyphony.

THE MAIN PURPOSE OF LIMITATIONS: OUR OVERCOMING

Jesus assumed human flesh not merely to die for our sins but also to show us the meaning of life. When we study His example, the continuity of the divine process cannot be questioned. His life certainly reproduced itself (the sign of life given above). He depended on His Father and the Holy Spirit. We are to learn from and imitate His example.

The main purpose of limitations is to teach us to overcome. Of all the purposes of the limitations God deliberately imposes, overcoming is the most difficult to realize and work out in our lives. Even the second person of the Trinity, in His incarnation, had to overcome formidable obstacles to prove to us that we really can surmount obstacles while in our flesh.

Jesus had to overcome temptation (Matthew 4:3-11). He had to conquer the lust of the flesh, the lust of the eyes, and the pride of life (1 John 2:16). Satan infiltrates the church and the kingdom with people who succumb constantly to all three enticements. Sometimes such people lure others into their weakness.

The incarnate Lord overcame the world (John 16:33). Jesus was referring primarily to the tribulation the world inflicts on us; He gives peace in the middle of it. But He also prevailed over the cultural boxes His fellow Jews were imprisoned in. These little jails hold people captive today when they interpret their relationship to God from a societal rather than biblical reading.

The Lord Jesus conquered one foe we do not have to face: spiritual death. "When He had disarmed the rulers and authorities,

He made a public display of them, having triumphed over them [in His resurrection]" (Colossians 2:15). No Christian need fear Graduation Day—or Transition Day, when we move from glory to the highest glory. The frightful second death we would have suffered has been forever vanquished. Stephen's death was not a shame; it was a glory (Acts 7:59-60).

Death can no longer threaten us, but we do have specific foes to conquer while we are still within our limitations. The most difficult enemies we face are ourselves. Self raised its ugly head in Lucifer's rebellion and in Adam's fall. The glory-to-glory believer prefers not to put self first in relationships, decisions, preferences, and tastes. Jesus never put Himself first; He put the interests of His Father and the Holy Spirit first.

Like Jesus, we also must overcome temptation. Being weaker than He and retaining a sin nature, we pray first for deliverance from it (Matthew 6:13; "temptation" could also refer to trial). The strength-to-strength Christian learns to think before he or she acts. The tenor of New Testament teaching tells us we can do that.

We are to overcome the world with the assurance Jesus gave us in John 16:33. Jesus claimed, "I am not of this world" (8:23). He could ask most of us that in the midst of our daily life: "Are you of this world?" The influence of the world can be readily seen in our checkbooks. We are also to overcome the tribulation that the world metes out to us. From Heaven's view, avoiding tribulation is of no consequence; overcoming it is.

The most difficult struggle we have is overcoming our own failure. We appropriate the grace of God for that terrible war. No other power is adequate.

In our limitations, we learn not to be threatened; God maintains control. Evidently, God attaches great importance to the drama of overcoming. There He demonstrates His glory, power, presence with us, and work with us.

On the day before I (T. W.) wrote this paragraph, a brief e-mail informed me, "Charles Williamson went to be with the Lord *in glory* at about 2:45 a.m. today." Charlie was a close personal friend during my years at Southwestern Seminary and one of the deepest Christians I have known. That evening his son informed me that his dad had anticipated this glory day eagerly.

If time were not linear, "history" and "future" would not allow progress. We cannot reverse time in order to correct our mistakes, but, in our own future, we can overcome previous mistakes. Only within our confines is development possible. Our daily walk demands close attention to each step at the time we take it; in development, we have a choice in what we are becoming. The two of us can prove it; in our illnesses we have been to the brink of death and back, for more "glory-to-glory"!

CHAPTER 8

How Heaven Views Evil

We are not wrestling with flesh and blood [contending only with physical opponents], but against the despotisms, against the powers, against [the master spirits who are] the world rulers of this present darkness, against the spirit forces of wickedness in the heavenly (supernatural) sphere.

EPHESIANS 6:12 (AMP)

Theologians and philosophers have spent centuries trying to comprehend the origin and nature of evil. The paradox strikes any thoughtful person as strange: God is good, yet He allows evil in His own creation. We would prefer that He create a perfect world to begin with, with perfect people obeying Him perfectly at all times. We would be more "efficient" if we could create a world.

Suffering in our world originates in one way or another from the presence of evil in it. Greedy people suppress the poor. Abuse is common. Dictators serve their personal whims. Malicious men torture the innocent. Christians are persecuted. Certain diseases spread from evil sources. Terrorism means none of us is safe. Most ordinary people become victims of cruelty or of gossip at some time during their lives. The pervading presence of wickedness and its consequences perplexes all of us.

Not all suffering comes directly from current evil actions. We can catch a cold or inadvertently miss a step. Few of us get disturbed about the accidents of life, especially minor ones. Suffering does not always indicate the presence of evil, but evil results in suffering. It is the monstrous presence of intentional evil that perturbs us.

THE PRESENCE OF EVIL IN THE WORLD
Evil's First Appearance

We have a few scriptural givens. Often, having to remain in ignorance, we must accept the fruitlessness of seeking full and satisfying explanations. We find it more practical to accept the few hints that are given in Scripture: Evil originated in the angels, they can influence humans, and the present world is essentially evil. All of us are so inclined to wrong thinking by nature that the whole world system reflects that same nature. Moreover, a major problem lies in our own responsibility for some of the evil in this world and therefore for some suffering in it (Romans 5).

God in His goodness—and also in His intention to teach us overcoming—gave us laws and principles by His Word to guide us in the midst of all this trouble. He gave us a conscience that comprehends right and wrong and responds to it. Whether it is the law of the land or the social norms of our particular propriety, humans prefer to cling to an outer standard—a law—to make our judgments and conform to societal expectations. As it works out, our conscience usually agrees with that law.

The angels, on the other hand, had no Ten Commandments or Law to adhere to. Created as servants, they attend God out of their nature rather than adhering to an externally imposed standard. No doubt they currently conform to God's righteousness better than we do because it is their nature to obey and stay faithful to their Creator.

Although theologians disagree on the Isaiah 14 and Ezekiel 28 passages, we must assume they apply to Lucifer, or Satan, because the language is far too grandiose to apply to a mere human, regardless of his rank. It seems preposterous to think of the king of Tyre as an "anointed cherub." Moreover, these passages are the most plausible explanation of Satan's present nature that we have available. He was joined by a large group of angels (Matthew 25:41; Jude 6; Revelation 12:7,9; see also 1 Peter 3:19-20; 2 Peter 2:4) who became the demons of the New Testament.

Lucifer evidently was "the anointed cherub who covers" (Ezekiel 28:14), "blameless in [his] ways . . . until unrighteousness was found in [him]" (verse 15). His unfathomable decision to rebel against God (Isaiah 14:12-14) cannot be understood by humans. We have the clue that his "heart was lifted up because of [his] beauty . . . [and] splendor" (Ezekiel 28:17), yet to understand his decision to rebel against God, we would have to get *inside* his mind and observe the (to us) bizarre machinations that induced his mutiny. Obviously, we cannot do that.

Lucifer "corrupted [his] wisdom by reason of [his] splendor" (verse 17) and attempted to "make [himself] like the Most High" (Isaiah 14:14). Desiring such an exalted state, he *chose* to become the adversary of God.

Language limits us here. In any language, *absolute* tends to mean (among other things) "without restriction" or "complete in its totality." *Ultimate* indicates the final or topmost degree. Unhappily, both terms can refer to attributes in the created or the Creator. We need terms that differentiate between creaturely "perfection" and divine perfection, but those terms do not exist. A creaturely absolute would be susceptible to corruption; a divine absolute would not.

Lucifer's fall from perfection was a total fall, so he had no way back. All *moral* attributes were reversed. Love became hatred; goodness became malevolence. Because God Himself cannot be overthrown, deserting Him compromised *every* attribute the powerful angel had been given while he served God. Lucifer's new ethical system was totally opposite to the one he had prior to his sin.

The attributes given for *service*, however, were not lost, because they do not involve character but only the ability to operate. The service attributes do not express the justice or the moral nature of God; they were given to facilitate the *work* of God. Therefore, Lucifer lost none of his power, intelligence, or will—a will now bent to purposes utterly opposing God. These same reversed qualities, and also the conserved qualities, would apply to the angels who followed him: They are hateful and malevolent but also powerful and intelligent.

His attributes after his fall are absolute, as they were before the sin. His hatefulness now has no admixture of godly wisdom or affection. His and his followers' hatred is unconditional and unlimited; their fear is cringing; their malevolent intentions have nothing to mollify them. The demons that followed Lucifer have attributes like his and follow his pattern when tempting or trying us.

Incidentally, we must not assume that God forced Satan's fall to make possible the trials that would perfect us in our process. God cannot author any kind of evil, not even the suffering that renders our crucible a teaching opportunity for Him, although testing does indeed make available occasions for our learning and developing. Undoubtedly, God knew that Lucifer would fall, but He did not cause his fall. The great angel made his own decision, yet he did not tie God's hands. Appearances do not reveal to us the bottom-line truth that God remains sovereign.

The Personal Nature of Good and Evil

"Good" cannot be defined by behavior. Although "good people" are likely to perform good acts, their deeds do not make them "good." Evil people can perform good acts. They give to charities, participate in demonstrations for right causes, and often pride themselves for "being on the right side," yet Heaven views their nature as essentially wicked.

The opposite is true too. People whom the Bible portrays as "good" do wrong things. Abraham lied about Sarah being his wife; David committed adultery; Mark deserted Paul and Barnabas. If we believe the Bible at all, our definition of goodness cannot refer to outer behavior because the outer behavior of humans is not consistent.

The Bible does not present good as an abstraction, realized in vaguely "good" acts. Real good is personal; it derives from a personal relationship with God through Christ. Biblical goodness is Christ living out His life within us and through us. Because of this, we who seek Heaven's view will seek Christ's *personal* desire for every individual we meet.

We also seek God's personal good collectively. Throughout most of history, it has been Christians who built the hospitals and established the schools, at least in the Western world. However, like individual Christians, collective "Christians" sometimes also do monstrous wrong—establish inquisitions or carry wars and crusades into pagan areas in order to "Christianize" territories. Today much of the evil committed by Christians comes from "Christians" who do not have the personal Christ controlling them (such as those who kill abortion doctors). Whether it is individuals or nations, the test for goodness is not the nature of the act or even the result of the act but rather the presence of the Spirit of Christ in that act bringing the kingdom of God.

If bad people can do good works, good people can also perform bad acts; the definition of goodness or badness cannot lie in the essential nature of the act. Obviously, the converse of good being personal necessarily asserts itself. Evil, too, is personal.

The personal nature of good and evil does not imply dualism, the belief that Satan and God are equal. It only implies the basic nature of good and evil. The Bible clearly teaches that God is infinitely greater and will triumph.

Many people do not believe in a personal devil. Our conviction derives from (1) the fact that the Bible teaches it and (2) the fact that the twentieth century manifested evil in a personal way never seen before in history through the mass murders by *persons* such as Hitler, Mao Tse-tung, and Joseph Stalin, not to mention a host of minor dictators. The malevolence in the enormous numbers of mass murders could hardly be impersonal; it had to result from personal choice. Christians defeat evil by looking only to God in a profoundly *personal* relationship.

Non-Christians are not furtively hiding their evil natures: The whole world lives (often unconsciously) in the grip of the evil one. Good people can even be "carried away . . . by [their] own lust" (James 1:14), and lust results either from personal interaction with an evil angel or from a nature corrupted by evil. If every human represents a desire of God, he or she also represents a desire of Satan.

The incarnate Lord, who understood evil from Heaven's perspective, regarded evil as personal. He instructed us to pray, "Deliver us from the evil one" (Matthew 6:13, NKJV). Jesus prayed for His disciples, "Keep them from the evil one" (John 17:15). While pain or suffering may result from accident (even bacteria in the air), intentional good or intentional evil comes from personal sources.

However, we must never forget that God can bring good, even nobility, out of suffering, regardless of its source (Romans 8:28). He who is essential goodness can reweave even evil consequences for His larger purposes. He would not be sovereign if He could not do that.

Despite this, the crucial contest in our psyches is basically a personal one: Good is personal, and evil is personal. Neither is abstract. The Christian committed to overcoming regards the conflict between the two as essentially personal and depends on a personal relationship with God for victory.

How a Reversed Nature Acts

Satan does not create (bring something out of nothing), but his extraordinary intelligence acts with cunning and subtlety. Because

Satan now represents the opposite of God's character, his every work will either pervert or corrupt an opposite quality in God. Just as God works according to His nature, Satan works entirely out of his nature.

God wants to facilitate our kingdom work; Satan will obstruct it or put obstacles in our way. God promises; Satan threatens. The Holy Spirit leads us; the Enemy distracts us. The Lord wants to open our understanding; the Devil wants to seduce us. One of the names of God's Spirit is Helper; His enemy is the Adversary. God encourages us; Satan discourages us.

Satan controverted absolute reality. Therefore, he is the father of lies. One of his main works is to obscure the truth. He will disillusion our hopes, distort our understanding, confuse the issue, deceive us, disorient our path, accuse us wrongfully, exaggerate the problem, and flatter our vanity. He makes us think the mirage is real.

As the father of lies, Satan will pervert the things that most point to God. Music is perverted when its style suggests worldly desires to the listener. God intends for intimacy to be a delightfully unifying factor within marriage; Satan makes it so obsessive that it destroys marriage. God made the world beautiful; Satan concentrates on a neurotic hard-to-resist "attractiveness." The Creator made wholeness; His enemy fragments. God allows us to experience Himself. Satan makes experience an end in itself and convinces us that we must duplicate every experience, godly or ungodly, by the same route as we did the last time.

From Heaven's view, all lies are transparent and every sin is deadly. Heaven knows no "little" lies or "harmless" misrepresentations. A man or a woman cannot entertain an "innocent look." No sin can be "just this once." Absolute holiness does not justify the "peccadilloes" (petty sins).

From Heaven's view, all excuses are invalid. Excuses work for people but not for God. We can make the excuse "Daddy will understand" but not "God will understand." Therein lies our problem: God really does understand. Human forgiveness can come from sympathy, but the forgiveness of unimpeachable holiness can be granted only with genuine repentance.

Heaven's View of Satan

When the disciples returned from their missionary trip exulting that even the demons were subject to them in Jesus' name, Jesus responded, "I was watching Satan fall from heaven like lightning" (Luke 10:18). In Satan, Heaven sees the instigator of all hatred and evil. Heaven sees the mastermind of hurt strike God's perfect creation. The world has chosen a number of counterfeits (what Satan wants us to believe) to deceive us about Satan's true nature. The Bible reveals to us what Heaven sees.

How Heaven Sees Satan	Satan's Deception
The evil spiritual ruler of wickedness "Our struggle is not against flesh and blood, but against the rulers, against the powers, against the world forces of this darkness, against the spiritual forces of wickedness in the heavenly places" (Ephesians 6:12).	Satan does not exist. He is not a real being, but a vague, nebulous force of evil in the universe.
A murderer and liar "[Satan] was a murderer from the beginning, and does not stand in the truth because there is no truth in him. Whenever he speaks a lie, he speaks from his own nature, for he is a liar and the father of lies" (John 8:44).	A life without God's restrictions gives excitement, pleasures, independence from authorities, and no accountability or responsibilities that I do not choose.

How Heaven Sees Satan	Satan's Deception
The accuser, adversary, and enemy of Christians "The accuser of our brethren has been thrown down, he who accuses them before our God day and night" (Revelation 12:10). "Your adversary, the devil, prowls around like a roaring lion, seeking someone to devour" (1 Peter 5:8). "If they persecuted Me, they will also persecute you" (John 15:20).	Christians are the enemy of tolerance and fair-mindedness. They are hypocritical and self-righteous.
Powerless before Christ "Since the children share in flesh and blood, He Himself likewise also partook of the same, that through death He might render powerless him who had the power of death, that is, the devil" (Hebrews 2:14).	Satan and God are two equal and opposite forces; I succeed when I choose the good more than the bad.
Conquered by Christ at the resurrection "When He had disarmed the rulers and authorities, He made a public display of them, having triumphed over them through Him" (Colossians 2:15). "The Son of God appeared for this purpose, to destroy the works of the devil" (1 John 3:8).	God is dead or doesn't exist.
Already judged by God "The ruler of this world has been judged" (John 16:11).	Tolerance and fairness demand that all religions and opinions be available and acceptable.
Facing eternal torment "The devil who deceived them was thrown into the lake of fire and brimstone, where . . . [he] will be tormented day and night forever and ever" (Revelation 20:10).	Hell is a holdover fantasy of the Middle Ages.

If we could consistently perceive this enemy the way Heaven sees him, we would never attend to his lies, excuse his murders, or side with our accuser. We would not align with a defeated ruler. Jesus warned, "He who is not with Me is against Me; and he who does not gather with Me scatters" (Matthew 12:30).

THE HEART AND THE SPIRIT DETERMINE OUR CHARACTER

The Heart as a Cognitive (Thoughtful, Reflective) Organ

The Bible indicates clearly that both good and evil originate in the heart (Jeremiah 3:17; Matthew 5:8). Because evil begins in the heart, we must understand what the heart is. The biblical concept of the heart has persisted to the present day in that in the twenty-first century, in spite of our emphasis on the physical organ of the brain, we still continue saying, "He has a hard heart. . . . She is tenderhearted. . . . He loves her with his whole heart." Many scientists have begun to suspect that not all cognitive processes take place in the brain.

With our lack of understanding of spiritual matters, it is impossible to talk about God who is Spirit without using anthropomorphisms — figures of speech that describe Him as though He were a material being. The Bible refers to God's "heart" (Genesis 6:6; Acts 13:22). The Bible necessarily also refers to our spirits with physical terms. Christ is our "bread of life" (John 6:48), as though we ingested Christ. We "walk" by the Spirit (Galatians 5:16). We could not communicate at all without figures of speech.

In both testaments, the "heart" holds such prominence that for our present purposes we define it as *the cognitive organ of the spirit*. Science, of course, is reluctant to dissect the spirit; what instruments could they use? The ancient wisdom of the Bible does not refrain from such constraints. The Bible talks about the heart as all that we are inwardly. The heart is where we exercise our will (2 Chronicles 12:14; Matthew 15:19; John 13:2), our spiritual understanding (1 Kings 3:9; Ecclesiastes 8:5; Matthew 12:34-35; 1 Corinthians 2:9), and our emotions (1 Kings 11:4; 21:7; Proverbs 15:13; Mark 12:30; John 16:22).

With this cognitive aspect of the heart, we choose to determine our own character for good or evil (Jeremiah 3:17; Colossians 3:22). We have control over our hearts. With them we can harden ourselves against God (Exodus 8:15; Mark 10:5), and with them we can also love God with all our being (Deuteronomy 6:5; Mark 12:30). We are cautioned, "Watch over your heart with all diligence, for from it flow the springs of life" (Proverbs 4:23). Jesus reiterated this warning even more strongly (Matthew 15:17-19).

Because the heart somehow functions in our thought processes but "is more deceitful than all else and is desperately sick" (Jeremiah 17:9), it will easily slip into wrong corollaries. We could better understand evil and suffering if we discarded the following invalid assumptions:

- God is good. *Therefore, my desires (what I think is good) represent His will. Also: My interpretation must represent His will.*
- God is efficient. *Therefore, nothing can go wrong.*
- God is delight. *Therefore, anywhere I find delight, God must be there.*

- God is beauty. *Therefore, anywhere I discover attractiveness, God is there.*
- God leads. *Therefore, all "impressions" must be from God.*
- God blesses. *Therefore, all luxury and comfort come from God.*
- God is in control this minute. *Therefore, I will never stub my toe or get a cold.*

As we mature, we trust less and less in circumstances as an indicator of the mind of God. We especially distrust traditional or obvious interpretations of circumstances. For example, illness does not indicate that God is angry with us.

Not living on automatic pilot, we determine our course by our own will—the trained heart, the heart that has learned to look only to God. The heart that is centered on God alone learns to interpret circumstances from the point of view of what will bring Christ's kingdom and give Him glory.

We cannot say that a supernova is evil or that a collision of galaxies is wrong any more than we can distrust the law of gravity. We *can* say that Satan has corrupted that part of nature that concerns us, especially our own temperament. We can say quite confidently that God overrules corruption to bring greater nobility to us by means of practice in overcoming.

The Relationship of Sins of the Spirit and Sins of the Flesh

Two general kinds of sins grieve the Spirit of God: self-satisfying sins and self-elevating sins. The Bible calls the self-satisfying sins "the lust of the flesh and the lust of the eyes" (1 John 2:16). It seems likely that John did not intend to cover all possible sins with the two lusts and the "pride of life." Rather, they are included in "all that is in the world," and a single list would be inadequate.

The lust of the flesh involves mental delights from within, in the fleshly pleasures from glands and appetites. They result from sensual desires divorced from the spiritual and are superficial pleasures in that they satisfy only physical needs.

However, in God's economy, the physical needs can satisfy the spiritual as well as the physical. The Bible does not divorce the two; Jesus lived a physical life that was profoundly spiritual. At times, the most spiritual moment of our day occurs when we praise God for His creativity in a sunset. Sin does not enter unless the "gratification" is isolated to the purely physical. God *intended* that we enjoy cashews, music, silk, and the delightful scent of a rose with all our being.

The lust of the eye comes from without and can include contemplating a physical temptation or a material possession. The sin nature enters when gratification becomes selfish.

The more dangerous sins are the self-elevating ones from the "pride of life" (1 John 2:16); for convenience we may designate these "spiritual sins," even though all sin affects the spirit. These include narcissism, pride, and lust for money or power, resulting in greed, envy, and jealousy. Self-consciousness can also assume the form of self-abasement.

David's downfall was physical (2 Samuel 11:4) and hence not as dangerous as Saul's (1 Samuel 15:1-9; 28:7-19), which was spiritual. Lucifer's first sin was spiritual; he had no flesh to appeal to. Satan tried the spiritual first with Eve and proceeded to the physical. Self-satisfying (physical) sin does not always lead to self-elevating (spiritual) sin: David (with physical sin) could recover; Saul could not, because spiritual sin is more blinding.

However, physical sin often reveals an underlying spiritual sin. Anger can indicate arrogance. Adultery can result from spite or hatred. Heaven's view reveals a larger whole that may be sick through and through. "As he thinks within himself, so he is" (Proverbs 23:7).

Spiritual sin (the pride of life) nearly always reveals and compounds physical sin (the lust of the flesh and the eye). Cain was first jealous (a spiritual sin), and then he became physical. The great tyrants of history became obsessed with power *and* sex. The spiritual sins have resulted in the greatest physical terrors, horrors, and violence of history.

What Are These Sins of the Spirit?

The spiritual sins poison Heaven's perspective and also blind us to their own presence. They are the roots of many outward physical sins. People can see these sins in our lives, usually in disgust. Heaven sees them as crippling to us, and they grieve the Holy Spirit (Ephesians 4:30).

Unbelief. Unbelief is serious sin; doubt may be infant faith trying to grow. Sincere, God-honoring Christians often wrestle with doubt. Doubt may be unwillful and even involuntary. It need not be helpless. Christians who have walked with God for a long time need to be sensitive to the honest inquiries of genuine seekers. God provides sympathetic answers and real help to anyone who seeks Him with all their heart.

Unbelief, on the other hand, is usually willful. It signifies an evil heart. "Take care, brethren, that there not be in any one of you an evil, unbelieving heart" (Hebrews 3:12). Unbelief is evil because it elevates our judgment over God's revelation, essentially making us "equal" with God. Jesus rebuked unbelief: "He reproached them for their unbelief and hardness of heart" (Mark 16:14). We must remain alert to the difference in the painful weakness of doubting and the diabolical temptation to unbelief.

Perversion of belief happens when we make God into the

kind of God we want Him to be. We may want Him to be lenient or indulgent. This perversion often results from culture, background, or training. Heaven's view seeks to rise above these constraints.

A related perversion arises when we choose what we prefer to believe about God's nature. Idolatry perverts the spirit nature of God. Racial or cultural bias fails to understand the all-encompassing nature of God's love. Limiting His grandness misses out on answers to prayer. We cannot conform God to our perception.

Self-centeredness. This most common of the sins of the spirit may involve self-righteousness, self-sufficiency, or being self-made. Self-centeredness contradicts the value of relationships more than any other sin. Satan did not fall because of the flesh; he fell because he centered on himself.

Self-righteousness happens when we evaluate ourselves in relation to others instead of in relation to Christ. Almost all of us can find someone we seem to be "superior" to. Pride is always of the world. When we see from Heaven's view, we can never find an occasion for pride.

Jesus commended love of self; we are to love others as ourselves (Mark 12:31). We may legitimately feed ourselves, protect ourselves, and care for all real needs. We are creatures of God, and we may love all that God loves.

However, the Bible condemns placing oneself at the center (Proverbs 21:2; 26:12; Isaiah 2:17). Jesus commanded us to love our neighbor *as ourselves*. God is totally other-directed; Jesus showed that quite clearly, and we are to become like Him.

Legalism. Legalism focuses on outer behavior, not on the inner spirit. Righteousness does not conform to rules; it conforms to Christ. Legalism exalts laws; obedience observes principles.

This sin nearly always results in self-righteousness because of what satisfies it. It places its faith in a formula or even in a culture instead of Christ. Christ alone is our righteousness.

Fanaticism. Fanaticism is belief without relationship. In fanaticism, we are more preoccupied with our personal "rightness" than with God's purposes as expressed in Christ. Fanaticism is intolerant and becomes cruel when the Spirit of Christ is left out. (This sin will be discussed more thoroughly in chapter 9.) Both legalism and fanaticism derive satisfaction from self-display.

Self-abasement. Self-abasement avoids self-revealing encounters. It can include discouragement, anxiety, depression, and reluctance. This sin paralyzes its victim. Bullying can come either from this weakness of spirit or, in other cases, from self-centeredness.

All these sins of the spirit originate from pride. Pride is impossible to detect in itself; the Spirit must convict and point it out. Heaven's view is totally obstructed by this sin. While we harbor pride, God resists everything we do (James 4:6). Desiring to understand Heaven's view of ourselves and those around us is the beginning of the cleansing process (verses 8-10).

A few years ago, I (Melana) went through an intense period of personal brokenness. I yearned to recognize pride in my life. Philippians 2:3 — "In lowliness of mind let each esteem other better than themselves" (KJV) — had gripped my heart, and I wanted to learn how to do that. My problem was, I honestly thought I knew some who were not "better than I."

A particular person at my church came to mind. I could not see much desire for growth in this individual. I saw worldly attitudes. I sincerely asked God, "How do I esteem _____ to be better than myself? He does not grow in Your Word. He is critical. I am trying to learn Your ways. How do I consider him to be better than I?"

My heavenly Father responded to me immediately: "Do you really want to know?"

That stopped me. I expected Him to say, "In this situation, you are right. You do not have to esteem him better than yourself."

I then knew that I had been wrong. I was still puzzled because I knew that this person did have some major attitude problems and did not appear to want to solve them. But God obviously had something in mind that I was clueless about.

I solemnly replied, "Yes, I do want to know how to honestly esteem _____ better than myself."

God showed me His view: This person had a genuine servant's heart. I had little desire at that point to serve others; I wanted to lead and be respected. God seemed to say, "In My kingdom, _____ is the greatest of all because I see his servant's heart. You need to learn this from him."

I knew God was right. This person was a true servant of His church. Now I could see it plainly. I learned that each person in my sphere has some strength that I need. Where they are strong, I am weak, so I truly do need their help and example.

THE INVASION OF SIN IN OUR LIVES
What Our Personal Sin Does to Us

No consequence of sin is as grim as the grief that sin gives to the Spirit of God (Ephesians 4:30). Once we begin to grow in Christ, our desire to please Him grows stronger. Conversely, our desire not to displease Him also grows. If we ever fully comprehend the enormity of our offense, our conscience becomes so sensitized that our first reaction to our own sin also becomes grief for ourselves.

Isaiah records a second result of sin: "Your iniquities have made a separation between you and your God" (Isaiah 59:2). Separation from God is hellish, a kind of death. The second death is eternal separation from the source of life. David begged, "Do not forsake the works of Your hands" (Psalm 138:8). Because God is omnipresent, He is wherever we are, but sin causes a *personal* disjunction of fellowship. We must never take God for granted; we purposely enjoy His person at all times.

Sin obscures Heaven's view. Peter should have known never to question Jesus, yet he rebuked the Lord when Jesus announced His impending death. Jesus' words to him chill us to the bone: "You are not setting your mind on God's interests, but man's" (Matthew 16:23). Peter did not have Heaven's view at that moment.

For us individually, the most dangerous aspect of sin is its tendency to compound itself (Romans 1:21-27). Just as virtue will compound itself in the first kingdom principle (see chapter 3), sin will also multiply rapidly. It is infectious (spreading rapidly, James 3:6) and contagious (Deuteronomy 20:8).

Sin dulls our spiritual senses (Romans 1:28-29). Pharaoh's heart was hardened by a lifetime of offenses. We can even develop to the point of completely searing our conscience (1 Timothy 4:2), which is to lose all that makes us human.

Sin takes glory away from us. God said of His own people, "The more they multiplied, the more they sinned against Me; I will change their glory into shame" (Hosea 4:7). Both glory and shame lie in the hand of God.

Our own transgressions interrupt the progress of the process of sanctification. Paul warned,

> This is the will of God, your sanctification; that is, that you abstain from sexual immorality; that each of you know how to possess his own vessel in sanctification and honor, not in lustful passion, like the Gentiles who do not know God; and that no man transgress and defraud his brother in the matter because the Lord is the avenger in all these things, just as we also told you before and solemnly warned you. For God has not called us for the purpose of impurity, but in sanctification. (1 Thessalonians 4:3-7)

The "slightest" sin has more lethal effect than appears at the moment of temptation. The dread aspect is that we usually do not enter it blindfolded. Sin happens when the *heart* chooses to turn the wrong way.

Misconceptions That Fetter Us

The father of lies would deceive us into a number of misapprehensions that cripple our growth and turn us further from God. Tragically, many believers turn from the Lord after they fall because of the misconceptions Satan whispers into our spirits. Some of the most obvious lies are:

Any fall is final and total. The cases of Jonah, David, and Mark will be cited later to show God's restoration. God assures us, "The LORD sustains all who fall and raises up all who are bowed down" (Psalm 145:14). That lie, that our failures put us past hope, seems to have special power over persons who fall into sexual sin.

I must earn forgiveness. God guaranteed Israel, "For a brief moment I forsook you, but with great compassion I will gather you" (Isaiah 54:7). John reassured all believers, "If we confess our sins, He is faithful and righteous to forgive us our sins and to cleanse us from all unrighteousness" (1 John 1:9). It is *righteous* of God to keep His end of the bargain, the covenant He made at Calvary.

We do not remove the guilt; it cannot be our works that clear us. God's faithfulness to His covenant ensures forgiveness. Repeating a theme of this book, if God does anything, how "done" is it? If *God* forgives, how thorough is His work?

I must punish myself. This insidious falsehood is extremely hard to unmask because a guilty conscience gets such satisfaction from making its own atonement. People who labor under this misconception seem to develop an emotional attachment to their own penitence, as if they could do a better job of reparation than Christ. Only God knows how to discipline us. The psalmist had a healthier attitude: "It is good for me that I was afflicted, that I may learn Your statutes" (Psalm 119:71). We cannot punish ourselves, but we can learn from our mistakes.

When we sin, God becomes our enemy. The Scriptures answer this lie most eloquently: "You forgave the iniquity of Your people; You covered all their sin" (Psalm 85:2). "You, Lord, are good, and *ready to forgive*, and abundant in lovingkindness to all who call upon You" (86:5, emphasis added). "Though your sins are as scarlet, they will be as white as snow; though they are red like crimson, they will be like wool" (Isaiah 1:18).

When it is reset, a broken bone grows back stronger than a normal bone. Wholeness of spirit, processed by confession out of the fragmentation of sin, is stronger than simple innocence. God can use even our sins and our mistakes to facilitate the process taking us to glory.

Shame and Glory

Adam and Eve felt shame (Genesis 3:10), as did Ezra (Ezra 9:6). This most uncomfortable of all emotions can have a constructive effect if we retain Heaven's view. God uses shame to turn us back to Him.

Shame is the opposite of glory, our life goal. At Graduation Day, we enter either into eternal, uninterrupted glory or into shame. It seems likely that the shame of hell will be more profound than any known on earth. Everlasting shame fills hell, the embarrassment compounded by the fact that hell's occupants will be forever incapable of turning back to God. Shame will become Satan's ultimate self-consciousness.

More shame attached itself to crucifixion than to any other mode of execution in history. Yet Jesus "for the joy set before Him endured the cross, despising the shame" (Hebrews 12:2). God transformed shame into glory, and that will be the testimony of many martyrs and saints in eternity.

Chapter 4 introduced us to three qualities imputed into us when we accept Christ: righteousness, holiness, and the resulting glory. Because these attributes are not earned or acquired, we do not lose them when we sin; we lose fellowship with God. The confession of our sin immediately restores the process of sanctification and the continuum of fellowship with our Maker.

THE TEMPTATION OF CHRIST

The fact that Jesus was tempted tells us that temptation itself does not corrupt us. In fact, the Holy Spirit led Him into the temptation (Matthew 4:1; Luke 4:1-2). The Holy Father deemed it important that the incarnate Son experience exactly the same problems we would face (Hebrews 4:15).

Satan had the freedom to test Jesus even in a fast (Matthew 4:2). We can be sure Jesus remained in unbroken communion with His Father throughout that fast. Therefore, Satan today can disturb our prayer or our witness. Jesus' example demonstrates this, and our experience validates it. We are not safe from the Enemy anywhere, though we also have the presence of God.

During the Last Supper, Jesus stated that "the ruler of the world is coming, and he has nothing in Me" (John 14:30). Jesus had no fallen fleshly nature to hook, no "old man" to respond. As the Second Adam, He had a chance to resist temptation in the same way the first Adam could have. We can say that from *Satan's* standpoint, the temptation was as real and valid as Adam's; from *Jesus'* standpoint, the temptation did not touch a responsive fallen nature. Jesus was tempted in all things as are we, yet did not sin (Hebrews 4:15). In the same way that Adam could have remained sinless, Jesus actually did.

The New Testament provides us with instructions for withstanding temptation. Jesus was successful because He appropriated every defense available. He overcame as a man in the same way Adam could have overcome and in the same we can. He modeled how to triumph over Satan's mightiest efforts, and our conquest over sin is waged in the same way and with the same weapons.

- **He knew His Father.** The closest relationship He maintained was with His Father (Matthew 11:27). Loyalty to His Father was paramount; nothing was worth compromising that allegiance (John 17:21). In the desert, He knew His Father, Jehovah Jireh, would provide for His intense hunger. Knowing God well and maintaining a close relationship with Him enables us to detect Satan's deceit in the same way (1 John 1:3-6).

- **He knew who He was.** (See Luke 22:70; Mark 1:11.)
  Jesus valued and respected His position as "[God's]
  beloved Son, in whom [God was] well-pleased"
  (Matthew 3:17). He knew that all authority in heaven and
  earth would be given to Him (28:18), so Satan's offer
  seemed paltry considering Heaven's view. Focusing on our
  own inheritance from Heaven's position makes the allure
  of earthly pleasures pale. We, too, are born of God and are
  to overcome the world (1 John 2:13-14). Our new nature
  cannot enjoy the estrangement sin brings.

- **He knew Scripture and could use it skillfully.** Jesus
  could tell when Satan misquoted a passage or took it out
  of context. He could use the Word of God to tear down
  Satan's arguments (Matthew 4:4,7,10). He was prepared to
  stand firm against Satan with truth, righteousness, peace,
  faith, salvation, the Word of God, and prayer
  (Ephesians 6:10-18). His weapons were spiritual
  ones — not of the flesh but divinely powerful for the
  destruction of (spiritual) fortresses (2 Corinthians 10:4).

- **He kept control of His mind (or heart).** Jesus took His
  thoughts of hunger and any desire for power that Satan
  could use against Him into captivity (2 Corinthians 10:5).
  He not only refused to focus on what Satan offered but
  also purposely concentrated on what His Father had
  already said about Satan's proposals ("It is written";
  Matthew 4:4,7,10).

- **He knew His enemy.** Jesus knew that Lucifer was cast out
  of heaven and already judged (Luke 10:18; John 16:11). He
  knew that Satan was a liar (John 8:44) and that what was
  being offered in the temptations could be retracted. He
  knew when to stop the confrontation ("Go, Satan!"

Matthew 4:10). Knowing that Satan is a liar, we do not give credence to him when he passes on fear, gossip, assumption, or slander.

- **He knew His purpose.** Jesus knew that He was to bring the kingdom of heaven (Matthew 4:23; Luke 4:18), bear witness to the truth (John 18:37), and seek and save the lost (Luke 19:10). Having such a clear purpose enabled Jesus to recognize what would help or hurt His mission. Paul also had purpose: "Brethren, I do not regard myself as having laid hold of it yet; but one thing I do: forgetting what lies behind and reaching forward to what lies ahead, I press on toward the goal for the prize of the upward call of God in Christ Jesus" (Philippians 3:13-14).

Early on, Satan made a seductive try at ensnaring Jesus in sin. The work of Jesus' human enemies in Judea tells us that Satan never gave up attempting to trap Him. When all else failed, Satan entered Judas and, in his evil mind, thought he put Jesus on the Cross. This tells us that if Satan cannot lead us astray, he becomes spiteful. That same pattern has been duplicated throughout the centuries in many believers and martyrs.

Yet Satan's spite became God's instrument of salvation for us. Evil is real and is all around us. But what was intended as the greatest evil of all time became the greatest good of all time, again demonstrating the sovereignty of God. The Cross of Christ proves that the Lord limits the most monstrous evil to His greater purposes. God allows trials and persecution, but He also holds the key to the greatest rewards we can know at Graduation Day. Sometimes He even brings a greater, unexpected good for us in the midst of our crucible.

Satan had nothing in Jesus that he could touch, but he has

much in us that he can lay his hands on. Therefore, we are to pray, "Do not lead us into temptation" (Matthew 6:13). For us, temptation is an abyss, the closest step to defeat. Once touched by Satan, it becomes difficult to extricate ourselves. In fact, 1 Corinthians 6:18 warns us to *flee* immorality. In temptation, Heaven's view becomes clouded. The slightest yielding, and the father of lies obscures our perception of God's perspective with his evil point of view. The safest place is as far from temptation as we can get.

God leads at all times, and perhaps occasions come when a strong Christian will step up the ladder of glory by a magnificent triumph over temptation. None of us should consider himself that strong. Only God knows how to take us up the ladder properly. Therefore, we should pray for deliverance from temptation.

HEAVEN'S VIEW IS ULTIMATE
We Adopt Either Satan's View or God's View

Satan cannot create, yet he believed that he could have a better purpose for himself than his Creator had for him. Satan makes this enticing offer to each of us, too. We fail when Satan successfully tempts us to embrace his desires as our own desires. He will face judgment before his Creator for disdaining the holy purpose of his existence. Most humans choose to meld with his position; therefore, his guilty verdict must also be theirs.

God's original intention to have a family with whom to share His glory and love was stronger than the grief He had to endure to secure our rescue from the wiles of God's enemy. God loved this world of helpless, shameful people so much that He gave His Son to be the only possible sacrifice for our sin so that every person who believes in Him will not perish in the hell prepared for Satan and his demons but will live forever in His presence, enabled to reach the full stature of glory that God originally purposed. "If . . . every transgression and disobedience received a just penalty, *how will we escape if we neglect so great a salvation?*" (Hebrews 2:2-3, emphasis added).

How Do My Little Daily Choices Affect My Eternity?

The choices we make have not only immediate results but also ultimate consequences. Our daily life—our breakfast, work, hourly relationships, fleeing from or resisting temptations—affects what we will be for all eternity. Book after book in the Bible tells us of the final triumph of good. Revelation 21 and 22 describe a new creation that will have no evil at all and also no suffering.

Spiritual maturity includes becoming conformed to Christ's image in the midst of suffering and evil. We grow to share His loathing of evil; we share His earnest passion that not one be lost; we share His desire for continuous, unbroken fellowship; and we rejoice in the growth and righteousness of others. Nothing Satan or the world can do will change God's glorious intention. Nothing else will give us satisfaction, peace, and purpose. We are learning hourly to distinguish between the temporal and the eternal. We master how to overcome the Evil One. One of the main purposes of this book is to examine what our responsibility is in reaching that spiritual maturity that will bring us to glory, even in an evil world.

CHAPTER 9

Heaven's View of Our Crucible

If anyone wishes to come after Me, he must deny himself,
and take up his cross and follow Me.

MATTHEW 16:24

The good angels need neither the grace nor the mercy we humans require. They do not overcome self as we must, although they overcome demons. We have to overcome hindrances to our own development; angels do not. They were created as pure spirits, fully mature. Our spirits begin immature, with possibilities for nurture and growth. God gives us some responsibility for our own growth. We have to concentrate on God to grow our spirituality to the maturity God wants.

UNIVERSALITY OF THE CRUCIBLE
Our "Hard Life"

In our straitened lifetimes, humans seem to lead a hard existence—one that militates against spiritual reality. Most people have had some kind of "problem" in life. Few realize that their difficulties direct their attention to this world instead of to a worthier, more distant goal. In Job's case, Satan succeeded in making the immediate hurt his primary preoccupation. He manages the same deception with us.

This week a friend has called us twice because her husband left her for another woman. Recently, I (T. W.) spent an afternoon with a father, a reserved and mature fellow, who wept bitter tears over his son's homosexuality. A lady handed me a slip of paper last week requesting prayer for a friend on drugs. In our Sunday school class, one lady is bald from chemotherapy and another is terminally ill with heart disease. Every one of the sons of the wealthiest person I ever knew (blessed fellow!) had severe birth defects (poor guy!). It seems impossible for human beings to avoid some blessings and some problems. The challenge cannot be to avoid troubles; it is to handle them in a way that will bring glory to God and, incidentally, to us.

Jesus did not try to gloss over our difficulties. He said frankly, "Your Father . . . causes His sun to rise on the evil and the good, and sends rain on the righteous and the unrighteous" (Matthew 5:45). Persecution comes specifically because we are like Him (John 15:18). The Son of God *expected* hard times to come.

What a Crucible Does

A crucible heats ore to a very high temperature in order to separate impurities from the desired metal. The Christian has the privilege of understanding all our trials as a crucible in which we are being refined and purified and of using that crucible to participate in his or her own process of being perfected.

If raw ore could talk, the slag and dirt (not the pure metal) would object to the process. To use a different example, if a mineral had feelings, the superfluous matter in the stone would flee the jeweler's tools. Raw clay would hate the potter.

On the other hand, the gold would be grateful that the workman separates and discards the useless, the non-gold. If the end product is jewelry, the main story of a rough stone is not the mining, refining, and fashioning; the *main* story is the beautiful necklace that adorns a woman at the end of the process. The diamond would be grateful for the chipping and cutting. If clay understood the process, it would love the potter for the elegant vase it is becoming.

Our life crucible exists for the purpose of discarding or chipping away useless (worldly or sinful) elements that distract from the glory of refined perfection. The main story of one's life itself is not really the crucible. God's ultimate aim in our lives directs us to that particular glory He is making out of us, the splendor that will emerge into eternity in unimaginable excellence.

These comparisons lead to a revealing insight: It is the rough, the impure, and the superfluous within us that object most to the purging work of God as He brings us to goals far beyond our normal purview. We can work with God by deliberately surfacing the good and the right ore He has placed within us, by exposing our inmost self to the tooling work of His cleansing Spirit.

This does not imply that the fire always pleases us or that His tools seem to be chipping at the "right places." We who have a mind have a distinct advantage over the ore, the stone, and the clay: God enables us to envision the gold, the diamond, and the vase that will come out after the refining and tooling. We do not know all about where we are headed, but we know that our final product is far superior to the ore, stone, and clay of this world.

WHAT GOES ON IN THE REFINING PROCESS

Becoming the Right Kind of People

Our advantages over the raw ore stagger us. Unlike lifeless minerals, we start by knowing our identity and then deliberately grow in that distinctiveness that God intends for each of us. All of us are *generically* "partakers of a heavenly calling" (Hebrews 3:1), "children of God" (John 1:12), joint heirs with Christ (Romans 8:17), and future royalty (Revelation 5:10). Beyond this, we have individually designed roles peculiar to each of us (Ephesians 2:10). The refiner's crucible reveals the gold, and our crucible helps bring our identity to the surface. We have the advantage of knowing this ahead of time.

Refining is a process, not an event. The crucible helps direct our attention vertically instead of horizontally. We learn to look to God. If we have Heaven's view, we cannot complain, "If I were God, I would see how desperate this situation is." Getting Heaven's view does not make God take on our desperation; it directs us to His view of the opportunities each current plight presents.

The crucible also tempers our attributes and virtues. We cannot have endurance without testing or patience without process. We learn through the crucible that our mercy must be judicious, our discipline has to be caring, and our love must reach further than we would prefer. We happen to be God's choice children, that He might "purify for Himself a people for His own possession" (Titus 2:14).

Lucifer proved that angelic perfection was not immutable, but our strength-to-strength growth, on the other hand, shapes in us an ever-growing stability. Not only are our attributes moderated but the crucible produces new and eternal qualities, such as constancy and wisdom. None of us would have expected the perfection of the beautiful necklace if we had studied the raw ore; only the refiner knows the end.

The Crucible and Our Emotions

The crucible inevitably produces strong emotions in those of us who are in it. The difficulties within the crucible can trigger good or bad feelings — resentment or cooperative participation in purposes too high for us to comprehend. Our cooperation does not depend on our understanding God; it depends on our trusting Him.

The fire can produce grief over our own sin or grief over the sin within Christ's body. Dietrich Bonhoeffer mourned deeply over the cooperation of the German church with Hitler. Many Americans have suffered severe heartache because of the sin of elected officials claiming to be Christian. The ever-increasing encroachment of worldly practices into the church distresses mature believers. The crucible helps us identify impurities.

Moreover, the crucible widens our God-given emotions. We are to love prodigiously what God loves, and it is legitimate to hate what God hates, provided we know the mind of God for a certainty. Part of the refining process removes from us illicit loves as well as unlawful hatreds. We also have to learn to temper our legitimate hatreds with the wisdom God gives. Our love grows greater and our hatred becomes more pure.

Many of us undergo the emotions of our culture rather than those of God. Cultural loves and hatreds vary enormously in different parts of the country and the world. Only by knowing God through His Word and through diligent prayer can we discover the *divine* preferences and tastes. (God really has preferences and tastes.)

The heat of the refining vessel can also intensify the Christ-likeness of legitimate emotions. It can make our love holy like God's. It can make our tastes spiritual rather than cultural. Through the crucible, we learn to really love the poor and the repulsive. We respect those with whom we disagree. Even God does that; if He did not, we would all be dead. The fire can make even our anger unselfish, a rare purity among God's people.

We never judge the presence of God by circumstances. We accept His word that He is with us always and that circumstances can unexpectedly produce a witness for Christ, encourage the down-and-out, and even establish a church. We have experienced all of these events in the last six months with close friends and relatives; in each case, adversity led to higher nobility.

We have a friend who was fired from his job because he was so disrespectful. The terrible trial forced him to reevaluate his whole approach to life. He rededicated his life to becoming like Christ and is now a fruitful missionary. In his case, the crucible served a useful purpose for him and for the kingdom of God.

The Crucible Can Help Us Discern God's Will

Trials tend to rectify our needs and wants; we have a hard time distinguishing the two. For most of us, a want is a need and it quickly turns into a craving. God prefers that we identify our wants and needs with only that spiritual direction that leads from glory to glory.

In the deepest part of us, we want what God wants, and few of us realize it. All of God's "wants" are holy; ideally we use *His* standard to evaluate *our* desires. He envisions for each of us the highest nobility possible in the present life and in the future life. Our dilemma surfaces when we admit that we do want the nobility for the *future* life, but in *this* one, we prefer the comforts and trappings of temporary satisfaction. We prefer the future throne without cost.

God works ceaselessly to give us His best, and few of us accept that. It takes spiritual insight to believe that:

- Discipline is kindness.
- Testing results in real proof.
- Martyrdom is glory.
- Sharing the persecution of Christ is sharing the glory of Christ.
- Graduation Day is really better.

The Bible furnishes us with examples of cooperative obedience. The examples that follow, believing the five principles above, chose the will of God when it was difficult to choose it:

- Isaiah: "Here am I. Send me!" (Isaiah 6:8).
- Mary: "Behold, the bondslave of the Lord; may it be done to me according to your word" (Luke 1:38).
- Peter: "I will do as You say and let down the nets" (Luke 5:5).
- Jesus: "Not as I will, but as You will" (Matthew 26:39).

In the crucible, we learn how to identify our will with God's will. Our attributes come as a gift from God; the will is our gift to Him. Once again, the cognitive can function at our bidding. Satan decidedly confuses our feelings by means of circumstances.

Only the will can function independently of feelings. In each of the biblical examples above, the choices became strongly deliberate, without regard to personal understanding in Peter's case and without regard to cost in the other three. The choices were intentional under difficult (or frightening) circumstances.

The most difficult—and most determined—of the choices quoted on the previous page was that of Jesus in Gethsemane. He established the validity of His earlier statement, "I always do the things that are pleasing to [My Father]" (John 8:29). Jesus was harder on Peter's trying to deflect Him from God's will (Matthew 16:23) than He was on Peter's denying Him (Luke 22:31-32). Jesus' determination furnishes us with the example we are to follow. His will was inflexibly identified with that of His Father.

The Crucible Invigorates Our Growth

As we saw in chapter 2, the Son of God, perfect from birth, had to grow. Growth is itself an imitation of Christ. We play a role in choosing how to grow.

Growth will also bring newness (more of this in chapter 12), which is to say that we add new facets to our spiritual selves. Human physical growth adds new cells; the child increases in size. The Christian also grows in spiritual stature. With Christian maturity, we handle our irritations better (that is new). We understand biblical concepts with greater depth. The Holy Spirit provides fresh insights and fresh meaning to old insights. Our relationship with others in the body of Christ becomes more profound. The Lord applies His wisdom more thoroughly and directly in the difficulties of the crucible.

Much of *The Mind of Christ* (a book by T. W.) resulted from our struggles because Laverne's father left her. Newness came out of brokenness. The death of a beloved friend and profound prayer warrior prompted a flood of new insights on prayer. And this book grew out of my (Melana's) cancer. In our lives, at least, the newness that the crucible produces always proves surprisingly welcome and timely.

The growth is upward—from faith to faith and glory to glory—in spite of outward appearances. Consider the amazing progression *upward* in the following cases:

- Joseph: His upward growth took him from home to a prison.
- Moses: It was upward from a palace to a desert.
- David: He progressed from tending sheep to fleeing Saul.
- Daniel: He was promoted when he went from a palace to the lions' den.
- Paul: He advanced when he went from being a lawyer to being a prisoner.
- Stephen: His upward progress was from being a deacon to being a martyr.

In the crucible, God helps us move from the demanding nature we have in babyhood to the maturity of self-sacrifice. After childhood comes adolescence, which is also a demanding stage. The difficult choices of Isaiah, Mary, Peter, and Jesus named on page 199 were not accomplished by self-centered adolescents. Even though Mary was quite young, she demonstrated mature adult choices. We also show maturity by the choices we make.

Fanaticism is another characteristic of adolescence. The total commitment demonstrated in the biblical examples had nothing to do with fanaticism. God demands total commitment (Matthew 19:21), and this dedication includes everything in life. True fanaticism, however, tends to be destructive. Jesus and His disciples were not fanatics; the Pharisees were dogged in their pursuit of Jesus. Fanatics do not act out of knowledge; they act out of uninformed but sincere conviction. One of the functions of the life crucible is to educate us; maturity includes knowledge.

Christian maturity does not indicate the *end* of a process; we arrive at maturity by staying on the right road. Maturity, in its stability, constitutes one of the steps toward our eventual immutability. God uses the crucible to achieve noble ends by (sometimes painful) development, a progression in maturing.

THE CRUCIBLE REQUIRES TIME

Learning to Use Time for Eternal Purposes

God lives outside time, in eternity (Isaiah 57:15). His vantage point grants a wide-ranging view of our crucible that we cannot see. Our only security is the certainty of His grace as events unfold before us. Because of His perspective, God does not focus or concentrate on our "current" distress, regardless of its effect on us. From *our* perspective, His actions toward us are indeed "current." But because we want to view our process from Heaven's view, we bear in mind continually that we are responding to unchanging eternity and wide perspective.

Eternity is a sea; time is the river that leads to the sea. The swirling waters around us are taking us to a sea that cannot be very far away for any of us. God created time in order for His *modus operandi* in dealing with us to be in process. The terrifying floods or the uncomfortable heat of the crucible has a high purpose: our process. The tempestuous river and the melting flame do not surprise God. He was prepared to help us before we arrived at the problem.

God created time in order to use it for our growth. Time, for God and for us, is a tool. Guarding and watching us confined by time, God makes moments, hours, and centuries propitious for our progress, yet time may also become hazardous if it leads to regression.

In the Bible, God dealt directly with time. Before the biblical flood, God grieved, "My Spirit shall not strive with man forever" (Genesis 6:3). Time affects man profoundly. David barely passed the time test after his confession and acknowledged, "Let everyone who is godly pray to You in a time when You may be found" (Psalm 32:6). Isaiah cautioned, "Seek the LORD while He may be found; call upon Him while He is near" (Isaiah 55:6). Paul guarded his own time: "Be careful how you walk, not as unwise men but as wise, making the most of your time, because the days are evil" (Ephesians 5:15-16). God intends for time to help us; we can use it advantageously. Time is a major factor in the crucible.

Time and Eternity

When Jesus assumed human form, He did not leave eternity. Always thinking in terms of eternity, He stepped into time and showed us how eternity (as a state) could function "confined" by time. This is why having His mind is so important for us (Philippians 2:5-11).

Jesus oriented His life strictly to ultimates. His life centered on absolutes: the eventual good of His fellow human beings and the supreme glory of His Father. He never sought His own glory or the advancement of His cause. Although He, more than any person who ever lived, had reason to believe His business was imperative, He entrusted the course of His cause to His Father. He demonstrated eternal life within time. Jesus showed us what future eternity will be like and what present eternity as a state should be like.

We, too, have "eternity in [the] heart" (Ecclesiastes 3:11) — that is, in the deepest part of our being. In our hearts, we yearn for absolutes. Because God has placed eternity in our hearts, we have the advantage of a resident reference point, if only we will learn how to use it. For Jesus, eternity here was like eternity with His Father. It can be that way for us.

In our *future* eternity, the "present" will not be fleeting. We will live in an eternal "now." *Presently* confined by time, we cannot conceptualize a "now" that does not grow out of a "past" or wait on a "future." Because of this, we must trust now, in our present life, only what endures. In trial or in success, we center our attention on what will last. Our "now" has eternal ramifications, and we fill our present moments with lasting attitudes and actions.

God does not expect the final glory today. Just as my (T. W.'s) wife's cake (chapter 2) had to go through steps, we have to proceed as Jesus did in His incarnation. He was perfected through suffering, and we are too, in precisely the same way. Jesus never went backward (the kingdom principle of forward movement in chapter 3). Today's glory is the next step.

The Crucible's Joy

This chapter and the next chapter on suffering could easily convey the impression that the Christian life consists basically of hard trials. But all people go through ordeals of varying difficulty, and a book on Heaven's view would be incomplete without addressing suffering.

Still, we must never forget that the *earth* is the Lord's; the *world* usually refers to Satan's domain. We live *on* the earth *in* an environment often distressing. Our challenge lies in appreciating the wondrous gifts of God on every side (His earth) and at the same time passing the inevitable tests that evil presents (the world).

Occasionally, we receive a letter sent from a persecuted Christian in a prison—amazingly full of joy. Our greatest joy must not be merely in the physical glories that surround us (although we honor the Lord for the gift of them). The highest joy we can know is the presence of Christ, which never leaves us. A large part of our maturing depends on placing our values in the spiritual realm. The highest joy is found there.

PURPOSES OF THE CRUCIBLE

God does not *make* the crucible terrible; God *uses* the crucible for our glory. This means that we can turn to Him for meaning in the most appalling life situations. He used pain mightily in the lives of Joseph, Daniel, Paul, and, above all, the Lord Jesus. None of these men censured God for their difficulties. They used trial to surface nobility.

It must have been beautiful to Heaven to see Jesus pass through the crucible with no dross to slough off; blamelessness entered at the beginning and high perfection emerged at the end. Nevertheless, Jesus' life was a crucible like ours (Hebrews 4:15; 5:8). From beginning to end, Joseph, Daniel, Paul, and Jesus perceived God in control and trusted Him completely.

Think of the most Christlike people you have known. Were they young and inexperienced, or were you able to observe years of seasoning as they advanced in the image of Christ? Almost universally, they confirm that their growth came through trials — through the crucible.

God utilizes the crucible to *process our identity with Christ.* Romans 8:30 (following the verse that tells us we will be conformed to Christ's image) presents a progression: "Whom He predestined, He also called; and these whom He called, He also justified; and these whom He justified, He also glorified." The call comes at the beginning and leads to glory at the end.

The continuation of our life in Christ must progress in the exact same image of the Christ that we received at the beginning. We are not to be a caricature of Him but an image (Romans 8:29). The picture must be exact, without distortion. Our purity cannot become pharisaical; we do not use power for display. "As you have received Christ Jesus the Lord, so walk in Him, having been firmly rooted and *now being built up in Him*" (Colossians 2:6-7, emphasis added). Paul claimed that his life exemplified the Christ in him: "I found mercy, so that in me as the foremost, Jesus Christ might demonstrate *His* perfect patience as an example for those who would believe in Him for eternal life" (1 Timothy 1:16, emphasis added).

God brings into play a second purpose as we pass through trials: He so manages our difficulties that they *make us pleasing to the Lord.* Because God does this, our lives will take twists and turns we prefer to avoid. What pleases us may not please the Lord. Jesus affirmed this more strongly than we would like: "That which is highly esteemed among men is detestable in the sight of God" (Luke 16:15).

No one can impress God, but anyone can please Him if he or she knows what to work for. The Bible makes clear several "superiorities" that do not thrill God:

- **Brilliance.** (Jesus speaking) "I praise You, Father, Lord of heaven and earth, that You have hidden these things from the wise and intelligent and have revealed them to infants" (Matthew 11:25).
- **Good looks.** "The LORD said to Samuel, 'Do not look at his appearance or at the height of his stature, because I have rejected him; for God sees not as man sees, for man looks at the outward appearance, but the LORD looks at the heart'" (1 Samuel 16:7).
- **Earthly power.** "Some boast in chariots and some in horses, but we will boast in the name of the LORD, our God" (Psalm 20:7).
- **Physical strength.** "From the mouth of infants and nursing babes You have established strength because of Your adversaries, to make the enemy and the revengeful cease" (Psalm 8:2). "He does not delight in the strength of the horse; He does not take pleasure in the legs of a man" (147:10).
- **Wealth.** "Every beast of the forest is Mine, the cattle on a thousand hills. . . . If I were hungry I would not tell you, for the world is Mine, and all it contains" (Psalm 50:10,12).

What, then, pleases the Lord? The Bible, again, tells us plainly how we can make God happy:

- **Obedience.** "Has the LORD as much delight in burnt offerings and sacrifices as in obeying the voice of the LORD? Behold, to obey is better than sacrifice, and to heed than the fat of rams" (1 Samuel 15:22).
- **Loyalty and knowing God.** "I delight in loyalty rather than sacrifice, and in the knowledge of God rather than burnt offerings" (Hosea 6:6).
- **Fear of the Lord.** "The LORD favors those who fear Him, those who wait for His lovingkindness" (Psalm 147:11).
- **Compassion (or mercy).** "I DESIRE COMPASSION, AND NOT SACRIFICE" (Matthew 9:13).
- **The sweet aroma of Christ in us.** "Thanks be to God, who always leads us in triumph in Christ, and manifests through us the sweet aroma of the knowledge of Him in every place. For we are a fragrance of Christ to God among those who are being saved and among those who are perishing" (2 Corinthians 2:14-15).

We display the first of these factors by submitting to Him and cooperating with Him. These make it possible for Him to work with us. The last two please God because in them we are becoming like Him so that He can share His glory with us.

A third purpose and useful benefit God can bring into our crucible is that in this way we *bring eternity (as a state) into our world.* Because it is implanted in the hearts of all humans (Ecclesiastes 3:11), many people are yearning to encounter a person whose genuine otherworldliness opens up to them what they really want. Jesus brought eternity into His every encounter, and the result was that multitudes were drawn to Him (Matthew 12:15; Mark 5:24). When we demonstrate eternity, we are demonstrating Jesus, the eternal.

A final and similar purpose or result God can bring out of our crucible is to *demonstrate to the world the power of the Lord.* In showing His power, we incidentally evidence His glory, a facet that draws people to Him. Who could have failed to perceive the glory of God when Jesus spoke? The officers sent to arrest Jesus returned without Him, reporting, "Never has a man spoken the way this man speaks" (John 7:46).

Jesus promised this same power to us in our need: "It is not you who speak, but it is the Spirit of your Father who speaks in you" (Matthew 10:20). Peter had it at Pentecost (Acts 2:37). Stephen's power was irresistible: "They were unable to cope with the wisdom and the Spirit with which he was speaking" (6:10). Jesus, Peter, and Stephen remained in the crucible, and the power and glory in their speech changed the course of history.

God is our refiner, our potter, even our jeweler. He aims for a glorious masterwork at the end of the process: "We are His workmanship" (Ephesians 2:10). No other beings in the universe have as high a destiny as the one He has chosen for redeemed humanity. God's artistry can be shown only as we cooperate with His intentions and methods. Within the crucible, we keep our eyes on the imagination and skill of the Creator, even looking at our tragedies from Heaven's view!

CHAPTER 10

Heaven's View of Suffering

I consider that the sufferings of this present time are
not worthy to be compared with the glory that is
to be revealed to us.

ROMANS 8:18

An observer on the corner watched slave owners dragging two men into the public marketplace before the chief magistrates, shouting slander and lies. After being humiliated and stripped, both were severely beaten with rods. Hurling them into a dark prison cell, a coarse jailer chained their feet in cold, jagged stocks to the wall and then abandoned them with no hope of trial or release. When they were limited to earth's view, their suffering had no purpose.

An observer in heaven also monitored Paul and Silas's suffering in prison while He cared for their needs. He watched tenderly as endurance and longsuffering developed hidden glories in their spirits. Heaven's view gave meaning to their suffering, both from their standpoint and from God's view.

EARTHBOUND VIEWS OF SUFFERING

Earth's View Is Limited

Nowhere are the opposites between Heaven's view and the world's view so clearly delineated as in suffering. From the world's view, the Bible's coupling of suffering with joy seems baffling. How can we honestly "consider trials to be joyful"? The pairing does not even appear to be logical.

Though not on the same plane as Paul's suffering, our family's pain and emotional agony certainly did not resemble any *past* pleasant sensations. Nothing in this world had taught us that joy could result from pain. The only solution seemed to be that there must be nobler dimensions of joy and glory in the process of suffering that were beyond our previous experience.

> Consider it all joy, my brethren, when you encounter various trials. (James 1:2)

> I am overflowing with joy in all our affliction. (2 Corinthians 7:4)

Assigning nobility to suffering is incomprehensible apart from Heaven's view. Both the redeemed and the unredeemed instinctively yearn to know God's intentions in allowing loss, torture, emotional agony, and death. We know that as Creator, God owes us no explanations for His ways and has even emphasized that His ways are not our ways. "As the heavens are higher than the earth, so are My ways higher than your ways and My thoughts than your thoughts" (Isaiah 55:9). Yet He has invited us to search: "Make me know Your ways, O LORD; teach me Your paths. Lead me in Your truth and teach me" (Psalm 25:4-5).

In the afterword, we share an e-mail from a friend near

Chicago directing us to search for God's glory in our suffering. That encouragement took root, and we watched carefully. Many others have had much greater pain than we have experienced, and we are the grateful beneficiaries of their insights. We are simple learners sharing how God has taught us to see suffering so far. We have come to understand that though He has great compassion with our grief, from His vantage point, He sees vistas of glory that result from proving ourselves on earth.

Our "Why" Questions Attempt to Equate Us with God

Suffering from the world's perspective begins with assumptions that actually put us on a level with God: "A good God would be more caring than this." "If God allowed this, then He is neither just nor good." We may become even more presumptuous, "If I were God, I would stop this," or questioning, "What did I (my child, and so on) do to deserve this?"

In fact, Satan has so manipulated our world's perceptions that we blame God for Satan's work. Drunk driving, street violence, deadly diseases, ruptured marriages, child abuse, floods, and genocide beg the question "For what purpose, Lord?" Most of us do not look for Heaven's view of the trial but rather seek only some possible blame. The question cynically implies, "God, You'd better come up with something spectacular to justify this tragedy."

Within Christian groups, worldly views of suffering often intensify personal grief rather than alleviate it. An implication that suffering indicates sin in the lives of the wounded may be valid but may not always indicate the reason for distress. Those who assume that suffering must indicate personal sin divert focus from God's grander plan and sometimes cause unnecessary additional pain. Other "Christian" opinions hold that God's children have special protection above other people or that enough faith will deliver us from any misery. Christians with these views assume that their understanding equals God's.

Sometimes the world (or Christianity) tries to "make the best" of our trials. The best justification the world's view can offer for floods, hate crimes, bankruptcy, verbal abuse, and the like is that it brings out unity in neighborhoods or charitable organizations — "the best of the human spirit." But privately, personal agony and frustration with "Why?" lingers. The truth is that suffering is unjustifiable and purposeless when seen only through the viewpoint of time on earth. We see devastation and think, *What a waste*. When seen from Heaven's view, suffering assumes higher purposes that may not be immediately evident.

THE OPPOSITE VIEW: HEAVEN'S PERSPECTIVE

The Hidden Joy That Heaven Sees in Suffering

Jesus led a sinless life, yet Hebrews 2:10 makes the startling assertion that He was perfected through suffering. This Greek word *teleioo* carries the understanding of reaching total maturity, being perfected and finished, and accomplishing and completing God's final, ultimate purpose or goal. James 1:2-4 makes clear the connection of suffering and perfecting: "Consider it all joy, my brethren, when you encounter various trials, knowing that the testing of your faith produces endurance. And let endurance have its perfect result, so that you may be *perfect and complete, lacking in nothing*" (emphasis added).

As we saw in chapter 4, we cannot share some of God's attributes, such as His transcendence, here or in eternity. Others of

His qualities we can share both here and in heaven, including His joy and peace. Still other virtues are possible only here on earth—virtues that perfect in us unimaginable character for heaven. Endurance, longsuffering, and patience will not be needed in heaven, but we develop the glory of immutability (without being static) by exhibiting them here and now. God uses them to carve our character into a maturity that cannot be attained through comfort.

Chapter 3 explained that we have a role in developing the degree of nobility we will eternally retain. The principle underlying the growth of nobility is that the more rigorous our training, the higher our nobility will eventually be if we utilize the opportunities in our training.

The higher glory achieved through the training of suffering can be reached by no other route. We attain to the resurrection through the fellowship of Christ's sufferings (Philippians 3:10). From Heaven's view, the joy there is worth whatever suffering we go through here: "The joy set before [Jesus] endured the cross" (Hebrews 12:2).

Therefore, we consider it all joy when we encounter various trials. If we could envision the indescribable jubilation in heaven for those who have developed endurance, patience, and longsuffering, we would embrace trials here. Our "light affliction" is exchanged for "an eternal weight of glory" (2 Corinthians 4:17). "We also exult in our tribulations, knowing that tribulation brings about perseverance; and perseverance, proven character; and proven character, hope; and hope does not disappoint, because the love of God has been poured out within our hearts" (Romans 5:3-5).

The contrast is grander than comparing grains of sand to storehouses of diamonds. Suffering exposes us to the reality of ultimate worth: The highest joy in suffering is that through it we become conformed to Jesus' character.

Suffering Causes Us to Appeal to the Higher Power of God

Jesus knew the agony of Mary and Martha, His own physical torture, and denial and betrayal by His own. He not only feels compassion for our pain, He Himself became acquainted with grief (Isaiah 53:3): "We have not an high priest which cannot be touched with the feeling of our infirmities" (Hebrews 4:15, KJV). As Jesus entered the testing of Gethsemane, He agonized, "My soul is deeply grieved to the point of death" (Mark 14:34).

In that garden, Jesus showed that the most significant achievement suffering accomplishes in our lives is the help it gives us in acknowledging the immeasurable difference between God and man. God's "otherness" becomes most obvious when we need Him most. We need someone to appeal to who is greater than we, and our appeal to God places His glory above ours (Ezekiel 38:22-23). All suffering has the potential to glorify the Father because it enables us to recognize our own vulnerability and His readiness to understand and help.

In addition, suffering causes us to cease from sin (1 Peter 4:1), which also glorifies God. We are to "arm ourselves" with the purpose of the suffering Christ.

Suffering is for our glory too. If we suffer, we will reign with Him (2 Timothy 2:12). As Christians suffer, they start by knowing that "God causes all things to work together for good to those who love God, to those who are called according to His purpose" (Romans 8:28). Our family had to learn some of that good through the ordeal of cancer.

DIFFERENT KINDS OF SUFFERING

The Bible distinguishes between the suffering of the rebellious and that of God's children. Because He is God, He *can* use all kinds of suffering in all people for noble purposes.

Suffering of the Rebellious

The sufferings of the rebellious are multiplied and are often sudden, like a whirlwind: "Many are the sorrows of the wicked" (Psalm 32:10). "Fools, because of their rebellious way, and because of their iniquities, were afflicted" (107:17). God allows calamities to flare with no promised help or compassion from above. When the unrighteous cry out, "Oh God!" as distress overwhelms, He will not answer their call for relief from trial (Proverbs 1:24-33). He *will* answer a repentant plea for mercy and salvation, which then moves the sufferer into His care as a member of His family. Seen from eternity, painful impetus toward sonship on earth is much more merciful than everlasting anguish in hell.

Suffering by the rebellious may induce a yearning for God. That is certainly His heart in their trial: From Heaven's dimension, He explains,

> My anger will be kindled against them in that day, and I will forsake them and hide My face from them, and they will be consumed, and many evils and troubles will come upon them; so that they will say in that day, "Is it not because our God is not among us that these evils have come upon us?" (Deuteronomy 31:17)

But too often, those who revolt against God use suffering as a justification for bitterness. Their hearts harden, as impenitence becomes habit. "You have smitten them, but they did not weaken; You have consumed them, but they refused to take correction.

They have made their faces harder than rock; they have refused to repent" (Jeremiah 5:3). Stubbornness destroys. "A man who hardens his neck after much reproof will suddenly be broken beyond remedy" (Proverbs 29:1).

The Suffering of Discipline

Heaven's goal for the suffering involved in the chastisement of His own is brokenness over personal sin. (Suffering is not punishment. Christ took the punishment for sin at Calvary.) We can limit brokenness by hardening our hearts (Jeremiah 5:3). Normally, brokenness involves a process, which may require crushing heartaches over personal failures. Every time we take offense, retaliate (even inwardly) against criticism, or flare with resentment, we show shreds of our old flesh that are alive and sensitive. Learning to see self-justification, irritation, lack of appreciation, self-defense, exaggeration, and discontent as God sees it—Heaven's view of our old fleshly nature—facilitates the process toward genuine brokenness.

Jesus provided one of the most important insights into the nature of His work when He claimed, "I can do nothing on My own initiative" (John 5:30). "Nothing" means zero; everything He did was under the direction of His Father. Having made that clear, He said of us, "Apart from Me you can do nothing" (15:5). This may be the most neglected of all His instruction. Our failures themselves account for our self-defense and exaggeration. We never seem to realize our inadequacy without God until He applies the discipline that we need.

Brokenness over sin—the work of chastisement—is central to usefulness in God's kingdom. Satan's ploy to keep us from that grief or brokenness is to accuse us (Revelation 12:10). Guilt makes us run from God. Brokenness makes us turn to Him. With His children, God always wants repentance and restoration to follow conviction of sin quickly. He does not deal with us harshly, angrily, or in a belittling way when He corrects. Often God reassures that His correction toward His children is a proof of His love and our relationship (Deuteronomy 8:5-6; Job 5:17-18; Proverbs 3:12; 1 Corinthians 11:32; Hebrews 12:4-15; Revelation 3:19).

His kingdom does not advance while we spend time either avoiding God or endlessly agonizing in penance. Begging over and over for forgiveness indicates our failure to believe in the immediacy of God's promise in 1 John 1:9 to forgive. He forgives and moves ahead.

Brokenness becomes joy when we see from Heaven's view how faithfully God keeps the covenant He made at Calvary. Our responsibility is to move on into more service (the kingdom principle of forward movement in chapter 3).

Our initial repentance involves grief; the burning away of dross may also become painful. In chastisement, most of our personal grief has been in the realization of the hurt we have caused God and others. The grief of chastisement ripens into the beauty of restoration. In restoration (as in a fine antique), the flaws become part of the beautiful patina as God sands down the pockmarks.

We are tempted to doubt the validity of complete restoration because of our limited view of grace. We know how hard it is for us as humans to forgive completely, and unwittingly we apply that handicap to God. A restored antique is more valuable than when it was new. Every child of God becomes at one time or another a divine work of restoration.

Though repentance and restoration occur quickly together, the consequences can go on for a lifetime. Consequences are not part of a "punishment." (Remember, the sin was punished and paid for on the cross.) Consequences are simply that: the subsequent effects of an action that become part of the fabric of our lives. They may be frustrating, aggravating, demanding burrs that consume time and emotion, but the results of *all* suffering—including innocent suffering and persecution—often have many difficult, lifelong consequences. Consequences also become tools in the process of perfecting (completing, maturing) our faith. Grace enables consequences to become part of the beauty of the restoration.

From Heaven's view, eternal values emerge from brokenness. Suffering breaks the grip of selfishness, allowing God's different kind of love to grow within our spirit. Humans are not likely to love with the divine love of the Father without brokenness. Additionally, suffering clears our eyes to see spiritual reality: Our relationship with God is all that matters in eternal values. Circumstances become a vehicle for trusting Him more, and even tragic ones assume unexpected worth.

> I now rejoice, not that you were made sorrowful, but that you were made sorrowful to the point of repentance; for you were made sorrowful according to the will of God, so that you might not suffer loss in anything through us. For the sorrow that is according to the will of God produces a repentance without regret. (2 Corinthians 7:9-10)

BEYOND RESTORATION: SUFFERING ALLOWED BY GOD TO TEST, PROVE, AND TEACH

When Christin, our oldest daughter, was approaching her second birthday, my husband and I (Melana) happily discovered that another baby was on the way. A few months into the pregnancy, I miscarried. As many women know, the physical pain was horrific, but the emotional grief was worse. In long-night seasons of prayer, Steve and I struggled, first pleading for comfort and later asking for another baby. I told God as circumspectly as I knew how that I did not want to go through the pain of another miscarriage. Steve was in the Navy during this time, and after he returned from another cruise, I became pregnant again.

A few months into this new baby's life, I miscarried. During the same week, Iran declared war on Iraq, and immediately Steve's ship was sent to the Persian Gulf for an indefinite deployment. This time we had no opportunity to grieve or heal together, and to make it worse, Steve's life was now in perilous territory. We could have no communication except for delayed letters.

I prayed, but I could not make out what God was doing. Gradually a fear grew in my heart that I was doing something wrong; God had already taken two babies, and now my husband was in danger. I grew afraid that if I didn't learn my lesson, God might take more extravagant measures. I saw God as a heavenly Father with a very large "spanky stick" disciplining me, but I didn't know what for.

My father came to Virginia Beach while he was in the area on a ministry trip. Over lunch he asked how I was holding up, and I shared my fears. He asked, "Have you lost your faith?" I looked up and replied, "No, not at all. I know that God wants my best, and I'm afraid that if I don't figure out what I'm doing wrong, He will have to keep disciplining me in order to conform me to the image of Christ."

My father thought for a moment and then asked, "Have you ever considered that this may be a test?" That was a totally unexpected thought for me, and I sat back in my chair, puzzled. We finished lunch, he returned to Texas, and I started a search for God's ways in my life.

Early one morning before dawn, I was praying with my Bible by a dim lamp beside my bed. Young and alone, my grief over the loss of the babies and my fear for Steve's life poured out of my heart onto my pillow. Suddenly I sensed God's near presence, and I rose up in the bed. He probed my heart: "Melana, what is your ultimate goal for Christin?" I thought for a moment and then responded as thoughtfully as I knew how: "As clearly as I can understand, I want her to go to be with You at the end of her life and in the meantime know as little personal sin as possible." His Spirit quietly illuminated my heart: "That goal is exactly what you got for your two little ones. They are here with Me, you can know them in eternity, and they never *personally* knew *any* sin."

All of the pain and fear of the last months was in one moment dispelled—finished—and was worth it for the explosion of joy and light in this revelation. He had tested me, melting away the dross of thoughtless parenting. In the testing, He purified my desires and defined my purpose in my motherhood. Without the suffering, Steve and I could not have perceived His better plans for our little family and may not have even wanted them. From that day, we made our plans and choices for Christin and the other children with the goal that each personally know as little sin as is possible on earth, not in an effort to "be righteous" but because God, through our suffering, gave us eyes to see goals for our children from His viewpoint.

Testing or proving validates our relationships. When Christin got married, she was a beautiful bride. At the moment she and her new husband, Brian, walked down the aisle after the ceremony, Christin could in truth make the statement "I have been 100 percent faithful to my husband." But that would mean nothing because she hadn't had a chance to be anything else. Years later, that statement means something. Twenty-five or fifty years later, it will mean even more because there will have been opportunities to prove the commitment. We authenticate our promises with the proof of time.

In the Bible, testing or proving has several distinguishing marks. First, the person being tested has an established relationship with the one doing the testing. They have a history together, and they know each other well. Their strong prior relationship provides the source of the faithfulness or loyalty of the one being tried (tested).

Second, during the trial, the One giving the test appears from earthly circumstances to be acting contrary to what the tested person *knows* Him to be. If God never appeared to act contrary to our human expectations (what we think He ought to be), He could not test our loyalty to our understanding of His true nature as Scripture and prayer have revealed Him. Testing removes limitations in our understanding of Him.

This is how testing worked in Scripture and how it works with us today. When God appears to be silent or distant while we suffer or seems to require something out of character for Him, He appears to be acting contrary to what we would expect. But if His wisdom so deals with us that we have to think or ponder His purposes, He can lead us into a deeper understanding of Himself.

Unless His dealings prompt us to question and investigate His purposes, He cannot test us to see if we will remain true to what we already know. From Heaven's perspective, He has not changed at all, and after the test, that becomes clear to us as well. We can safely say then that testing makes us probe further into God's nature and that probing usually establishes the validity of His revelation of Himself. Sometimes the probing also adds to our knowledge of Him.

Third, the person who passes the test emerges with greater spiritual stature, purified, and knows God more intimately.

Therefore, he or she has more trust in His veracity and more love for Him personally. These distinguishing marks characterize the trials recorded in Scripture. Once they are recognized, they enable us to walk through our own fiery trials with unwavering faith. We studied many individuals in Scripture whom God tested, and found this pattern consistently repeated.

Job. Job was blameless and upright; he feared God and turned away from evil. He had ten children for whom he continually offered sacrifices. It takes several years to amass the family and the wealth Job had, and from this we can infer that his relationship with God had developed over time (process). God called Job "My servant" and said there was no one like him on the earth. God knew Job, and Job knew God.

When Satan spoke with God, he demanded that God bring suffering to Job. God would not personally touch Job. But knowing the great good that would come from the purifying of Job's faith, He allowed Satan access to all that Job had. From earth's perspective, Job lost everything and suffered intense pain and humiliation. Three of his friends filled his ear with their stunted perspective. Although God appeared to be acting contrary to what Job would have expected, Job clung to what he knew of his God. He did not doubt God's love or sovereignty. He affirmed, "Though He slay me, I will hope in Him" (Job 13:15). Later Job had the assurance to tell his friends, "He knows the way I take; when He has tried me, I shall come forth as gold" (23:10).

Job's trial purified him radically. Early in his test, Job had presumed to answer for God to his friends. Yet at the end, he grievously confessed, "I have declared that which I did not understand, things too wonderful for me, which I did not know. . . . I have heard of You by the hearing of the ear; but now my eye sees You; therefore I retract, and I repent in dust and ashes" (42:3,5-6).

The first six weeks of Laverne's first cancer treatments were an agonizing attempt not to question God. Finally I (T. W.) realized that when I stand in the presence of Jesus and see the ineffable glory of His face, I cannot possibly have any "why" questions. God Himself satisfies every desire, every question, every search we can possibly have.

Job also came through his trial with the realization that God Himself was his answer. God did not answer Job's questions; He revealed Himself. When we stand in God's presence, we will stand before absolute wisdom; when we see Him as He is, we will understand all. At that time, in the confrontation with absolute Wisdom, we will have no questions. Absolute Wisdom is Himself the answer to all questions. If we will have no questions then, by seeing from Heaven's view, we can reach the point where we have no questions now; we can see God Himself as the answer to everything we want to know. Faith becomes "completed," "finished," "perfected."

Abraham. Abraham had walked with God for many years. He had watched God's ways, heard God's promises, been given God's covenant, and seen God's miracles. God knew Abraham, and Abraham knew God well enough to be called "the friend of God."

Abraham had seen God's value of human life in His willingness to spare Sodom and Gomorrah for the sake of only ten righteous people. He had seen God keep His word as brimstone rained on the doomed cities. He had seen God's promise fulfilled as elderly Sarah became pregnant. Each time he saw God act, his understanding of God became deeper. His lifetime was a process of learning God's ways in ever-increasing measure.

Then God tested Abraham. He appeared to command a thing that seemed totally out of His character: a human sacrifice of the promised heir, Isaac. From earth's perspective, it was untypical and cruel. The world's view on that rocky path up the mountain would have been, "This is out of control," "A good God would not let this happen," or "If God requires this, He is neither just nor good."

Here was the test: Would Abraham cling to what he *knew* of his God in the face of seemingly opposite circumstances? Would Abraham be loyal to God, believing only the best about Him, never doubting His integrity or veracity for a moment, even in the face of a horrible, incomprehensible situation? Would he trust his Friend?

No proof exists that we believe God unless we are faced with the appearance of the opposite yet hold to what we know. Abraham passed his test: "ABRAHAM BELIEVED GOD, AND IT WAS CREDITED TO HIM AS RIGHTEOUSNESS" (Romans 4:3). Joshua also knew: "Not one word of all the good words which the LORD your God spoke concerning you has failed; all have been fulfilled for you, not one of them has failed" (Joshua 23:14).

Abraham's test led him into a deeper understanding of his Friend. God showed him that He would always provide, sharing with Abraham another of His defining names, Jehovah Jireh (The Lord Will Provide). God bestowed on Abraham one of the most magnificent promises and heritages in the Bible: The Messiah would come from his seed, and the entire world would be blessed because of his obedience.

Abraham could obey because he knew God well enough to trust Him with the life of his son. Our obedience comes much easier when we realize that God loves our lives more than we do. We can trust Him with them more than we can trust ourselves. In fact, as Heaven's view takes root, we fear not to trust Him more than we trust ourselves.

The Syrophoenician woman. From earth's view, this story is one of the most difficult to understand in the New Testament. From Heaven's view, it is a beautiful portrayal of pure gold passing out of a fierce crucible.

> Jesus went away from there, and withdrew into the district of Tyre and Sidon. And a Canaanite woman from that region came out and began to cry out, saying, "Have mercy on me, Lord, Son of David; my daughter is cruelly demon-possessed." But He did not answer her a word. And His disciples came and implored Him, saying, "Send her away, because she keeps shouting at us." But He answered and said, "I was sent only to the lost sheep of the house of Israel." But she came and began to bow down before Him, saying, "Lord, help me!" And He answered and said, *"It is not good to take the children's bread and throw it to the dogs."* But she said, "Yes, Lord; but even the dogs feed on the crumbs which fall from their masters' table." (Matthew 15:21-27, emphasis added)

This woman understood well who Jesus was: She called Him "Lord" and "Son of David." She recognized His capacity for mercy and His authority to deal with demons. She clung to her understanding of Him, even though it was not as deep as Abraham's intimacy. Her faith was greater than that of Jesus' disciples at that moment.

Jesus acted toward her in a way that seems opposite to all we know about Him. He first ignored her and then equated her to a dog (albeit a diminutive form of the word *kunarion*, verse 26). How *not* "like Jesus"! In testing, God often acts in a way that seems contrary to what He would normally do. Jesus *knew* her, and He knew what her faith would bear. If He had said yes immediately, the woman's faith would not have been tested, both for her benefit and for the benefit of His watching disciples.

As in Job and Abraham's story, this woman came away with a deeper relationship with Jesus than she'd had at the beginning. He told her, "O woman, your faith is great; it shall be done for you as you wish" (Matthew 15:28). This Canaanite woman was given one of only five compliments from Jesus recorded in the Gospels (Matthew 8:10; 15:28; Mark 14:9; Luke 7:28; John 1:47). Her tenacious faith and Jesus' unusual compliment were recorded for all of history to admire. She would not turn loose of what she believed.

Jesus on the cross. Jesus' ultimate test arrived as His last hours on the cross waned. The most horrifying aspect of His suffering began when the sin of the world overshadowed His tormented body. The intimate unity that Jesus and the Father had shared for eternity were severed. Everything of heaven that is pure, right, just, bright, loving—all that is good—abandoned Jesus in the presence of everything in hell that is loathsome, hateful, dark, malignant, vile—all that is evil. God had to turn His back on His Son as He, who had never personally known sin, became the embodiment of sin. Hanging on metal spikes in immeasurable agony, Jesus cried out, "My God, My God, why have You forsaken Me?" (Matthew 27:46, NKJV).

Jesus and His Father had enjoyed a perfect relationship in a unity unknown to humans. God did have to act in a way seemingly "out of His character" when Jesus, voluntarily and with the agreement of His Father, took upon Himself the sin of the world. He had never been separated from His Father throughout all eternity. But though God in His holiness did have to turn away from the guilt now borne by His Son, in the trial Jesus could not turn away from His Father. His cry was still *My* God, *My* God. (Jesus was actually quoting verse 1 of the crucifixion hymn, Psalm 22.) He clung to what He *knew*. Emerging from His sufferings, He then was exalted above every name, given a throne above every throne, conferred with glory above all other glories.

This pattern of knowing God in an intimate relationship—when suddenly circumstances appear to show God contrary to what we know of His nature, followed by greater spiritual stature for the one tested—is repeated throughout Scripture. Joseph, Jeremiah, Daniel, and Stephen passed these horrendous tests. In fact, it really is not out of God's norm to test or prove us. Knowing "what is on the exam" prepares us to cling to God as tests come.

In the suffering associated with trials and testing, the basis for faith is what we already know God to be and the resolute determination to cling to what we know to be true, regardless of circumstances (Joshua 23:8). In the last stanza of "It Is Well with My Soul," Horatio Spafford wrote, "And Lord, haste the day when the faith shall be sight, the clouds be rolled back as a scroll." Spafford saw from Heaven's view. There, faith becomes the finality of sight—every point clear, no fuzzy edges, no shadows obscuring details. For us, "Faith is the assurance of things hoped for, the conviction of things not seen" (Hebrews 11:1). Looking at trials from Heaven's view keeps our attention on the reality that God sees.

Suffering in Innocence

Satan appears to have the upper hand with the question "Why do the innocent suffer?" His ignoble lie tells us that God is wrong, impotent, or at the least apathetic. This worldview of suffering perplexed Abraham. Wrestling with the information that Sodom would be destroyed, Abraham requested that God reconsider His decision, pleading, "Far be it from You to do such a thing, to slay the righteous with the wicked, so that the righteous and the wicked are treated alike. Far be it from You! Shall not the Judge of all the earth deal justly?" (Genesis 18:25).

However, his request was given from a limited perspective. Abraham assumed there were at least fifty righteous men in Sodom. One major problem we have with innocent suffering is that we fill in blanks with assumptions. Our assumptions appear valid because we do not realize our ignorance.

Thoughts like this are unjust toward God. He is being judged unfairly (without all the facts), and our rejection causes Him intense sorrow. We become hypocrites, we ourselves causing undeserved pain. God has suffered innocently more than any mortal can imagine.

God cannot normally give us anything that costs Him. The Creator of the universe owns everything He made (Psalm 50:10-12). Giving lavishly out of His bounty cannot diminish His wealth. God, through Christ, could give us only one gift that would truly cost Him: the life of Christ Himself. No human ever suffered so much on behalf of others as Christ did.

If assumptions deceive us, what is Heaven's perspective of innocent suffering? The greatest need of a sufferer is not relief; it is the Comforter Himself. I (Melana) was in almost daily cancer management for exactly one year. When the final burst of the last radiation treatment stopped, I lay on the table almost incredulous that the therapies were over.

Suddenly, a very unexpected soberness overwhelmed me: My heavenly Father had carried me closely and tenderly all during the illness, and I now did not want that nearness to end. The worst thing I could imagine was going back to a "life as routine" mentality. Though I wanted my health back very much, I also had come to realize that the intimate presence of my Comforter was worth more than what had been routine.

Surprisingly, His closeness had, over time, made the trial seem not like a trial. Though I hope for years of good health, I have no fear of a recurrence because if it happens, I know how good it is to be held so gently in His hand. "This I recall to my mind, therefore I have hope. The LORD's lovingkindnesses indeed never cease, for His compassions never fail. They are new every morning; great is Your faithfulness" (Lamentations 3:21-23). "Do not let your heart be troubled. . . . I will not leave you as orphans; I will come to you" (John 14:1,18).

To see Heaven's view, the sufferer must want to know God and His ways more than he desires a justification for the trial. This shifts the focus from the pain to the Comforter. In my treatments, I perceived God more profoundly than I had ever known Him before.

Innocent suffering has an amazing potential to glorify God. In unexpected ways, it reveals all that He is. It strips away all fleshly desires (1 Peter 3:14), making a dependent walk preferable to a false sense of self-satisfaction. It perfects (completes, matures) our desires, perspective, prayer life, and faith. Suffering is the direct path to spiritual maturity (Romans 8:17). No wonder the first-century Christians rejoiced when they were considered "worthy to suffer" (Acts 5:41).

Paul expressed joy like this when He saw his "thorn in the flesh" from Heaven's view:

> There was given me a thorn in the flesh, a messenger of Satan to torment me—to keep me from exalting myself! Concerning this I implored the Lord three times that it might leave me. And He has said to me, "My grace is sufficient for you, for power is

perfected in weakness." Most gladly, therefore, I will rather boast about my weaknesses, so that the power of Christ may dwell in me. (2 Corinthians 12:7-9)

Most of our innocent suffering results from someone else's sin (a drunk driver, rape, abusive mate or coworker, rebellious child), disease, death, financial setbacks, or a catastrophic event of nature often called "an act of God." The destruction of the World Trade Center and all terrorism seem the most senseless of all human tragedies. Yet these painful situations can resolve themselves into the "afflictions" referred to in 2 Corinthians 4:17: "Momentary, light affliction is producing for us an eternal weight of glory far beyond all comparison." An affliction brings painful pressure. It hurts. It is consuming. Yet it gives the ability to cry out to God honestly.

Failure by yielding to resentment, depression, or rebellion wastes an opportunity from God to let endurance have its perfect work. (As our friend Paul Billheimer put it, "Don't waste your sorrows.") What seems unbearable produces nobility greater than the pain. Ultimately, we discover that the pain is temporary and nobility is eternal.

Suffering from Persecution

"All who desire to live godly in Christ Jesus will be persecuted" (2 Timothy 3:12). History verifies this. Currently, huge numbers of Christians around the world are suffering religious harassment and martyrdom. Persecution is now increasing in Western countries from growing hatred and violence in society.

The two of us have experienced some heated reactions only when a strong stand on a personal conviction was necessary. Others have known more severe vilification for their faith. In the Sermon on the Mount, Jesus prepared His followers to go through this intense trial by focusing ahead to their great reward in heaven (Matthew 5:11-12).

God has called us to pray daily for our persecuted brothers and sisters. Both of us have more than forty countries listed in our prayer notebooks where intense persecution continues daily. The Lord's instruction to bear one another's burdens makes their suffering our concern. Love for our brothers compels us to pray for their faithfulness, courage, hope, pure testimony, basic needs, and deliverance. Suffering with the persecuted church in prayer also has eternal value.

> He who receives a prophet in the name of a prophet shall receive a prophet's reward; and he who receives a righteous man in the name of a righteous man shall receive a righteous man's reward. And whoever in the name of a disciple gives to one of these little ones even a cup of cold water to drink, truly I say to you, he shall not lose his reward. (Matthew 10:41-42)

Jesus knew the connection of innocent suffering and the process of perfecting that results in glory. He went through His greatest trial with His will intentionally unified with the will of His Father. In His high priestly prayer before His crucifixion, Jesus' first request was "Glorify Your Son, that the Son may glorify You" (John 17:1). His second request amplified the first: "Now, Father, glorify Me together with Yourself, with the glory which I had with You before the world was" (verse 5). The unity with the Father that we share when everything temporal is burned away is the glory attained through innocent suffering.

HEAVEN'S INSTRUCTIONS FOR GOING THROUGH SUFFERING

Obeying the Scripture

Suffering is so important to God's kingdom that He gives us specific guidelines. The following list comes from 1 Peter:

- Endure it with patience.
- Do not revile in return.
- Utter no threats.
- Entrust yourself to Him who judges righteously.
- Do not fear their intimidation.
- Do not be troubled.
- Sanctify Christ as Lord in your heart.
- Be ready to give a defense for the hope within you.
- Keep a good conscience.
- Keep fervent in your love for one another, being hospitable.
- Do not be surprised at the fiery ordeal coming upon you.
- Keep on rejoicing.
- Entrust your soul to a faithful Creator in doing what is right.
- Humble yourself before God.
- Cast all your anxiety on Him.
- Be of sober spirit.
- Resist Satan, standing firm in your faith.

At the end of his epistle, Peter summarized, "After you have suffered for a little while, the God of all grace, who called you to His eternal glory in Christ, will Himself perfect, confirm, strengthen and establish you" (1 Peter 5:10).

Much suffering within the body of Christ would be lightened if collectively and individually we obeyed Matthew 25:35-40. We are to feed those who are hungry, give water to those who are thirsty, befriend strangers, clothe the naked, and visit the sick and imprisoned. When we carry out these instructions, Christ credits these ministrations as being given to Him personally. We are given a charge to minister with love and compassion to widows, orphans, and the poor. When one member in the body of Christ suffers, all suffer with him or her (1 Corinthians 12:26). We really are a body.

Jesus emphasized the importance of continuous prayer to avoid temptation and trial. He warned us to "keep watching and praying that you may not enter into temptation" (Matthew 26:41; the word for "temptation" can also mean "trial"). He instructed us to ask for deliverance from evil (Matthew 6:9-13). We are to love and pray earnestly for our enemies and for those who persecute us (5:44). How much heartache do we bear because we didn't ask for what He told us to? Joseph M. Scriven wrote in 1855, "Oh, what peace we often forfeit, oh what needless pain we bear, all because we do not carry everything to God in prayer" (from "What a Friend We Have in Jesus"). James 5:13 gives the answer: "Is anyone among you suffering? Then he must pray."

Surprising Outcomes of Suffering

God's intention is to surprise us in our suffering with the highest joys possible. Paul reported in 2 Corinthians 7:4 that he was "overflowing with joy in all [his] affliction." The night before He was crucified Jesus told His disciples in John 15:11, "These things I have spoken to you so that My joy may be in you, and that your joy may be made full" (complete, lacking nothing). Some joys are accessible only through suffering. For example, the resurrection morning would not have been possible without the suffering of the Cross. Suffering enabled Jesus to finish His work (John 17:4; 19:30). Mary, the mother of Jesus, had intense personal agony as her Son was rejected and tortured. Salvation was secured, and millions of redeemed individuals eternally benefit, but the *process* pierced her heart. What an unknowable joy must have filled her heart on Easter morning!

Moreover, suffering creates compassion for others. We can receive comfort from those who have been through similar trials, and we can give hope to succeeding generations from our experience (2 Corinthians 1:4). Suffering lifts us to a perspective beyond ourselves. Jesus explained that the blind man in John 9:3 was born with his affliction (and suffered through years of blindness) so that the works of God could be displayed through him.

Suffering also opens to us the realm of spiritual reality and enables us to recognize the deceitfulness of flesh. It makes God's grace vivid and practical. Paul laid out the interplay of grace with suffering in 2 Corinthians 4:8-9:

- We are afflicted (physical reality) but not crushed (spiritual reality).
- Perplexed (physical reality) but not despairing (spiritual reality).
- Persecuted (physical reality) but not forsaken (spiritual reality).
- Struck down (physical reality) but not destroyed (spiritual reality).

Suffering molded the giant saints in Scripture. We reach spiritual greatness in the same way.

Ultimate Suffering and Ultimate Glory

"If any man will come after me, let him deny himself, and take up his cross, and follow me" (Matthew 16:24, KJV). The common denominator of all biblical suffering is a willingness to deny self and embrace whatever "cross" God allows. The essence of denying self lies in our willingness to give up what we love most. God gave what He loved most. But after the suffering, God had the joy of honoring His Son with the highest glories that infinite creativity can devise. From Heaven's perspective, an eternal panorama of glory develops for us as we suffer. "You have been called for this purpose, since Christ also suffered for you, leaving you an example for you to follow in His steps" (1 Peter 2:21).

CHAPTER 11

The Noblest Miracle of Heaven: Grace

As sin reigned in death, even so grace would reign through righteousness to eternal life through Jesus Christ our Lord.

ROMANS 5:21

The one factor that enabled us to "get through" Laverne's and Melana's experiences with cancer was the grace of God. Nobody told us how important it was or how to appropriate it. The Holy Spirit simply led us to this one major solace. We did not begin Laverne's illness in 1983 with a full-blown understanding of our privileges under grace. Understanding and application grew slowly while Laverne was sick; that provided us with an advantageous background when Melana's suffering began. With Melana's illness, our comprehension grew rapidly and explosively. This time we knew to be diligent in working into our lives what God was teaching. God used both learning periods to bring us to this book.

WHAT GRACE IS
The Grace of God Is Unique
Grace has as many definitions as there are passages on it in the Bible. For the most part, in the discussion that follows, we

leaned strongly on the Pauline passages and one in Hebrews because they applied to the other parts of our lives as well as to the illness.

So far in this book, we have studied attributes and emotions of God. Grace does not properly qualify as an attribute or an emotion, although it taps into God's attributes and affects His emotions. Grace is rather a disposition of favorableness to humans that remains resident in God and colors what He thinks and does.

God never has to struggle to apply any aspect of His nature to our needs; He remains ever available to us. He is always propitious to His creation and especially to humankind. The Bible never speaks of God becoming reconciled to anyone. Instead, it tells us that we are to "be reconciled to God" (2 Corinthians 5:20). We never need ask God to have good intentions toward us or anyone. God stays favorable to us; we are the recalcitrant adversaries who run from God and resist Him. If we only knew the cost of our resistance!

Grace, reflecting God's love, is that factor in God that overrules the necessity that His holiness destroy us. Few of us understand the difference in our native disposition and His. If God were only holiness, all of us would all be deservedly dead. Grace works with holiness to bring us to acceptability with God.

The good angels evidently have no need of grace. The fallen angels cannot appeal to it. Grace seems to be reserved for humans alone for two reasons: (1) those of us in process need that big a resource to appeal to in all our ups and downs, and (2) grace is especially a *spiritual* (not physical) need for those able to access it.

God has pity on His creation (Job 38:41; Psalm 147:8-9; Matthew 6:26-30; Romans 8:20-21). After each creation day, He saw that it was good (Genesis 1:4,10,12,18,21,25). His good pleasure has sustained the universe for millennia (Colossians 1:17). Grass, lilies, crocodiles, and deer depend on the ever-supplying Lord for their sunshine, water, and life. But nature has no need of a *spiritual* resource.

However, after God made man, He pronounced creation "*very good*" (Genesis 1:31, emphasis added). God has grace only for humankind, for us who are made with a spirit in His image. Paul tells us that the grace of God in Christ "abound[s] to the many [persons]" (Romans 5:15). God's most astounding gift to the human race is not our upright physical walk or our incredible brain but rather the grace — the unearned, undeserved love — that He reserves just for us.

Grace means that His acceptance of the redeemed is unqualified. God accepts without reservation our efforts and our repentance. Considering our sinful background, grace is far kinder than we could have hoped for. The grace of the Lord guarantees the continuity of our process, regardless of our falls and our failures: "The LORD sustains all who fall and raises up all who are bowed down" (Psalm 145:14). God accepts both winners and losers.

Grace knows that our deepest desire reaches to God, regardless of how much Satan may warp our wants by his lies. Time after time, new converts describe how they have finally found the true desire of their hearts.

Grace pictures the bigness, goodness, and generosity of God. Paul describes Heaven's view as us being "seated . . . in the heavenly places in Christ Jesus, so that in the ages to come He might show *the surpassing riches of His grace* in kindness toward us in Christ Jesus" (Ephesians 2:6-7, emphasis added). Grace exceeds all our imagination — a spiritual bounty, a nobility arching over all His attributes to place them at the disposal of our need.

God Applies Grace to Us

When Paul states that "God is *able* to make all grace abound to you" (2 Corinthians 9:8, emphasis added), he is implying that God's grace works with His will. God *wills* to show us favor. His will becomes synonymous with His grace. The entire mind of God is "on our side."

God's *attitude* can be affected by our sin, as occasion demands from Him some specific function or action. In anger or displeasure, He must discipline us. His *grace* remains unaffected by hardship or emotion. Even when He disciplines, His eye is on achieving some result of grace.

Speaking temporally (the only way we can speak), God's grace precedes every other work or quality of God. In his salutations, Paul always places grace at the beginning, before every other quality (peace and mercy). In the beginning, grace created; in our sin, grace redeemed. Grace will bring us to glory.

The one aspect of God's nature that He cannot express mutually is His grace. We cannot show Him grace. It pleases God when we utilize or return His love and care, but grace is one-sided. God shows *us* the glory of His grace; it is all of Him.

We can be "gracious" to someone else, but none of us knows how to forgive in the breadth that God does or to love on the scale that He does. Whatever grace we show others is so dwarfed that this chapter will concern itself only with the cosmic grace of God, His resource that we need for our suffering.

Although He created us, God does not owe us anything. If creation obligated Him, all people would be redeemed. While we did not ask to be created, we did receive Christ of our own volition. Yet God took the initiative even in our redemption. All we had to do was accept a finished work of Christ. We owe God; He does not owe us. This makes grace even more amazing. It really is one-sided.

Refusing the Grace of God

Some persons do not appropriate the grace available to us. Some are carnal and simply do not want the work of God. However, many Christians also fail to grasp what God wants to give them. Either they are ignorant of the scope of grace or they misapprehend the nature of God.

A man once confessed to me (T. W.) that God could not forgive him because he had committed a heinous sin as a teenager. He had never told this sin before for fear of being excluded from society, but he also had never been able to make peace with God. I spent hours describing the enormity of God's grace, and finally the man saw what he had never seen before: how great the reach of Calvary extended.

Among the former are many people who think their sin is too great for God to forgive. They refer to 1 Peter 2:20: "What credit is there if, when you sin and are harshly treated, you endure it with patience? But if when you do what is right and suffer for it you patiently endure it, this finds favor with God." These persons focus on the second sentence instead of the first. The context indicates that this passage refers to servants who are punished for some misdeed; they are admonished to remain submissive in order to please God. However, this passage does not treat sin in general or in the dimensions of sin.

The tenor of the New Testament states that grace remains always available for *any* repented sin. Satan deludes us with the misconception that God will not forgive by fastening our attention on the size of the sin instead of the size of God. These deceived people have never grasped either the limitlessness of infinity or the enormity of the price Christ paid at the cross. We have seen that nothing is too difficult for God. The blood of Christ covers heinous sin and determined perversion. "The blood of Jesus . . . cleanses us from *all* sin" (1 John 1:7, emphasis added).

A second reason individuals refuse to accept the grace of God lies in their secret desire to punish themselves. In their hearts, they know that wrongness must be punished, but they do not realize that Jesus accepted *all* our punishment on the cross. In punishing themselves, they sometimes feel they are helping God. They "get what they deserve" (although we must face civil authorities if we break the law). God *disciplines* in grace, usually for our glory, but the *punishment* was completed two thousand years ago. We will probably realize the enormity of the payment Jesus made on the cross only after Graduation Day.

We are warned not to come short of grace. This includes all human situations, including suffering and sin. "See to it that no one comes short of the grace of God; that no root of bitterness springing up causes trouble, and by it many be defiled" (Hebrews 12:15). Paul gratefully acknowledged, "By the grace of God I am what I am, and His grace toward me *did not prove vain*" (1 Corinthians 15:10, emphasis added). Paul did not fall short; he seized the grace available to him.

He urged the same church, "Working together with Him, we also urge you not to receive the grace of God in vain" (2 Corinthians 6:1). The grace of God is too big for us to understand, but this does not mean we limit it.

Although we can reject grace, our refusal does not affect the fact that God's grace is unlimited. Grace is unlimited favor. If it were not infinite, God would not be God. We do not comprehend the scope of grace because we are so limited. In our limits, we accept on faith the enormous scope of grace.

THE NATURE OF GRACE
Qualities of Grace

The single most striking factor in grace is its price: It costs mankind nothing. We do not earn it or deserve it. Romans 3:24 tells us that it is a *gift*—it is absolutely free. Paul should know; his history shows that he certainly did not merit his salvation, no more than you do or we do. Our only responsibility is to take what is offered to us.

A second factor to help us all is the *universality* of God's grace. It is available to all: the rich, the poor, the gifted, and the ungifted. God's potential grace does not vary from person to person, although the appropriation of it does. Paul tells us, "The free gift is not like the transgression. For if by the transgression of the one [Adam] the many died, much more did the grace of God and the gift by the grace of the one Man, Jesus Christ, abound to the many" (Romans 5:15).

The availability, this abounding, applies to the sins and the failures also. Jacob seized it, and so did David. Both of us can name dozens of personal friends who "came back" after failure. The distinguishing marks of grace are its freeness, its universality, and its huge scope.

Grace is total and unconditional. When God picks us up after we fall, the new start is truly fresh from Heaven's view. Sometimes earthly consequences do not allow others to see the newness that God establishes, yet His work in our lives matters more than any earthly view. When He forgives a sin, that sin no longer exists in His mind (Jeremiah 31:34). After thirty chapters of calling Israel a prostitute, God declares that when He renews her, she becomes a virgin (verse 4)! A dog may return to its vomit (2 Peter 2:22), but the Christian does not have to do that.

The more grace you appropriate, the more you get. God gives liberally (James 1:5); His nature calls for Him to give and keep on giving, far beyond what we know to ask (Ephesians 3:20; James 1:17). In the kingdom of God, the key to receiving more and more is to take all that God will give you, the kingdom principle of compounding.

The Interplay of Grace, Holiness, and Mercy

Grace covers any repented sin (1 John 1:9). Only holiness— through grace, sin, and God's disposition—waits eagerly on our confession. Because He is God, because He is infinitely nobler than we, because His grace is bigger than any of our wrongs, He is more anxious to restore fellowship with us than we are.

For the believer, the referent for our sin is not its quantity, quality, or size but the great Forgiver. Grace refers to the generosity of God, which cannot be measured. Only God knows how big it is. We humans *must* simply go on assuming that we will never reach the end of it so long as the Holy Spirit continues His convicting work in us.

Grace removes the *guilt* of our sin. Mercy removes the *misery*. Grace comes from God's generosity. Mercy comes from His compassion. We do not pray for grace; we pray for mercy in the midst of God's ever-flowing grace. Grace keeps mercy always available, simply for the asking.

Grace and mercy overrule all human actions. Nehemiah understood how God worked. In spite of Babylon's cruelty and Israel's apostasy, Nehemiah prayed, "In Your great compassion You did not make an end of them or forsake them, for You are a gracious and compassionate God" (Nehemiah 9:31).

APPLYING THE GRACE OF GOD
Practical Living

Grace rules our Christian life from the first to the last. At the beginning, it is a salvation event. We are "justified as a gift by His grace through the redemption which is in Christ Jesus" (Romans 3:24). "By grace you have been saved through faith" (Ephesians 2:8; see also Titus 3:7). We can start only with grace.

Then our salvation life remains under grace forever, again, from beginning to end. Paul said we stand in this grace (Romans 5:2; see also 1 Thessalonians 5:23). God gives it; we appropriate it. God extends grace not just for the forgiveness of sins; He gives it for the living of life. Grace is for any child of God who needs it in any way.

Each member of our family, from the youngest to the oldest, found some measure of the grace of God illuminating our walk during chemotherapy, surgeries, baldness, nausea, and nightmares. In our darkest moments, we learned to cry to God, "Lord, we need to see the glory of Your grace in higher measure." God never failed to grant us a new vision of Himself. It was always the vision of God that reassured us and gave us new vigor—strength to strength—along the way. We can assure you: Grace works!

The Bible names four areas in which Christians may apply grace directly: in suffering, weakness, overcoming sin, and good deeds. In each case, God intends that we draw directly from His supply in order to continue our progress from glory to glory.

Most Christians feel that they need grace more desperately in *suffering* than in any other area of their lives. The most reassuring promise in the New Testament tells us, "Let us draw near with confidence to the throne of grace, so that we may receive mercy and find grace to help in time of need" (Hebrews 4:16). God uses the discomfort of desperation to drive us to Him. Some become bitter in pain; some blame God and turn from Him; some cry anxiously for relief. God wants to present us with a gift far greater than answers or relief: God wants to give Himself—the gift of grace.

We apply to God for grace in *weakness*. A major theme of this book has centered on our advancement from strength to strength. When God refused to remove Paul's thorn, He said, "My grace is sufficient for you, for power is perfected in weakness" (2 Corinthians 12:9). Grace functioned under trial. Paul made headway in strength to strength through rejection, imprisonment, court trials, and shipwreck. We need strength when God allows a trial. At the end of his life, Paul reassured his young disciple, "You therefore, my son, be strong in the grace that is in Christ Jesus" (2 Timothy 2:1). Paul knew where to turn. He had been there.

We draw on grace in *overcoming sin*. A dreadful tragedy occurs when sin overcomes a Christian. Paul (him again!) informed the Roman church, "As sin reigned in death, even so grace would reign through righteousness to eternal life" (Romans 5:21). The world does not see grace ruling in the lives of many Christians. Either grace rules or sin rules.

Grace supplies the fodder for our *good deeds*: "God is able to make all grace abound to you, so that always having all sufficiency in everything, you may have an abundance for every good deed" (2 Corinthians 9:8). The entire work of the church rests on the supply of God's generosity, on His grace.

The Makeup of Grace

Grace is so grand that it includes many components. Not one of them hints at all that comprises grace. In our prayers, we can call on God's grace through any of these factors:

Favor	Kindness	Beneficence
Goodwill	Propitiousness	Attentiveness
Mindfulness	Watchfulness	Greatheartedness
Thoughtfulness	Heedfulness	Generosity
Considerateness	Regard	Help
Alertness	Care	Concern
Painstakingness	Diligence	Vigilance

Use these twenty-one factors as you pray. We do not intend to make the list exhaustive, only evocative. Meditate on each one. As you meditate, the Holy Spirit may suggest other factors as viable as these. Grace is much too grand to limit it to lists.

HOW GRACE WORKS

The Realism of Grace

God is the only genuine realist in existence. Satan's tactics fool the rest of us on every hand, no matter how wise and discerning we may be. As we approach God, we always remember that He alone is ultimate reality and can guide us to what is genuine and what is false.

Grace does not deny our mistakes and misdeeds. That denial would step into unreality. Grace, unlike our enemy the Devil, will never tell us, "What you did was not really *that* bad." If God were not God, His mercy might give that very encouragement. In all its perceptiveness, only grace understands how bad our misstep really was. We do well to agree with grace.

Instead, grace covers all our demerits with the merits of Christ. Christ in us "really is *that* good." Although Christ will judge our works (2 Corinthians 5:10), He will not take away our established status as redeemed people. He will reward our deeds for Him, which resulted from the kind of heart we had.

Grace does not regard our sinful condition but rather our receptivity. God will not dispense any gift to an unwilling recipient. A believer achieves the most penetrating insight when he or she recognizes how desperate is our need of grace. God sees merit, not in our condition but in what grace itself gives.

Grace knows that no one is innocent. The rest of us know that too. What we do not know is that grace never runs out of mercy.

Grace does not normally remove consequences. David understood the extent of God's forgiveness, but he still had to live out the cost of his sin. Many people fail to realize that the most important aspect of David's whole experience was not his baby's death or Absalom's rebellion but rather his restoration to fellowship with God (Psalm 32). Grace used David's consequences to make him more godly; it can use ours to make us more Christlike. Even in acknowledging the results of our own wrong, we can move upward through Christ from glory to glory.

Grace will not contradict the legal. One of the purposes of the law was to demonstrate the irrevocability of God's permissive limits. Realism recognizes the rightness of our confines; God will not go beyond them. But grace establishes the finality of the payment of the Cross. God confirms the legal by His own payment.

Grace never compromises holiness. The beloved child of God

never gets by or gets away with something. Those who seem to escape the discipline of God are likely not regenerate. We welcome correction because it proves who our Father is. We who know Him intimately know that grace obliterates the vilest sin and the most serious mistakes.

Although God leaves our will free, grace, being from God, forbids the most determined evil. It also prohibits the most "harmless" evil. Yet grace embraces all races, classes, mentalities, and cultures. It works inwardly and does not evaluate outwardly.

Grace is not God's "sweetness." When we know Him well, we comprehend the polarity of His terrifying holiness (an absolute) and His tender invitation (absolutely genuine) to us. Grace is thoughtful openhandedness.

These negatives, oppositions to grace showing what grace is not, tell us that God deals strictly, on His own terms, with the realism His character demands. We cannot move from sin to sin or from sin to glory. The wondrous realism of God helps us stay on the right track, onward and upward, from glory to glory.

What Grace Will Not Do

The previous negations of grace highlight the realism of God, but they show only how grace, with its kinder intentions, prevents wrong directions. In God's holiness, He still must place other limits on the meaning of genuine divine grace.

Grace will not accommodate us. Our determined preferences and tastes usually have little to do with Christlikeness, God's goal for us. Grace is quite strict; the road is narrow (Matthew 7:13-14).

Grace does not approve of us; it approves of Christ in us. We often feel we can rest on our laurels. So long as God leaves us on this earth, our goal remains those things that we will present to Him at Graduation Day.

Grace will not excuse us; it is not human propriety. Decorum may or may not enter into the fierce requirements of holiness. Grace is not grace if it does not work together with holiness. It cannot grant amnesty. Every sin must be so fully paid for that absolute holiness is satisfied. The only access to that payment is not pardon but the full compensation provided by the Cross.

Grace does not exonerate us. It cannot relieve us of any obligation placed on us when we received Christ. Grace will not clear us of any guilt; only Calvary does that (remembering that grace, utilizing Calvary, removes the Christian's guilt when he confesses his sin).

It will not exempt us. In Matthew 5:48, Jesus stated the goal for every Christian: "You are to be perfect, as your heavenly Father is perfect." We have seen, however, that perfection is not arrival at the final goal; it is being where God wants us to be at any given stage in our path of life.

Grace cannot "overlook" our weaknesses. God cannot overlook anything because His omniscience is unlimited. We submit our weaknesses to God in the humble expectation that He will turn them into strength to strength.

Heaven Sees How Grace Does Not Work

The limits God places on grace do not exhaust Satan's deceptions in deflecting us from the greatness and glory of grace. He also has four alternates, substitutes for God's demands that have turned Christians away from appropriating the grand freeness of grace: works, law, legalism, and license.

If we depend on our *works*, we are not depending on grace. Salvation comes "not as a result of works, so that no one may boast" (Ephesians 2:9). We have a subtle distinction between those works that produce the rewards of 2 Corinthians 5:10; we *do* work with God in achieving His goals. We do not *perform* to make an impression. For this reason, our heavenly rewards come from works that are out of our hearts.

Law will not achieve what only grace can achieve. Paul opposes the two ideas of law and grace in Romans 6:14: "Sin shall not be master over you, for you are not under law but under grace." God gave the law to restrict the limits; it had a useful purpose. Acting under grace calls upon our spiritual instincts, in direct communion with God, to understand God's limits and live within them.

A perversion of acting under the law arrived in the form of *legalism*. The Pharisees perverted truth by demanding increasing technical accuracy. God is precise, but only He can interpret accuracy in spiritual matters. The Pharisees did not become more and more spiritual; spirituality was what they missed (Matthew 6:16; Mark 2:18; Luke 11:42; 18:10-14).

License misrepresents grace. The gratuitousness of grace gives some people the liberty to insult holiness by their actions. Paul countered this deceptive argument:

> What shall we say then? Are we to continue in sin so that grace may increase? May it never be! How shall we who died to sin still live in it? Or do you not know that all of us who have been baptized into Christ Jesus have been baptized into His death? (Romans 6:1-3)

The Christian lives in the polarity of the absolute freedom of grace and the strict path of representing God through Jesus Christ.

WE APPROPRIATE GRACE THROUGH FAITH

The cautions mentioned keep us out of the pitfalls Christians fall into occasionally. Yet they are minor in light of the enormous accomplishments grace makes for us, achievements and character qualities unthinkable without divine help.

Satan does not care if we know God's power and omniscience. He remains indifferent to all our exhaustive knowledge of God, provided it remains merely an intellectual or indifferent apprehension. What he does not want us to discover is the grace — the favor — that God has for us. We are likely to respond to such good news! God's immeasurable grace will always be the happiest information ever broadcast to the human race.

Grace appropriates for us:

- Removal of all condemnation (Romans 8:1)
- Total forgiveness of all (not some) sin (Ephesians 4:32)
- An inheritance with Christ (Romans 8:17)
- Holiness (Hebrews 3:1)
- A seat in the heavenly places with Christ (Ephesians 2:6)
- Peace with God (Philippians 4:7)
- Acceptance with God in the Beloved (Ephesians 1:6)
- A reign with Christ (Revelation 5:10)
- Progression from glory to ever higher glory (2 Corinthians 3:18)

The lofty position that grace gives must be channeled to us through some agency. That agency has to be faith. Paul stated it more clearly than anyone else: We are saved *by* grace *through* faith (Ephesians 2:8). If I simply sat and looked at a plate of delicious food, it would not satisfy my taste buds; I have to put the food where the taste buds are. We "put" the goodness of God on our "taste buds" by *believing* what He says about Himself.

Grace, by virtue of its nature, will work only with faith, not performance. Satan does all he can to deflect our attention to our performance. We judge "how we are doing." Righteousness, though, is not an achievement; it is a gift: "Much more those who receive the abundance of grace and of the *gift of righteousness* will reign in life through the One, Jesus Christ" (Romans 5:17, emphasis added).

Satan has so corrupted our race that none of us can achieve perfection of performance, yet Satan convinces us to strive for that one goal. The world helps him along with that misconception. Achieving high performance usually represents the world's view, not Heaven's view. This does not rule out God's leading us to set high goals for our lives, provided we work with Him to achieve His purposes.

We cannot achieve a perfect performance, but we can achieve biblical faith. Faith is accepting the reality of God and the reality of His purposes. True belief cannot falter once it tastes the glory—glory designed for us by our Creator, nailed down (or nailed up) for us by our Redeemer, and finished for us by the Perfecter of our faith (Hebrews 12:2). To develop faith, we go to Jesus, its author and finisher.

The Lord Jesus will perfect your faith as He does His other great works: in process. Peter admonishes, "Grow in the grace and knowledge of our Lord and Savior Jesus Christ" (2 Peter 3:18). We may grow in the grace we show others, but, supremely, we appropriate more and more of Jesus' grace for our suffering, weakness, temptations, and good deeds. Growth implies process, and it may proceed slowly.

We have seen many complements in the course of this book.

We saw the importance of overcoming in chapter 7; overcoming has a complement: grace. Death, loss, tragedy, hurt, temptation, trial—we have much to overcome. Whatever we overcome is trivial alongside the magnificent grace of God, which helps us in every life situation. It really is amazing.

CHAPTER 12

Heaven's View of Glory

*The Spirit Himself testifies with our spirit that we are
children of God, and if children, heirs also, heirs of
God and fellow heirs with Christ, if indeed
we suffer with Him so that we may also be
glorified with Him.*

ROMANS 8:16-17

Most of us think of heaven as a state of alleviation—the final taking away of our burdens and sorrows. God did not design heaven to be a negation of our earthly problems but rather a positive state of assumption. In eternity future, we will become absorbed in and reflective of unimaginable glory.

FROM HERE TO ETERNITY
Our Present Glory and Our Future Glory
God will certainly wipe away all tears, but that is only the beginning. Even in our present negativism, we would not boast, "I don't have a bad cold right now." We do not brag about negatives. When we "graduate," we will take into eternity future what we have been *becoming*—in our nature, in our attributes, and in our glory. The

difference in our being or our nature will not be in kind but in degree. On that magnificent occasion, we will take all our accumulated glories into the presence of Christ to share glory with Him forever.

We must therefore give diligent attention to the glories we are presently adding to the original glory God gave us in our salvation. We develop our present glories by cooperating with God in realizing the character of Christ in us. We saw in chapters 5 and 6 that we can grow in the specific attributes He demonstrated in order that we might understand and imitate Him. In chapters 7 through 9, we learned the ways in which Satan and our culture inhibit the growth of these attributes.

We share Christ's glory now in part by working them out in our daily walk in eternity present. Soon, in eternity future, we will share His glory throughout our total being and life. Peter states graphically that we have glory both now and in the future:

> In this you greatly rejoice, even though now for a little while, if necessary, you have been distressed by various trials, so that the proof of your faith, being more precious than gold which is perishable, even though tested by fire, may be found to result in praise and glory and honor at the revelation of Jesus Christ; and though you have not seen Him, you love Him, and *though you do not see Him now, but believe in Him, you greatly rejoice with joy inexpressible and full of glory*, obtaining as the outcome of your faith the salvation of your souls. (1 Peter 1:6-9, emphasis added)

Peter's goal was not to "tough it out." He constantly maintained his eyes on the present and future glory.

The Meaning of Glory

Glory, like grace, is not an attribute. Glory is the aura emanating from God that contains the totality of all His attributes. Glory, in God or in us, will always involve a sum of all that He is or all that we are.

In the Old Testament, God is called the "King of glory" (Psalm 24:7,10). He rules over all glory. Presently, "The heavens [among many other factors] are telling of the glory of God" (19:1). His glory also shows currently in our lives: "Much more does the ministry of righteousness abound in glory" (2 Corinthians 3:9; see the entire passage, verses 7-11). In the future, "The earth will be filled with the knowledge of the glory of the LORD, as the waters cover the sea" (Habakkuk 2:14; see also Isaiah 11:9).

The basic idea of the Old Testament word for glory (*kabod*) was weight. "All the kings of the earth . . . will sing of the ways of the LORD, for great is the glory of the LORD" (Psalm 138:4-5). This meaning (weight) implies great importance (as Habakkuk 2:14 implied importance). The seraphim called out, "The whole earth is full of His glory" (Isaiah 6:3). The tone of these (and many other) passages indicates that the highest importance of all is assigned to God alone.

Second Corinthians picks up this idea of heaviness, although other connotations of glory in the New Testament reveal even more sublime meanings. Still, the importance of its context elevates the idea of weight to a lofty position in the New as well as the Old Testament: "Momentary, light affliction is producing for us an eternal weight of glory far beyond all comparison" (2 Corinthians 4:17).

The New Testament specifically calls Jesus "the Lord of glory" (1 Corinthians 2:8, as opposed to God being the "King of glory" in the Old Testament), perhaps because the lordship of Christ assumes such significance throughout the New Testament

(Matthew 12:18; John 13:13; Philippians 2:11). All glory stems from God alone, and Jesus is the Lord of all of it.

In the New Testament, a connection with light or splendor assumes more prominence than any other connotation among the various descriptions of glory. When the angel appeared to the shepherds to announce the birth of Christ, "the glory of the Lord shone around them" (Luke 2:9). At the transfiguration, "[Jesus'] face shone like the sun, and His garments became as white as light" (Matthew 17:2). The writer of Hebrews tells us that Jesus "is the radiance of [God's] glory" (1:3). The New Jerusalem "has no need of the sun or of the moon to shine on it, for the glory of God has illumined it, and its lamp is the Lamb" (Revelation 21:23).

God's glory is also rich (Ephesians 3:16). According to Paul, those riches are worth waiting for: "I consider that the sufferings of this present time are not worthy to be compared with the glory that is to be revealed to us" (Romans 8:18). Paul's next chapter tells us that God is making known "the riches of His glory upon vessels of mercy, which He prepared beforehand for glory" (9:23).

Second Corinthians 3:9-11 also brings in the idea of importance, as does the passage cited from 4:17, with its emphasis on weight. Both testaments demand recognition of the prestige that God assigns to those He glorifies.

When Jesus changed the water to wine, He "manifested His glory" (John 2:11), indicating that God also associates glory with power (seen also in Psalm 19:1). Interestingly, God connects this assignment of power to glory also with the making of our new bodies:

> Our citizenship is in heaven, from which also we eagerly wait for
> a Savior, the Lord Jesus Christ; who will transform the body of
> our humble state into conformity with the body of His glory, by

the exertion of the power that He has even to subject all things to Himself. (Philippians 3:20-21)

God, then, assigns His own personal qualities of splendor, riches, prestige, and power to those of us He has prepared for eternal glory. We have it now, it can grow during our time on earth, and it will take on unimaginable proportions in eternity.

The Uniqueness of God's Glory

The Bible never speaks of attributing to God the holiness due His name or the worth due Him alone, although His holiness and worth are ultimate and beyond anything we humans can have or become. But the Bible does tell us to ascribe to God the glory due His name (Psalm 29:2). The aura that represents God in His totality eternally sets Him apart from all He created.

The glory of God is unique in degree. All of us fall short of it (Romans 3:23) now and forever—now because of our sin, and forever because of His stature as Creator. The tenor of the book of Revelation puts Him far above all He redeemed. Our joy is to worship Him alone forever.

The glory of God is unique because it is eternally ultimate and absolute. Although our limited glory will become complete at Graduation Day or in eternity future, we develop our glory through a time process. God never had to develop glory. He was all that He now is before He created the universe. His glory had no beginning and will have no ending; it is eternal.

Because His glory differs from ours in degree and in its eternity, no one can appropriate God's glory. He rightfully claims, "I am the LORD, that is My name; I will not give My glory to another, nor My praise to graven images" (Isaiah 42:8). We are given glory because He specifically states that He created us for

His glory (43:7). Our glory, wondrous as it is, comes from Him for the purpose of glorifying Himself.

Actually, it could not be any other way. When, before creation, God planned a family to share His glory, by definition it would have been impossible to create for us a glory different from His own. We are made in His image and then conformed to the image of Christ in order to magnify all that He is. Only those who have His kind of glory can glorify God, as Christ did in John 17:1.

The New Testament, as well as the Old Testament, places the glory of God first, above ours. "Christ also accepted us to the glory of God" (Romans 15:7). The birth of Jesus occasioned angelic attribution. They cried, "Glory to God in the highest, and on earth peace among men with whom He is pleased" (Luke 2:14). Our material existence is to glorify God: "You have been bought with a price: therefore glorify God in your body" (1 Corinthians 6:20). The angel of the Lord struck Herod because he failed to glorify God (Acts 12:23). Everything in creation is to glorify God.

In chapter 3, we introduced three principles of the kingdom of God. This chapter will bring in two more. The fourth kingdom principle is that *we glorify God, our Creator and Redeemer, above all other glory.* The two kingdom principles in this chapter rank above those given earlier. We gave them at that point in order to refer to them in later contexts. Now we come to the sublimity of God's infinite glory and our finite glory and explain some of the principles that apply to glory.

GOD SHARES HIS GLORY WITH US
His Original Purpose Was to Bring Many Children to Glory
As comprehensive, indescribable, and grand as God's glory is, His desire is to share portions of it with those of His creatures who

accept Christ. "It was fitting for Him, for whom are all things, and through whom are all things, in bringing many sons to glory, to perfect the author of their salvation through sufferings" (Hebrews 2:10). The main emphasis of the Bible is the glory of God. Secondary to that important theme is the glory He is bringing us to. Everything else in the Bible contributes primarily or secondarily, directly or indirectly, to these two most important concepts.

We can be glorified only *with Christ*. "It was for this He called you . . . that you may gain the glory of our Lord Jesus Christ" (2 Thessalonians 2:14). Remembering always that God's glory comes first and must remain primary, we need not fret about accepting glory from Him. If infinity gives glory, it loses nothing. What we have is joint glory with Christ (not independent glory).

> The Spirit Himself testifies with our spirit that we are children of God, and if children, heirs also, heirs of God and fellow heirs with Christ, if indeed we suffer with Him so that we may also be glorified with Him. For I consider that the sufferings of this present time are not worthy to be compared with the glory that is to be revealed to us. (Romans 8:16-18)

Paul also makes it clear that our glory derives from our justification, also a work of Christ:

> Those whom He foreknew, He also predestined to become conformed to the image of His Son, so that He might be the firstborn among many brethren; and these whom He predestined, He also called; and these whom He called, He also justified; and these whom He justified, He also glorified. (verses 29-30)

Whereas Jesus' glory did not grow or develop, we, His joint heirs, progress "from glory to glory" (2 Corinthians 3:18) — that is, in process. We are *becoming* what God wants us to be when we are with Him in eternity future. The "becoming" is progression in Christlikeness.

A striking aspect of Jesus' life that seems often neglected is the fact that He was always other-directed. His teaching was on behalf of others. The healings showed deep compassion for others. He came to the disciples in their distress in the storm (John 6:17-20). Most of the Sermon on the Mount treats how we relate to others. Even on the cross, He prayed for His tormenters and cared for His mother.

Now we are ready to grasp the fifth kingdom principle: *True members of the kingdom of God are other-directed.* This is the highest indication of heavenly nobility we can demonstrate in this life. It is one of the glories of Jesus that is most neglected. Jesus' gaze was consistently outward and upward.

This glory, other-directedness, cannot be compared with physical manifestations of glory (expressed in figures of speech), such as weight, light, riches, and power. Therefore, it will not be as obvious as the other expressions of glory. Other-directedness is a spiritual glory, and just as all spiritual matters are more remote to our this-world consciousness, it will seem an inaccessible glory. Natural man does not know the things of God. No one is naturally oriented to others.

The members of the Holy Trinity are other-directed within their unity. We, on our diminutive scale, can imitate the compassion, mercy, pity, and love of the Trinity as spiritual glories, often unseen and not appreciated. We saw in chapter 3 that Christianity is based on relationships. In this chapter, we have seen that in the same way that we first love God above all else, we also first glorify

Him above all other glories. Now we begin to perceive that because Jesus' second command was to love our neighbor as ourselves, we can also defer to others in humility, respect them with wisdom, and care for them with love. "Render to all what is due them: . . . honor to whom honor" (Romans 13:7). These are manifestations of nobility.

Jesus did not call attention to Himself. He chose the unknown and the poor for His followers. He labored in districts far from the great and famous of His day, never seeking for Himself fame or wealth. The Gospels record the most unstinting self-giving ever recorded: the Creator giving Himself to His created. Jesus did not come to earth to be honored; He came to minister to others (Mark 10:45).

He entrusted the church of the book of Acts to the recipients of His giving. They who had observed His other-directedness gave to one another generously (Acts 2:44-45; 11:29-30; 20:35). Because such self-sacrifice does not come easily, we have to labor and pray earnestly to acquire this little-known and seldom-observed glory of self-sacrifice.

We are headed toward a glory that defies description; God will share His glory with us. Paul rejoiced in the indescribable glory that awaits us: "Having been justified by faith, we have peace with God through our Lord Jesus Christ, through whom also we have obtained our introduction by faith into this grace in which we stand; and *we exult in hope of the glory of God*" (Romans 5:1-2, emphasis added).

Relating to God's Glory

In chapter 3, we learned three frames of reference that help us love God first, above all else: mutual occupying, relationships, and proximity. Now these categories facilitate even further our honoring God supremely. They relate us not only to His person but also to His glory. In mutual occupying, we become love and holiness (glories themselves) because God really is in us. In relationships, we are love and holiness because God continuously shares them with His children. The frame of proximity helps us as we reflect the love and holiness of God to His world (2 Corinthians 3:18).

God's glory is original; ours is derivative but nevertheless real. God generates the glory; we receive it; what He gives is solid and substantial. The glory emanates from Christ, and although we reflect it, it becomes an essential part of us. God shares His glory; we partake of it, but, living a spiritual life, it becomes an integral part of us. God's glory is part of His essence; ours is participating yet intrinsic to our nature. As we progress in our process, Christ in us more and more becomes our hope of glory (Colossians 1:27).

ELEMENTS OF GLORY

Up to this point, most of this book has been concerned with glories we may have in this life and, at the same time, with those we will assume at Graduation Day or eternity future. The rest of this chapter will mainly pertain to the new glories God has planned for us when we are eternally and uninterruptedly with Him. The occasional mention of our present glories is incidental to what they occasion in eternity future.

The Glory of Humanity

When the Incarnation introduced humanity into the nature of Christ, it established humanness as a permanent part of His being. A human body was born, died, and resurrected. A human Jesus ascended. "There is . . . one mediator also between God and men, the *man* Christ Jesus" (1 Timothy 2:5, emphasis added).

Few people realize the glory of humanness. We excuse our mistakes and sins with "I'm only human," as though humanness made us weak. Humanness did not weaken the Lord Jesus. He showed us the full meaning of God's intention for us in making us human.

Most Christians secretly think of the image of Christ as unattainable and therefore not worth the effort. For this very reason, God imputes to us the attributes of righteousness and holiness when we become Christians. We do not develop these; we are given them. And because of these imputed gifts, we also have glory at the beginning. In other words, our Lord has provided us with a magnificent starting place for becoming fully human!

As we become human in the way Christ is, we discover a new dynamism in each attribute. We are not "trying to love"; we are allowing God to love through our minds. Only in eternity will we understand the depth of what God calls love. In eternity, we will finally have wisdom, purity, knowledge, and even humility with a vigor and zing that would shock us if we grasped it.

Our senses will be expanded and our capacities greatly extended. Although we do not yet know much about extra-dimensionality (scientists have discovered at least ten dimensions) and especially its relation to the spirit world, we know that Jesus was able to enter a locked room (John 20:19), eat (in what kind of measure did He enjoy that?), physically touch (John 20:27), and ascend on a cloud (Acts 1:9). The truth is that God formed an incredibly complex machine in our old bodies. What would His generosity have in mind for our new bodies?

Our New Position: Royalty

The twenty-four elders and the four living creatures sang, "You have made them to be a kingdom and priests to our God; and they will reign upon the earth" (Revelation 5:10). The Bible speaks often of our crowns (1 Corinthians 9:25; 2 Timothy 4:7-8; Revelation 2:10). Even today, in our present state, we are "A CHOSEN RACE, A royal PRIESTHOOD, A HOLY NATION, A PEOPLE FOR God's OWN POSSESSION" (1 Peter 2:9). The children of God are the nobility of all creation. We must learn nobility of spirit and action as Heaven views them, not as exampled by earthly royalty (with wonderful exceptions). We practice our nobility by all the reverence, humility, and love in the fourth and fifth kingdom principles.

As royalty, we will have dominion. "The King will say to those on His right, 'Come, you who are blessed of My Father, inherit the kingdom prepared for you from the foundation of the world'" (Matthew 25:34). Jesus assured His disciples, "Do not be afraid, little flock, for your Father has chosen gladly to give you the kingdom" (Luke 12:32).

The question arises, "Whom will we reign over?" God has it planned, and He has the power to create for us whatever He wishes. At this point, if we trust God, we do not need to ask the question.

The Splendors of Eternity Future

The vein running through Paul's writing and of the book of Revelation almost dares us to guess the inconceivable outer glories ahead of us. (For convenience, with reference to heaven, we have used "outer" glories and "physical" glories synonymously; the Bible speaks of physical features in eternity, but no one knows what they mean.) How much were Paul and John unable to put into words? God Himself has limited our present understanding and by doing that has placed great value on our faith and the potentiality that faith has. Only faith can guide us beyond our present limitations.

In this life, pleasure ends in itself. When the meal is past, the enjoyment of taste and smell ceases. When the symphony ends, no audible harmonic vibrations remain. When the ride finishes, we "want to do it again."

In eternity future, joy will be a continuum that never ceases. That joy will include within itself peace, expectation, beauty, and sublimity. Our present understanding of pleasure only hints at the dimensions of enjoyment in the sheer outer joys of heaven. The environment alone is worth the anticipation.

However, our greatest joy will not be in the external but in the realization of the final perfection of the inner. Because at present much of our delight comes from the physical, we have to struggle to comprehend complete happiness in being—being completely like Christ in every detail and aspect of our lives.

Not only will our inner qualities be dynamic, they will be complete. What, in this life, would love, joy, and peace be like if they were whole? We will know very soon!

The Company We Will Keep

We know the presence of Christ in us right now, but with the impediments of a resistant nature and poor spiritual eyesight. In eternity future, we will at long last have our Lord without any kind of hindrance from the world or Satan. "We know that when He appears, we will be like Him, because we will see Him just as He is" (1 John 3:2). We will ever be with Christ and be like Him!

The highest joy of heaven will be the uninterrupted fellowship with our Redeemer. Being with Him will remove all difficulties occasioned by our earthly process. Seeing His glory will make all doubt impossible. The thought of sin will be intolerable. We will not deal with any crankiness or worry about any of our possessions. These are only the negatives that can no longer preoccupy our thoughts. Our minds will be forever on the positive glory we see in the highest of all kings.

From time to time, we also experience worship and praise in some public service that lifts us out of our mundane life. It almost seems as though we have been transported into heaven itself. We have not learned how to anticipate when a worship service will reach that high joy, although we yearn for it. But in heaven, we will have uninterrupted worship and praise. We will not look forward to it; we will live in it.

We will also have the company of other perfected saints — those who feel just as we do about our Lord! Right now we can hardly imagine a world with no griping, scolding, anger, or bitterness. In that future glory, every perfected saint we meet will be exactly like the Lord Christ: all positive!

We will also participate eternally and continuously in the activity of God. Now so much of our activity does not take Him into account. Some of us should have discovered long ago that working with Him (1 Corinthians 3:9) is such high joy that we would want to do it continuously.

Newness

Perhaps the most unexpected element of glory will be the constant newness we confront. If we are alert, newness should characterize this life. The Lord's mercies are new every morning (Lamentations 3:23). Considering the lives most of us live, we need different mercies every day.

Renewal is God creating. In his repentance, David prayed, "Create in me a clean heart, O God, and renew a steadfast spirit within me" (Psalm 51:10). Paul could boast, "The old things passed away [when we are new creatures]; behold, new things have come" (2 Corinthians 5:17). Paul mentions creation again in Ephesians 4:24: "Put on the new self, which in the likeness of God has been created in righteousness and holiness of the truth."

The passing of the old informs us that newness is often unexpected and may even seem strange. Jesus came to an unexpected place, chose unexpected persons, and taught unexpected concepts. We do not tell God how to do His new thing; we enjoy His gift.

Newness occurs in the mind; we are to be renewed in the spirit of our minds (Ephesians 4:23). Newness has nothing to do with age. A basic law of science is entropy: the continual decay of all things. But in the spiritual world, the basic law is renewal: "Though our outer man is decaying, yet our inner man is being renewed day by day" (2 Corinthians 4:16). The brain wastes away; the mind (the heart) renews.

The only way we can become immutable is in our spirits. The body remains subject to entropy. Our physical resources tire, our step slows, and our skin wrinkles. But the qualities of the spirit—love, compassion, humility, grace—can be greater and wiser as we obey in deeper measure Romans 12:2: "Do not be conformed to this world, but be transformed by the renewing of your mind, so that you may prove what the will of God is, that which is good and acceptable and perfect."

Earlier we referred to the Hollywood technique of building suspense on ever-increasing tension. Plots and subplots introduce "newness" that ties our stomachs in knots. Usually the denouement relieves all the anxiety with a resolution of the pressure. Our earthbound culture likes mysteries and ghost stories.

That attitude has caused some persons to complain that heaven sounds like boring harps endlessly sounding eternal sameness. Some of them even claim that they prefer the liveliness of hell to the dullness of monotonous uniformity. The truth is that the series of startling new ecstasies in heaven will be far more dynamic than any paltry earthly drama. Heaven will be anything but static! Infinity cannot ever "run out." We will know inexhaustible, constant newness.

THE GLORIES OF ETERNITY FUTURE (OR GRADUATION DAY)

The Surprises of Eternity (or Graduation Day)

One of the greatest surprises when we face our Lord will be how much more we could have known and practiced on earth if we had been willing. We will be shocked at how much divine revelation in the Bible we failed to explore. Although the entrance into eternity future will be joyful and (we believe) without regret, we surely will realize that others around us achieved greater nobility. We will witness the burning of our useless works (1 Corinthians 3:12-15).

We will not carry any bad body chemistry. Recently a friend of ours "graduated" into the presence of Christ. She had a lifetime of lithium imbalance that doctors had never been able to correct. Because of her chemical imbalance, facing life and normal behavior were extremely difficult for her. Yet she loved the Lord with all her being; she simply did not have the physical resources to do what some do. We are convinced that our Father is going to give her a "super" body as a reward for all she overcame in this life.

At that point, we will also understand how ungrateful we were. We will finally know that God was always acting in our lives, even when we ignored Him or failed to perceive His purposes. Facing Christ will produce a gratitude for the enormous amount of work He constantly carried on for us that we did not appreciate. God's kind intentions all along will amaze us. We may even be able to see how much of Himself He manifested at times when we thought He was not there.

The unimagined greatness of God will surprise us. Only then will we grasp how inadequate our worship and praise of Him were. We will be astonished at how much joy true worship and praise give us.

What We Carry into Eternity

We will carry no wrong associations with people or words. Although few of us understand Christly forgiveness, once we see the face of Christ, old resentments cannot persist. His glory will erase all grudges and hurts.

All our inferiorities, complexes, and painful memories will be erased when God Himself wipes the tears from our eyes. Any action of God is total; imagine *God* cleaning your tear-stained face! We repeat: If God does anything, how "done" is it?

We *will* carry into eternity all our accumulated glories. Jesus made His instructions clear:

> Do not store up for yourselves treasures on earth, where moth and rust destroy, and where thieves break in and steal. But store up for yourselves treasures [glories!] in heaven, where neither moth nor rust destroys, and where thieves do not break in or steal; for where your treasure is, there your heart will be also. (Matthew 6:19-21)

Our glories are all the joys we can now share with Christ. Many of those glories we collect in the process of our life crucible. Peter knew suffering intimately, yet he penned the words at the beginning of this chapter in 1 Peter 1:6-9. If Peter knew this kind of joy on earth, what happened when he "graduated"?

We will almost certainly carry into eternity new senses, probably with coordination between them that is only hinted at here. Our senses of taste and smell work closely together, but our senses of touch and hearing have a different relationship. We coordinate information in our brain among all the senses, but can we imagine that it might feel good physically to enjoy a lovely cloud bank or a shapely tree?

New concepts are going to delight our intellectual apprehension, which itself will be more acute with faculties now undreamed of. Eternity cannot exhaust infinity. The joy of learning will not be limited to a few. Both simple fishermen and wily tax collectors rabidly devoured the teaching of the greatest teacher of all. That joy was denied the "wise and prudent" (Matthew 11:25, NKJV) of earth, but in heaven we will all explore the refreshment of our Lord's ways forever.

Obviously, the enormous difference between earth and heaven will require a new and expanded language. As we have read the Bible in various languages, we have learned more of God simply through the "slant" that culture places on our concepts.

For example, the Hebrew word for "worship" (*shacah*) carries the basic idea of bowing down or prostration. (In all languages, any word will have a number of connotations, and a number of different words may express the same idea; here we are talking about only the basic connotation of "worship.") The Greek word implies honoring or paying respect (*proskuneo*) and literally means to kiss toward or do obeisance. The German word implies honoring or paying respect (*Verehrung*; we are not referring to the word *Gottesdienst*, the word for "service"). The Romance languages (*adorer*, *adorar*, and the rest) convey the idea of intense devotion or love. The English word comes from the old Anglo-Saxon *weorth-scipe*, or "worth-ship," with its emphasis on valuing.

No one language includes all these concepts, but reading them in the various contexts and languages, we begin to realize that "worship" includes (at least) submission, adoration, reverencing, and valuing. We have actually learned that reading the Bible in various languages and in many different translations ultimately adds up to a deeper understanding of the biblical ideas than if we limit ourselves to one language or one culture (or even one subculture; certain translations reveal the translators' predispositions, and that, too, sometimes contributes to our understanding).

Is it possible that in heaven, we will have a word or words for "worship" that will include all the connotations from all the languages of the world? If that is true, we can see that "graduation" will broaden us prodigiously, and that broadening will make us more Christlike. We will have such capacities that we would wonder in amazement if we understood our own future.

Many of our present words (that is, ideas) will disappear. We speak of the "blessed dead" and the "afterlife" as though our "graduated" form were less alive than our present existence! Just as "worship" will mean more, nearly all our words will take on unimaginable proportions. A word such as *holy* will suggest far greater beauty, and a word such as *righteous* will suggest more "rightness" (or "fitness") than we can now understand.

The attributes of God (and ourselves) will assume dimensions inexpressible in present languages. All affirmative nouns (wonder, beauty, consciousness, life, thrill, rapture, music — no list could contain them) will assume a positiveness that will enhance every conversation. The positive adjectives and adverbs (great, utter, wondrous, humbly) will have a degree of finality that we cannot now express. The great divine verbs will contain actions not now conceivable: praise, worship, adore, love, enjoy, and on and on.

Some words useful in time and space will persist in new meanings.

"Fear of the Lord" will become an adoring reverence that we will crave and enjoy instead of tending to reject. We have no way of envisioning what "obedience" will become.

Parenthetically, we inject the fact that the unregenerate will finally understand such words as *shame* and *dread*. (They may even wish they could be "disciplined," as the regenerate were on earth.) If they use language at all, these words will be appropriated with an eternal, hateful purpose.

The new language of heaven will have no use for many important words in our earthly vocabulary. We simply list examples of words that will be dropped:

- Nouns: death, stain, sorrow, revenge, hatred, rivalry, sickness, wrong, war, anger, hurt, pretense, hypocrisy, perversion, compromise, blame, peril, danger, opinion, treason, crime, shame, embarrassment
- Verbs: compete, subdue, annoy, bother, pretend, disturb, disagree, quarrel, fight, criticize, belittle, scorn
- Adjectives: separate, tawdry, dirty, cheap, repulsive, arrogant, ugly, wounded, persnickety, tired, bored

All of us at times feel frustrated that we cannot put into words what we feel. In heaven, we will never be frustrated about anything!

Perfected!

The greatest joy for us in eternity future will be that we are totally conformed to the image of Christ. That inevitably will bring in many perfections that are now inconceivable.

We will have a perfect environment. The physical (if that is the appropriate word), or the outer, will show God's glory on every hand. Those around us will help and never hinder. With the best of our efforts, our Christlikeness is presently frustrated by evil and sometimes by intended good.

We will have perfect relationships. At that "point" (we have no better word because we do not fully understand spiritual reality), all relationships will derive from our primary love for God. His supremacy in all points will unite us in a bond never experienced on earth. All of us humans will bond in the way the Holy Trinity now bonds.

God is going to provide us with perfect bodies. No allergy, imperfection, crippling, or physical defect will be possible in the unrestricted presence of Christ. Our faculties and senses will always respond appropriately to every opportunity.

Our minds will be perfectly sane. Every deed and word will make sense. Activities such as investigation, comprehending, and probing will never be necessary. Our understanding will be complete.

Have you ever realized how your mind darts from one subject to another? Have you been aware that you might be thinking about the Lord one minute and then, five minutes later, your mind was absorbed in a hellish thought? If you have, your mind is fragmented, at war with itself. One part of the mind fights against another part. We find it quite difficult to maintain a direction of thought that is consistently godly. In eternity future, one's mind, always in tune with God, will be an integrated mind—a perfect mind. In our eternal state, one's mind will be single, ever at peace with itself.

At long last, we will enjoy the beauty of holiness: perfect beauty. As glorious as our new environment will be, the outer glories will pale in comparison with our new appreciation of the inner (possibly manifested outwardly).

Our communication will be perfect. On earth, many fights and quarrels originate in our failure to communicate properly. In eternity, not only will we say it right but our fellow royals will hear what we are saying. All faculties will function in a totality not now known.

We will have perfect consciousness. At rare times in prayer, we now become conscious of the unhindered presence of God. This has happened enough to us that we have begun to yearn for more consciousness. Perfect consciousness is that which perceives God faultlessly.

In our present lives, we find it easy to see Heaven's view in retrospect — sometimes clearly, sometimes regretfully, sometimes wistfully, and sometimes gratefully. For most of us, Heaven's view is harder to perceive in prospect. To do that, we must look to the example of Christ, depend on the Holy Spirit, and plow forward to bring the kingdom of God and give Him glory.

To know Heaven's view, we do not merely ask, "What would I do if I were in God's place looking down?" The appropriate question is "What would Christ do if He were in this situation?" Heaven sees us as representing Christ where we are. Our job is to manifest Christ in each life situation, as He manifested the Father in each of His earthly circumstances.

Still, even if others see Christ in us, we do not rejoice in where we have arrived; we rejoice in our progress along the road. God's eyes are on the goal He is taking us to. Therefore, we never take our eyes off Him who is guiding us on the road.

It is true that we have the Father, the Son, and the Spirit of God with us now. But we are still in the crucible, or the oven. The day will arrive more quickly than we realize when the Lord Jesus will take us out of the oven and present us to the Father, finished, beautiful, pleasing to perfect holiness, ready for unceasing, eternal glory with Him — *graduated!*

Even so, come Lord Jesus!

Afterword

DEATH AS A THREAT — OUR FIRST CANCER

As I (T. W.) wrote this, I was preparing to drive from Houston to Fort Worth for the funeral of a beloved friend of many years, Dr. Ernest Byers. Dr. Byers, a physician, had critiqued my medical facts and documentation for the account of the crucifixion in *The Mind of Christ*. His death had a strange impact on me, one that results from a series of new insights beginning when Melana developed cancer at the beginning of 1999. I now identify with Paul's desire to "depart and be with Christ" (Philippians 1:23).

Yet, like Paul, I am convinced that it is better to remain than to go on to the glories that I now understand await me, as exciting as we know them to be. I never expected to look forward to Graduation Day as eagerly as I do now. Why is the death of His saints "precious in the sight of the LORD" (Psalm 116:15)? And why has Graduation Day now become so glorious to all of our family? In this book, we hope we have helped you see our new paradigm as we introduced you to life and death as God sees it: from Heaven's view.

Although I had lost uncles, aunts, and grandparents to death, I never had to live in the same house with the immediate threat of the death of a loved one until I was married. When my wife's mother developed cancer at the age of forty-three, I faced a new horror I had never known before. At the time, our financial condition meant that we had to move in with her and care for her during her last year of life. Being a devout Christian, she did not fear death, but, facing its immediacy, I developed an unhealthy attitude toward it. As we approached her last days, death seemed somehow unfit for the stature of redeemed human beings, for real children of God. Blessedly, her faith steered us through the dreadful seeming finality of death. After she died, we had the assurance that she was quite literally better off, in a better place, with Christ Himself.

COMFORT IN THE MIDST OF THE THREAT — OUR SECOND CANCER

We added another increment to our understanding of life and death (and also our prayers) when my wife, Laverne, had cancer, surgery, and chemotherapy in 1983. Treatment was not as advanced then as it is now; the oncologist gave her a fifty-fifty chance of survival. When I first heard that dreaded word *cancer*, I had the same reaction most men do when faced with the awful brutality of the possibly terminal illness of a wife. Once again there returned the horror of the finality of death. All these thoughts were below the level of my conscious mind. When they surfaced, I would not give them voice, although my conscious mind was aware of the ugly facts with which our fallen race has to deal. I was horrified and very frightened — terrified at the idea of losing my life companion. The finality of that loss was a bottomless pit I could not face.

God gently led Laverne and me to study together that profound book on suffering, 2 Corinthians. I canceled all my engagements during her chemotherapy. Each evening after dinner, she and I would sit down together with our notebooks and Bibles in hand. We worked our way along very carefully, word by word, phrase by phrase, verse by verse. As we studied and prayed together, we began to sense the leadership of the Holy Spirit bringing new insights and, more important, the ability to appropriate the indescribable comforts that God's Spirit can give during suffering. A new glory entered our relationship with each other and especially with the Lord, who was enlightening His Word.

The turning point came when we began to comprehend the enormous significance of chapter 3, verse 18: "We all, with unveiled face, beholding as in a mirror the glory of the Lord, are being transformed into the same image from glory to glory, just as from the Lord, the Spirit." Yes, the suffering was still there. Yes, the dismal prospects of nausea, weakness, baldness, and death were still threatening. But now we entered in a new glory with God's own Spirit each night as we studied together. The unhappy aspects of our plight no longer intimidated us so much; we somehow understood the comfort of the Holy Comforter on a scale we had never known before. We had a oneness in our marriage that was new and different.

When we reached the end of the chemotherapy, Laverne declared that if she had the choice of not having cancer and therefore not learning what we had learned, or of having cancer with the new glories we now knew, she would prefer the latter. And I actually agreed with her! The awfulness of the reality was still there, but we had somehow achieved a new glory in our relationship with each other. We had discovered that spiritual glories (new insights and the comfort of the Holy Comforter) are far greater than any physical comfort. Yet we did not know at the time that God would be taking us far deeper into an understanding of His purposes when our daughter later developed cancer. We were destined to go through this yet again.

GROWTH OUT OF THE THREAT — OUR THIRD CANCER

As a child, I (Melana) gradually became aware that, unlike most children, I had only one set of grandparents. Soaking up family history from conversations and traditions, I realized that my mother had endured an adolescence and young adulthood of great suffering. This gradually became part of the warp and weave of my perspective. Abandonment and humiliation by her father, nursing her mother through the year of cancer with virtually no funds for medical intervention, the death of her mother, and her young husband's (T. W.'s) induction into the army to serve in Korea were the precursors in her life to my entrance into the world.

As I reached adolescence myself, I marveled that despite all the pain (and even anger) my mother had daily coped with throughout my childhood, she had never once presented these trials in any sort of negative light. I was blissfully unaware of any hurt from her father's rejection. Although I knew that my grandmother had died of cancer and that my mother had nursed her through the year it took to waste away, this was related to me in such a way as to give me the impression that it had given her tremendous comfort to care for her. Therefore, my early impressions of cancer were that it can kill but can bring blessing as well.

My parents both earnestly sought to be people after God's own heart for many years. Every time a blow would come to our family, it consistently dropped us to our knees to seek what God was teaching. Moreover, God regularly used the setbacks to give us blessings of unexpected design. When I was in my thirties, my parents approached me one crisp autumn morning with the news that now my own mother had cancer. Because the groundwork had been prepared, I had absolute calmness within the first second that our heavenly Father had some more insights into His kingdom for us that would come through this suffering, and I had no fear for her life at that point. My father has already described how these dark threads became part of the lovely tapestry of our lives that God has planned.

Knowing that both my mother and grandmother had battled cancer, the idea that it could and maybe would visit me in my "golden" years was in my mental file drawer, but I was stunned to encounter this disease at the age of forty-two, with six children still at home. Late on a gray January evening, my husband and I sat in red vinyl chairs in a chilly examining room, waiting for the surgeon to come in with the report from my breast biopsy and mammograms. At one point, I left the room for a brief moment, and when I came back, my chart was on the door. I made the quick decision that I wanted to encounter this news alone with my husband. A glance at the first page made me rush in to him, and we held each other and cried and prayed together before the doctor came. Our first prayer was for faith to go through this in a way that would please Him and give Him glory, no matter the outcome. We asked Him to use this for our best and for the betterment of our children.

Steve and I had a solid marriage. We had been high school sweethearts and were best of friends as well as marriage partners. After twenty-two years, though still in love, we had reached the take-you-for-granted stage, with many little irritations that were insidiously taking root ("I thought *you* were going to go to the bank!"). The first thing this news did was burn away everything petty with a flash of white-hot fire from the flame that eternally burns away dross. Every priority in our lives immediately lined up in order, and we had eyes to see the importance — or insignificance — of almost every detail in our lives.

Very soon, Steve and I were walking hospital corridors from one battery of tests to another. Each one weakened and frightened me more because of the seriousness with which the doctors were approaching the diagnosis and management. As we walked down the halls, Steve and I held each other up, praying for the faith to take the next step. The faith we were asking for was to see this cancer from God's perspective.

Soon a medical plan was formulated. I would take three months of chemotherapy to try to shrink and control the large, aggressive mass before surgery. When we sent out e-mails asking for prayer, Gary Fraley, a dear pastor friend living near Chicago, replied with a profound note:

Dear Melana,

Marina told me yesterday of your cancer and we have prayed. I have come to see that even though there are three types of sickness — for chastisement, the glory of God, and to death — the only ones we should focus on is to the glory of God. If it is to chastisement, then the Lord needs to communicate to us what for. If it is to death, we may not know for some time. However, if we focus on giving glory to God, then, whatever the situation, He will be praised.

In times like this, the nearness of our God is what we seek. May His grace be with you and your family.

This short note became our anchor. Everything we were encountering was new and strange, even vocabulary we didn't understand yet. However, one phrase, "Focus on giving glory to God," I could understand. This became our prayer: for faith to see Him, to focus night and day on His glory. I literally would repeat the phrase over and over as painful procedures were performed and the news became increasingly grim. My extremely aggressive cancer occupied three separate foci within one breast—not a hopeful sign. My young age was not a good factor. The medical emphasis (and therefore our perspective also) was on fighting for my life. For this reason, the idea of losing a breast, with all that this implies and entails, was on the back burner of my thoughts for several months. I couldn't think about that three months ahead of time.

My greatest sorrow at that point was losing my hair. Baldness was almost obscene to me; it had a nakedness about it that stripped me of any feelings of femininity and made me feel unworthy of Steve's love and attention. Nevertheless, he cared for me tenderly and kept me focused on the future and on God's glory. Baldness was the instrument God used to strip me of the illusion that there was little beauty in me for Steve to enjoy or be attracted to. This, oddly enough, would become the greatest part of our love and joy in a few months.

After the months of chemotherapy were completed in April, surgery was scheduled for May 7. One of the goals of chemotherapy had been to control the disease prior to surgery if it had already spread into my lymph system. There was no test to check for this, but the assumption was that because it was so aggressive, we needed to proceed as if it had already metastasized locally. I was beginning to "hope" that it was not in my lymph system. Because of much suffering in chemotherapy, I "hoped" that it had done its job. The more I "hoped," the more insecure I became with just what "hope" was supposed to mean.

"Hope" to me tended to indicate the desire that the future here on earth will change. "I hope that I'll get a new bike for Christmas" meant that I hoped Christmas morning would bring a change in my material possessions. "I hope that it won't rain tomorrow" meant that I desired the circumstances of the next day to be different from what the weatherman promised.

As I read the book of Philippians, I began to grasp that I was using the word *hope* in a different way than the Bible does. In conversation, I usually followed my word *hope* with the word *that* ("I hope that there is no cancer in my lymph nodes"). Used this way, hope is nothing more than a very intense wish. In fact, I found that because this hope has no basis in fact, there is a slim, disconcerting line between this use of *hope* and the word *dread* ("I dread that they may find it").

The Bible's concept of hope has nothing to do with past, present, or future circumstances as we habitually use the word. Instead, Scripture speaks of hope *in* someone or something. "Lord, for what do I wait? My hope is in You" (Psalm 39:7). I understood that hope is the peaceful anticipation gained through a relationship with someone who is trustworthy. The prepositions that follow *hope* in the Bible require a firsthand relationship with Him.

I began to understand that I realize hope by centering on God's personality and character. When I focus on Him, I gaze into dependable love and stability. Hope is related to the future in that He holds the future. I found that this is why hope is an adjunct to faith. Through hope, I was able to settle my concentration on God rather than on medical prognoses and friends' opinions.

The first mastectomy was scheduled. As the day approached, the realization and dread of having a breast removed consumed me. Even though I knew this was for God's glory, the steepness of the personal price crushed me. The morning of the surgery, I was very cold and trembled uncontrollably in the preparation room, mostly from the personal grief of what was going to happen in the next hour and what that would mean for whatever time I had left as Steve's wife. Much of a woman's grief in losing a breast is interwoven with her personal identity and what she means to her husband.

A first lesson in love from Heaven's view awaited me in recovery. I awoke from the surgery in a special unit because I was struggling to recover from the anesthesia. Steve brought me to consciousness by holding my hands and telling me how much he loved me. He never left me and became my nurse through the first hard week, emptying drain tubes, charting information the doctors needed, feeding me, holding me as I began to try to move or get up and walk. From the beginning, Steve took total charge of absorbing the information from our medical team. He had done all the research on our options and the procedures and was still my shield and strong support as he nursed me and prayed with me through the first hours.

The doctors told us not to remove the bandages for several days after leaving the hospital. I began to loathe the time when I would have to look at the scar. I didn't want to see it, and I didn't want Steve to see it. One part of my mind still knew that God was working a greater glory in our lives this way than we could have in any other way. But at the moment, what consumed my attention was the loss for Steve and our marriage, how incredibly ugly I was, and the incredulity that we could ever be happy or normal again.

An afternoon came when all six of our children were not home. Steve and I found ourselves alone in the house, and we both knew the time had come to go through the torture of taking off the bandages. As we went into the bathroom, I suddenly knew that I could not go through with it. I collapsed in grief so intense that I couldn't even cry. Breathing was almost impossible. How could I ever be his wife again? How could he go on with me bald, maimed, eaten up with cancer? I was as ugly as a woman could be. No hair, eyebrows, or eyelashes; swollen lips and eyes from the grief; helplessly weak; physically worthless. I had nothing whatsoever to offer him that a wife would want to give her husband. I managed to utter that I was so sorry that I could never again be for him a bride as in the Song of Solomon.

In the next moments, God was about to reveal love as I had never understood it before. Steve put his arms around me and held me. He, too, was overcome, but for a very different reason. Holding me up, he whispered hoarsely, "Melana, I love you because that is who I am."

In that moment, my universe changed. I saw in my husband a live picture of the Lord Christ, the Bridegroom of the church, who loves us, we who have nothing to offer Him, ugly with deception and manipulation and pride — *because that is who He is.* Steve's personal identity is "the man who loves Melana and is giving himself and everything he has for her." Christ's personal identity is "the one who loves His church, His bride, and has given Himself and everything He has for her."

Steve and I found a new relationship in the bathroom that afternoon. I had feared that we were losing our marriage relationship. Instead, God gave Steve the deepest, grandest godlike love a human can experience, the exact love (*agape*) Christ has for His bride. When I became the recipient of that kind of love, I learned the true heavenly meaning and application of submission. Joyful, ready submission comes with absolute trust. Even mutual submission is possible only in the certainty of genuine love's trustworthiness.

After this surgery, we found that my lymph nodes were extensively involved. I went through five more months of chemotherapy, another mastectomy, and six weeks of radiation. The cancer was discovered January 7, 1999, and I finished the last treatment December 22, 1999. The perspective that God began giving us with Gary Fraley's letter of focusing on God's glory made 1999 the best year of our lives. Steve realized as the year drew to a close that God began our year calling us to walk in faith, seeing this trial from His viewpoint. He next took us through a new understanding of hope. As we walked on through the valley of the shadow of death, He gave us the unspeakably wonderful gift of *agape* love. We learned that "the greatest of these" really is love.

Many years have passed since that afternoon in our bathroom. Our marriage continues to be literally heaven on earth because we share the *agape* love of heaven. God has shown us hundreds of facets of love, delight, and joy in each other that we never would have known if life had gone on "as usual" without the trial of cancer.

God has used this immeasurably for our best, and I can now say "it was good that I was afflicted." His desires have become our desires. Each of our children has been confronted with serious issues and experienced the imperative grandeur of seeing life from God's perspective. God is continually working all things for good for those who love Him and are called according to His purpose. We are—in every way—more than conquerors when we see from Heaven's view.

A NEW PARADIGM

Strangely, when Melana told me (T. W.) the seriousness of the cancer, God began waking me up every morning between two and four. I kept careful notes of the new way of life to which God was introducing me, and from time to time, Melana and I would compare notes. We finally realized that the Holy Spirit was leading us both in the same direction: to view all of life from God's perspective (which is really the basic biblical perspective). At long last, we became aware that our mutual insights formed such a perfect pattern of a whole new paradigm for us that we knew that God wanted us to write it all down for our brothers and sisters in Christ.

One man who heard me teach this said, "This teaching has made me get outside my box, and that has been good because I understand the Lord's viewpoint so much more clearly than I did before." When he said that, I realized that our "boxes" are too often drawn culturally rather than biblically. As we have written this book, we at first thought we might be "coloring outside the lines" but slowly have realized that the true *biblical* lines are much broader than we had imagined.

The new paradigm is not new biblically; it is new only culturally. Jesus Himself rebuked Peter for seeing from the world's point of view: "You are seeing things merely from a human point of view, not from God's" (Matthew 16:23, NLT). The problem has been that sometimes the lines are drawn by a particular societal orientation rather than from the Bible. The passing of time exposes the truth of the Bible in deeper meanings than our ancestors may have suspected. The newer discoveries of science do not conflict with the Bible; they harmonize with it. The Bible does not discuss gravity, relativity, quantum theory, or the size of the universe, yet Psalms 19 and 104 mean more to believing scientists today than they did to Isaac Newton.

With the growth of knowledge and understanding, the Bible should mean more to us. This does not change eternal truths, always emphasized by the church of the Lord; it makes them clearer and clearer. The Spirit of God wants to broaden our horizons, and this is usually accomplished in *process*.

We have had to learn through Melana's illness to "get outside the box." We found the ideas we are writing about actually in the Bible. Moreover, they may make much clearer the importance of seeing life from a spiritual perspective—from Heaven's view. Christianity itself learns new approaches as we near the time when the bride of Christ must be ready for her great Bridegroom. It has been advancing for two thousand years, just as you will be developing until your Graduation Day (earthly death). God is giving us more and more of Himself as we seek Him diligently (Hebrews 11:6).

We must emphasize that the "new concepts" we now practice are derived from the Bible. Our environment tends to put us into a fixed mold that is very difficult to break out of. We have come to believe that Joseph, Daniel, and especially David approximated seeing life from Heaven's view. Most of the New Testament leaders—particularly Paul—followed Jesus in seeing all things from Heaven's view. For example, they thought in terms of eternity rather than the confines of their little world, one of the major themes of this book.

We also realized that this paradigm has been known to many of the great saints of history—Madame Guyon, Oswald Chambers, C. S. Lewis, and others—even if not expressed by them as we would. We have enjoyed the fellowship of several peers who thought this way.

The insights that have opened us to this new way of seeing life have come mainly from memorizing Scripture or from consulting it diligently. In fact, both of our lives have been saturated since childhood with Scripture. Time reveals new vistas on Scripture, and, as we have learned, Scripture itself becomes more meaningful—for example, as we understand more and more the enormity and complexity of the cosmos in relation to Psalm 19 (and many others).

Seeing life from Heaven's view has changed the way we pray and the way we view suffering. It has changed our way of relating to others. It has changed the way we view the world and God's plan for it. In this book, we have recorded what God said to us. We hope that for you it will be an exciting new adventure in seeing life from Heaven's view!

We emphasize that our concept of God's having a goal beyond redemption is not new with us. For many years, godly writers have emphasized a "deeper life" beyond redemption. It is central in the Keswick movement. Writers such as Ian Thomas, Charles Trumbull, and J. I. Packer have made enormous contributions to our lives. Our friend DeVerne Fromke saw an "ultimate intention" of God redemption (God-centeredness) many years ago. We are indebted to a legion of predecessors, but the ultimate goal of God's sharing His glory with us came, in our case, specifically through the anguish of a crucible we could not have invented. We hope God uses these insights from suffering in that crucible of life necessary for every believer.

About the Authors

T. W. Hunt is a former prayer specialist with LifeWay Christian Resources and also served on the faculty of Southwestern Baptist Theological Seminary. He is the author of *The Mind of Christ* and a contributor to the *Disciple's Study Bible*. Dr. Hunt received his master's and doctorate degrees from the University of North Texas. He lives with his daughter and her family in Conroe, Texas.

Melana Hunt Monroe has six grown children, whom she home-educated over the past thirty years. She has served the homeschool community all across the country and currently is curriculum supervisor for Paideia Classical Christian Education in The Woodlands, Texas. All six children and their families are committed to Christ and His church. Melana lives with her husband of thirty-six years, Steve, and her father, T. W. Hunt.

More powerful books from NavPress!

Seeing the Unseen
T. W. Hunt

Sometimes God seems a bit hazy or even imperceptible in our busy day-to-day lives. Experienced author and Bible teacher T. W. Hunt directs you to see and hear from God in the supernatural, no matter where you are: at work, in the kitchen, or on the road. You will come to see that God is always present.

978-1-61521-581-2

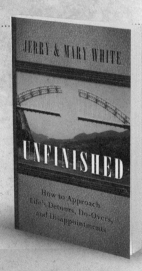

Unfinished
Jerry and Mary White

Learn to walk by faith, finish well, and accept without regret the things God has asked you to leave behind.

978-1-61291-268-4

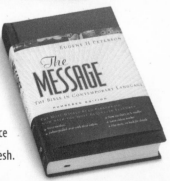

NAVESSENTIALS

Voices of The Navigators—Past, Present, and Future

NAVESSENTIALS offer core Navigator messages from Jim Downing, LeRoy Eims, Mike Treneer, and others — at an affordable price. This series will deeply influence generations in the movement of discipleship. Learn from the old and new messages of The Navigators how powerful and transformational the life of a disciple truly is.

The Triumph of Surrender
by William M. Fletcher
9781615219070 | $5.00

Meditation
by Jim Downing
9781615217250 | $5.00

Advancing the Gospel
by Mike Treneer
9781617471575 | $5.00

Laboring in the Harvest
by LeRoy Eims with Randy Eims
9781615216406 | $10.99

To order, go to **NavPress.com** or call **1-800-366-7788.**

 Facebook.com/NavPressPublishing   Twitter.com/NavPress

NAVPRESS
Discipleship Inside Out®